Approaches to Teaching Masterpieces of World Literature

Joseph Gibaldi, Series Editor

Approaches to Teaching Wordsworth's Poetry

Edited by

Spencer Hall

with

Jonathan Ramsey

The Modern Language Association of America
New York   1986

Copyright © 1986 by The Modern Language Association of America

Library of Congress Cataloging in Publication Data

Main entry under title:

Approaches to teaching Wordsworth's poetry.
  (Approaches to teaching masterpieces of world literature ; 11)
  Bibliography: p.
  Includes index.
  1. Wordsworth, William, 1770–1850—Study and teaching—Addresses, essays,
lectures. 2. Wordsworth, William, 1770–1850—Criticism and interpretation—Ad-
dresses, essays, lectures. I. Hall, Spencer, 1942– . II. Ramsey, Jonathan, 1942– .
III. Series.
PR5888.A66   1986   821'.7   85-21762
ISBN 0-87352-495-0
ISBN 0-87352-496-9 (pbk.)

Cover illustration of the paperback edition: iris motif from eighteenth-century lac-
querware (Joseph D'Addetta, *Traditional Japanese Design Motifs* [New York: Dover,
1984] 4).

Published by The Modern Language Association of America
10 Astor Place, New York, New York 10003

CONTENTS

HUM / EB & WB 5/24/90

PREFACE TO THE SERIES

In *The Art of Teaching* Gilbert Highet wrote, "Bad teaching wastes a great deal of effort, and spoils many lives which might have been full of energy and happiness." All too many teachers have failed in their work, Highet argued, simply "because they have not thought about it." We hope that the Approaches to Teaching Masterpieces of World Literature series, sponsored by the Modern Language Association's Committee on Teaching and Related Professional Activities, will not only improve the craft—as well as the art— of teaching but also encourage serious and continuing discussion of the aims and methods of teaching literature.

The principal objective of the series is to collect within each volume different points of view on teaching a specific literary work, a literary tradition, or a writer widely taught at the undergraduate level. The preparation of each volume begins with a wide-ranging survey of instructors, thus enabling us to include in the volume the philosophies and approaches, thoughts and methods of scores of experienced teachers. The result is a sourcebook of material, information, and ideas on teaching the subject of the volume to undergraduates.

The series is intended to serve nonspecialists as well as specialists, inexperienced as well as experienced teachers, graduate students who wish to learn effective ways of teaching as well as senior professors who wish to compare their own approaches with the approaches of colleagues in other schools. Of course, no volume in the series can ever substitute for erudition, intelligence, creativity, and sensitivity in teaching. We hope merely that each book will point readers in useful directions; at most each will offer only a first step in the long journey to successful teaching. We may perhaps adopt as keynote for the series Alfred North Whitehead's observation in *The Aims of Education* that a liberal education "proceeds by imparting a knowledge of the masterpieces of thought, of imaginative literature, and of art."

Joseph Gibaldi
Series Editor

PREFACE TO THE VOLUME

This is the first volume in the Modern Language Association Approaches to Teaching Masterpieces of World Literature series devoted to the work of a single author rather than to a single masterwork. Wordsworth does have his masterpiece, of course, and a volume given over entirely to *The Prelude* would not be out of place in the company of volumes on *The Canterbury Tales*, *The Divine Comedy*, and *Beowulf*. But Wordsworth is the poet of the *Lyrical Ballads* as well as of *The Prelude*, of "Tintern Abbey," the Immortality Ode, "Resolution and Independence," the Lucy poems, "I wandered lonely," "Elegiac Stanzas," "The Ruined Cottage," and scores of other lyric and narrative poems that have become part of the mainstream of undergraduate literary studies in this country and Canada. He is frequently taught as the representative English Romantic poet in introductory survey courses of English and world literature and as the central figure in upper-division surveys of Romantic poetry. He appears prominently in introductions to poetry, criticism courses, comparative literature courses, and specialized courses of every description. One contributor whose essay we were unable to include even uses Wordsworth's lyrics as texts for a remedial composition class. It seemed reasonable to devote a volume to Wordsworth's poetry in general and not to *The Prelude* alone.

This decision entailed certain consequences. Numerous essays would be required to do even minimal justice to the range of the poet's work and to the variety of pedagogical and critical perspectives that teachers bring to it. This requirement, in turn, would limit the space available to list editions, recommended readings, and teaching aids, as well as imposing restrictions of length on the essays themselves. Accordingly, the first part of the volume ("Materials"), which provides information on teaching and reference editions and on secondary readings for both students and instructors, has been kept comparatively short. It reflects the preferences of respondents to the questionnaire that preceded preparation of the volume, but it does not pretend to be a thorough bibliography. The second part of the volume ("Approaches") contains thirty essays of varying lengths, in which respondents to the questionnaire describe their approaches to teaching Wordsworth's poetry. A list of participants in the survey, a bibliography of works cited, and an index complete the volume.

The volume is directed to the beginning or nonspecialist undergraduate teacher. We hope, however, that even veterans and specialists will find parts of it useful. We should probably add that the selection and the arrangement of essays in the "Approaches" section have been influenced by a dissatisfaction with the conventional distinction between theory and praxis. The essays have been assembled in the belief that one of the most important challenges currently facing literary studies is to assimilate to the demands of undergraduate teaching the often highly specialized critical and historical interests of recent scholarship. Whereas much of the ground covered in the "Approaches" section will seem familiar to the general reader and will bear in fairly obvious ways on what happens (or can happen) in the classroom, some of this material may not be familiar, and its applicability to the classroom (at least to the teaching of undergraduates) may not seem immediate or direct. We hope readers (to echo Wordsworth) will "for themselves create" useful applications whenever such are not "created for them" and will keep in mind that critical and pedagogical disagreements, instead of being liabilities, can (switching now to Blake) "rouse the faculties to act."

We wish to thank the many participants in the Modern Language Association survey, whose commitment both to Wordsworth and to undergraduate teaching made this volume possible. We owe particular thanks to Joseph Gibaldi, general editor of the series, for his encouragement and helpful suggestions and to Beth Darlington and Carl Woodring for their thoughtful, informed, sometimes critical, and always relevant comments on the manuscript. We also wish to acknowledge with gratitude the Faculty Research Committee at Rhode Island College for its support of work on this project.

SH and JR

Part One

MATERIALS

Spencer Hall

Editions

Introduction

Modern editors and editing principles have served Wordsworth well, especially considering the number of his poems and the abundance and importance of his revisions over a long lifetime. Scrupulous editing has traced a history of Wordsworth texts revealing the poet's evolving epistemology, social and political perspectives, and style. Thus the standard editions often record the coexistence of phrases, passages, and entire texts that compete with one another for authority. These editions are generally too large, too expensive, and too specialized, however, to be assigned in the undergraduate classroom, even though more and more teachers have begun to explore Wordsworth's revisionary practices and to teach previously neglected poems.

In practice, the edition chosen by the teacher of undergraduates will depend on the class, and Wordsworth is taught in a wide variety of classes. One by no means atypical contributor to this volume says, "I use the Norton Anthology for freshman courses; Perkins's anthology for upper-division courses that are surveys; Stillinger's selection for more specialized courses. This current semester I am using Owen's edition of *Lyrical Ballads* and the Norton Critical Edition of *The Prelude.*" Presented below is a guide to the editions now used for teaching Wordsworth, as reported by respondents to the survey that preceded this volume. We have made no attempt to provide a complete list but have only noted the texts that respondents most frequently consult, require for class use, place on library reserve, and recommend to students.

These texts are divided into four categories: teaching editions of Wordsworth's poetry; teaching editions of individual works; anthologies; and standard reference editions. No out-of-print teaching editions or anthologies are included in the discussion that follows.

Teaching Editions: Selections and Collections

According to the survey, by far the most popular single-volume classroom edition of Wordsworth's poetry is Jack Stillinger's Riverside paperback *William Wordsworth: Selected Poems and Prefaces*. It was "enthusiastically recommended" by several respondents, one of whom described it as "more than ample, scrupulously edited, well-annotated." In particular, it was praised for its useful critical apparatus, which consists of a short introduction, a chronology, a map of the Lake District, and a large number of Wordsworth's own notes, as well as the editor's annotations and critical notes, which appear at the back of the volume. Stillinger's selection is quite generous: in addition to the entire *Prelude*, he includes most of the poems usually taught in undergraduate courses, many that are not often taught, and over fifty pages of Wordsworth's critical prefaces. Some respondents complained, however, that the edition is out of date and objected especially to Stillinger's editing of *The Prelude*, which involved, according to the editor (xviii), correcting and emending the 1850 version of the poem "in some eighty places mainly on the basis of manuscript readings." (All references to *The Prelude* in this volume, unless otherwise noted, are to the 1850 version.)

After the Riverside, the single-volume edition of Wordsworth's poetry most often mentioned by teachers was the Oxford Standard Authors paperback *Wordsworth: Poetical Works*, edited by Thomas Hutchinson and revised by Ernest de Selincourt. This volume has been for many years the most convenient collected edition of Wordsworth's poetry. The editors claim to have printed "every piece of original verse which we know to have been published by the poet himself, or of which he can be shown to have authorised the posthumous publication" (vii), as well as most of his voluminous notes, postscripts, and prefaces. There is also an extensive and informative chronology. The earlier versions of *The Prelude* and *The Recluse* are not included, since Wordsworth did not authorize their publication. Recent scholarship has rendered the Oxford edition out of date in a number of ways, and even those teachers who use it complain about its compressed two-column format, its "woefully small print," and its awkward arrangement of the poems (on this last point, see "Standard Reference Editions"). To quote one respondent: "I tried the Oxford complete edition for graduate students and hated it." According to another, however, "the advantages outweigh the disadvantages." Use of this edition seems pretty much restricted to graduate and to certain advanced undergraduate classes. A recent addition to the Oxford Authors series, Stephen Gill's *William Wordsworth*, which includes the 1805 version of *The Prelude*, may in time replace Hutchinson as a favored teaching edition.

Two other single-volume teaching editions of Wordsworth's poetry that have gained wide acceptance are Carlos Baker's Rinehart paperback *William Wordsworth: The Prelude and Selected Poems and Sonnets* and Mark Van Doren's Modern Library *William Wordsworth: Selected Poetry*. Van Doren's selection is extensive, including a number of lesser-known poems from Wordsworth's early and late periods, and is arranged chronologically, as the editor states, "to follow the story of one poet's development, high glory, and decline" (xiv). Baker's selection, which features *The Prelude* and a group of thirty-five sonnets, is less full, although it does include the most often taught poems and a good sampling of Wordsworth's critical prose. Both volumes are textually out of date, and neither Van Doren nor Baker provides notes or annotations to the poems. A third, more recent paperback teaching text is Geoffrey Hartman's *The Selected Poetry and Prose of Wordsworth*, which contains a valuable interpretive introduction, a fairly up-to-date select bibliography, annotations that appear on the page, and a few selections from Dorothy Wordsworth's *Grasmere Journal*. It also prints several works, both poetry and prose, found in no other selected edition, including recently established manuscript versions of "The Ruined Cottage" and "The Pedlar." A significant liability of the volume is that it heavily excerpts a number of the longer texts, most notably *The Prelude*.

Two recent collected editions of Wordsworth's poetry also deserve notice here, although neither is likely to be widely adopted in the undergraduate classroom. Both might be appropriate texts for graduate and for specialized undergraduate courses, however, and both could be important additions to a library reserve list. The Cambridge Edition of *The Poetical Works of Wordsworth*, revised by Paul D. Sheats, prints "all the poems Wordsworth chose to publish in the edition of 1849–50" (vii), plus *The Prelude* (in Stillinger's emended version) and *The Recluse*, the major critical essays, and Wordsworth's notes to the poems. Sheats has written a new introduction, revised both texts and editorial notes, updated the select bibliography, and included a useful chronology of the poems by date of composition.

John O. Hayden's two-volume paperback *William Wordsworth: The Poems* first appeared in England in the Penguin English Poets series. Because *The Prelude* occupies another volume in that series, it is the one work omitted from Hayden's collection. The poems are meticulously edited, with factual annotations and selections from Wordsworth's notes at the end of each volume, and are printed in a readable single-column format. Hayden places the poems by date of composition and includes a table of dates and a further reading section that lists editions, reference works, biographies, and selected criticism. The 1802 Preface to *Lyrical Ballads* is appended to volume 1, the Preface and Supplementary Essay to the 1815 edition of Wordsworth's *Poems* to volume 2.

Teaching Editions: Individual Works

A few respondents cited the need for inexpensive teaching editions of such works as the 1807 *Poems, in Two Volumes* and *The Excursion*. In practice, however, only two works are widely taught in separate editions: *Lyrical Ballads* and *The Prelude*. One teacher reported basing an entire undergraduate seminar on the former collection, while others reported teaching it as a self-contained, independent body of poems in courses on Wordsworth, on Romanticism, on literary theory, and on historically important poetry collections.

Two paperback teaching editions mentioned by respondents were R. L. Brett and A. R. Jones's *Lyrical Ballads: Wordsworth and Coleridge* and W. J. B. Owen's *Wordsworth and Coleridge*: Lyrical Ballads *1798*. Brett and Jones print both the 1798 and the 1800 editions of *Lyrical Ballads* (the latter contains a second volume consisting of thirty-seven new poems) and the variant readings of the 1802 and 1805 editions. Owen prints the twenty-three poems in the original edition of 1798 only. Both editions include useful biographical and critical introductions, moderately extensive notes and annotations, somewhat dated select bibliographies, and the Preface to the 1800 *Lyrical Ballads* with variants from the 1802 Preface in footnotes. Brett and Jones also include Wordsworth's Appendix on poetic diction from the 1802 edition and a representative sampling of contemporary responses and criticism.

The Prelude is, of course, Wordsworth's masterpiece. It is a work so rich in its own right, so influential on modern critical theory, and so protean that teachers often make it the focus of graduate and undergraduate seminars in the Romantic period and of specialized courses on such topics as the long poem, autobiography, and psychoanalytical approaches to literature. Many teachers in Romantic survey courses also supplement their anthologies with a complete edition of *The Prelude*.

The overwhelming choice for a teaching text among respondents to the survey was the Norton Critical Edition paperback *William Wordsworth:* The Prelude, *1799, 1805, 1850*, edited by Jonathan Wordsworth, M. H. Abrams, and Stephen Gill. Despite a few reservations about its being "biased, and sometimes inaccurate in its glosses," this volume has gained wide acceptance as a standard classroom edition. It gives readable, up-to-date, and accurate texts of the 1799, 1805, and 1850 versions of *The Prelude* (the latter two on facing pages), manuscript drafts and fragments from 1798 to 1804, a succinct textual history, copious and informative notes placed on the page, a chronology of Wordsworth's life, and a select bibliography. In addition, the editors print a number of representative nineteenth-century responses to the poem, as well as seven modern critical essays by Jonathan Wordsworth, M. H. Abrams, Geoffrey Hartman, Richard Onorato, William Empson, Herbert Lindenberger, and W. B. Gallie.

Another classroom edition mentioned by respondents was J. C. Maxwell's paperback *William Wordsworth:* The Prelude, *A Parallel Text*, first published in the Penguin English Poets series. "The purpose of this edition," according to Maxwell, "is to offer, in a form which will make comparison as easy as possible, the two main texts of *The Prelude*"—the 1805 and the 1850 (23). The two versions are printed on facing pages with rather cursory annotations at the end and a short textual introduction. The 1805 *Prelude* is also available by itself in the Oxford Paperbacks series, edited by Ernest de

Selincourt and corrected by Stephen Gill. This volume features a wide-ranging, informative introduction and extensive notes.

Perhaps because of the current interest in critical theory, Wordsworth's critical prose is being taught more and more in the undergraduate classroom. The most frequently cited teaching edition is Paul M. Zall's paperback *Literary Criticism of William Wordsworth*. Zall prints, with annotations on the page, the 1798 Advertisement and the 1800 and 1802 prefaces to *Lyrical Ballads*, the Preface and Supplementary Essay to the 1815 *Poems*, the "Essays upon Epitaphs," Wordsworth's prefaces and notes to several poems, and selected letters bearing on critical topics. Feminist studies have also increased interest on the undergraduate level in the relations between Wordsworth's poetry and his sister's journals. *Journals of Dorothy Wordsworth*, edited by Mary Moorman for the Oxford Paperbacks series, is a convenient text for those who wish to explore these relations, although it does not include all the journals.

Anthologies

Teachers differ about anthologies—about which texts should be included; about the number, character, and placement of notes; about the value of excerpting longer works. The respondents to the survey were no exception. At one extreme was the judgment that "no anthology has been satisfactory," and some teachers who use anthologies appear to rely heavily on the ditto machine to supplement the Wordsworth selections. For the most part, however, respondents found the available anthologies at least "adequate" (this word appeared again and again) to their needs. As one noted, most of the anthologies "include what I teach." Among the texts they would like to see included more often, respondents mentioned a greater number of early works—including the newly edited early versions of "The Ruined Cottage" and "Home at Grasmere"—and, in particular, parallel passages from the 1805 and 1850 versions of *The Prelude*. *The Borderers, Peter Bell, The White Doe of Rylstone*, the *Yarrow Revisited* poems, and the *River Duddon* sonnets were also mentioned as deserving more attention from anthologists, as were Wordsworth's poems on solitaries and the early drafts of poems normally given only in later, revised versions.

It would be impossible to list here all the anthologies in which Wordsworth is represented or all the kinds of courses in which they are used. Two courses, to which Wordsworth's poetry is central, however, appear, mutatis mutandis, in most English curricula across the country. One is the lower-division introductory survey of English literature, taken for general education credit or as part of the English major. The other is the upper-division Romantic survey for English majors.

Since the former course is often referred to as the *"Norton* survey," it should come as no surprise that the vast majority of respondents teaching it use volume 2 of *The Norton Anthology of English Literature*, the Romantic section edited by M. H. Abrams, who is also the general editor. Remarks on the Wordsworth portion of the *Norton Anthology* were generally favorable. Teachers praised Abrams's introductions and found the notes, which are printed on the bottom of the page, helpful without being oppressive. The *Norton* was also called responsive to recent developments in Wordsworth studies and textually up-to-date. Several respondents cited, for example, Abrams's decision to print the two-part *Prelude* (in addition to ample excerpts from the 1850 *Prelude*, also freshly edited by Jonathan Wordsworth) and "The Ruined Cottage," as well as a comparatively generous selection from Dorothy's journals. Others did object, however, to the omission of such traditional teaching favorites as "The Old Cumberland Beggar," "The Thorn," and "Anecdote for Fathers." Given the limitations of a collection spanning two centuries, the Wordsworth selection is substantial, although there is scant representation from the pre-1798 and post-1807 periods (the 1850 *Prelude* excepted). Abrams also includes the Preface to *Lyrical Ballads*.

Other anthologies that teachers reported using in the English literature survey or in comparable lower-division introductory surveys included the *Romantic Poetry and Prose* volume of *The Oxford Anthology of English Literature*, edited by Harold Bloom and Lionel Trilling; volume two of *The Norton Anthology of World Masterpieces*, the Romanticism section edited by Howard E. Hugo, with Maynard Mack as general editor; and *The Norton Anthology of English Literature: Third Major Authors Edition*, edited by M. H. Abrams. Volume two of Macmillan's *Literature of the Western World*, edited by Brian Wilkie and James Hurt, prints several of the best-known lyrics and substantial portions of *The Prelude*.

In the upper-division Romantic survey, a number of teachers devote more time to Wordsworth than to any other Romantic poet, using him as a focus for the course as a whole. The preferred anthology among respondents was David Perkins's *English Romantic Writers*. Perkins's selection is generous, including poems from all periods of Wordsworth's career, while emphasizing the work of 1798–1807. He prints fourteen poems from the original (1798) *Lyrical Ballads*; parts of thirteen of the 1850 *Prelude*'s fourteen books, with books 1, 2, and 4 entire; a large number of sonnets; book 1 of *The Excursion*, with excerpts from books 2, 3, and 4; the Preface to *Lyrical Ballads*, with the Appendix on poetic diction, an excerpt from the Preface to the 1815 *Poems*, and the Essay Supplementary to the 1815 Preface; and eight letters of Wordsworth and his family. There are also selections from Dorothy's Grasmere journal and comments on Wordsworth by such nineteenth-century figures as Francis Jeffrey, H. D. Rawnsley, Henry Taylor, and Thomas

Carlyle. Perkins's introductions to the Romantic period, to Wordsworth, and to specific poems were generally praised, although some teachers found his annotations to be few in number and unhelpful to students in understanding difficult passages. The Wordsworth bibliography is out of date.

Three other Romantic anthologies mentioned by respondents were Russell Noyes's *English Romantic Poetry and Prose*, William Heath's *Major British Poets of the Romantic Period*, and John L. Mahoney's *The English Romantics: Major Poetry and Critical Theory*. Noyes gives more extensive critical apparatus than does Perkins and prints more works from Wordsworth's later period. His selections from *The Prelude* and the prose are not as extensive, however, and the more than twenty-five years since its publication have severely dated the volume both critically and textually.

Whereas Perkins and especially Noyes seek to cover the Romantic period in depth by including selections from a number of secondary authors, Heath and Mahoney include only the six major Romantic poets (plus, in the case of Mahoney, a selection of Hazlitt's criticism). Heath's anthology is particularly noteworthy for the extensiveness of the Wordsworth selections. He prints the poet's contributions to the first edition of *Lyrical Ballads* as a unit and gives *The Prelude* and "The Ruined Cottage" entire, as well as complete texts of such less frequently taught long poems as *Peter Bell*, "Home at Grasmere," and *The White Doe of Rylstone*. He also prints over thirty-five sonnets and a significant number of Wordsworth's later poems. Prose works include the Preface to *Lyrical Ballads*, "Essays upon Epitaphs," and several letters.

Mahoney's Wordsworth selections are much less extensive and are directed toward a less specialized undergraduate audience. They include, among other texts, the Preface to *Lyrical Ballads*; seven poems from the original *Lyrical Ballads*; books 1, 2, 11, 12, and 14 of *The Prelude* entire, with excerpts from several other books; and book 1 of *The Excursion*. A major feature of the anthology is the inclusion of selected modern critical essays; the four on Wordsworth are by David Perkins, Douglas Bush, Willard Sperry, and Robert Langbaum. Only Mahoney's, among the Romantic anthologies, is available in paper.

Standard Reference Editions

Thomas Hutchinson's *Wordsworth: Poetical Works*, Paul D. Sheats's *The Poetical Works of Wordsworth*, and John O. Hayden's *William Wordsworth: The Poems* have already been mentioned under "Teaching Editions." While Hutchinson's is probably still the most often consulted complete edition of the poetry, the standard edition remains *The Poetical Works of William Wordsworth*, edited by Ernest de Selincourt and Helen Darbishire. This five-volume collection of poems, notes (historical, biographical, bibliographical, and critical), variant passages, and the poet's own comments and major prefaces is still invaluable to the teacher and to advanced students, even though several decades of Wordsworth studies have dated both its scholarship and its texts. A difficulty in using this edition—one shared by the Hutchinson volume—is that it preserves the arrangement of the poems in the collected edition of 1849–50. Although this arrangement reflects Wordsworth's own choice in the last edition he saw through the press, many teachers find that it is cumbersome for students, that it blurs the actual chronology of composition, and that it imposes misleading thematic and critical categories on the poet's work. *The Prelude*, published posthumously, is not included in the five volumes but was edited separately by de Selincourt and revised by Darbishire. Generally considered the standard edition until the appearance of the Norton *Prelude*, this volume prints both the 1805 and 1850 versions of the poem, accompanied by an extensive and valuable critical apparatus.

A number of teachers, especially those who incorporate early drafts and textual revisions in their teaching, report using the Cornell Wordsworth, a series of editions of the longer poems published by Cornell University Press under the general editorship of Stephen Parrish. These editions are models of the most informed editorial practices and provide a wealth of research opportunities for serious students, particularly on the graduate level. At the same time, they can prove intimidating to many undergraduates, majors and nonmajors alike. Each volume includes a reading text prepared from the available manuscripts and the editions published in Wordsworth's lifetime, photographic reproductions or facsimiles of the manuscript material, and an informative editorial and biographical introduction. Volumes in the series already published include *The Salisbury Plain Poems*, edited by Stephen Gill; *Home at Grasmere*, edited by Beth Darlington; The Prelude, *1798–1799*, edited by Stephen Parrish (this is the two-part *Prelude* first published in the 1974 edition of *The Norton Anthology*); "*The Ruined Cottage*" *and* "*The Pedlar*," edited by James Butler; *Benjamin the Waggoner*, edited by Paul F. Betz; *The Borderers*, edited by Robert Osborn; Poems, in Two Volumes, *and Other Poems, 1800–1807*, edited by Jared Curtis; *An Evening Walk*, edited by James Averill; and *Descriptive Sketches*, edited by Eric Birdsall. Several other volumes are in production as of this writing.

The standard edition of Wordsworth's prose is *The Prose Works of William Wordsworth*, edited in three volumes by W. J. B. Owen and Jane Worthington Smyser. Encouraged by the availability of accurate and well-annotated texts, teachers have begun to assign Wordsworth's noncritical prose with some frequency. Works such as the "Letter to the Bishop of Llandaff," "The Criminal Mind," and *The Convention of Cintra* offer interesting research possibilities for advanced undergraduate and graduate students. (Gordon Thomas's paperback facsimile edition of *The Convention of Cintra* makes this important political document easily available.) Owen has also done a reference edition of the Preface to *Lyrical Ballads* and has edited *Wordsworth's Literary Criticism*, a collection of the poet's critical texts culled from the three-volume *Prose Works*.

The preferred edition of Wordsworth's letters is de Selincourt's six-volume *The Letters of William and Dorothy Wordsworth*, revised (so far through 1839) by Chester Shaver, Mary Moorman, and Alan G. Hill. Hill has also edited two useful paperback volumes, *The Letters of Dorothy Wordsworth: A Selection* and *The Letters of William Wordsworth: A New Selection*. Beth Darlington's *The Love Letters of William and Mary Wordsworth* chronicles a neglected side of the poet that can make him more "human"—and thus more accessible—to many students. The standard edition of Dorothy's journals is de Selincourt's two-volume *Journals of Dorothy Wordsworth*. De Selincourt's text of the important Grasmere journals has been revised by successive editors, however, and is less accurate than the one printed in Moorman's paperback edition already mentioned.

Readings for Students and Teachers

Introduction

Specialists in Wordsworth and the Romantic period will find many omissions in the following list of readings. Nonspecialists may well find the list too long as it is. Our aim is neither completeness nor a scrupulous selectivity. Rather, we seek to present a limited yet representative listing of important titles for the study and teaching of Wordsworth that reflects as accurately as possible the results of the survey that preceded this volume. With a few exceptions, we have excluded articles that do not appear in book-length collections. We have also avoided detailed evaluative and descriptive comments, preferring simply to identify those works that teachers of Wordsworth most often use themselves, recommend to students, and suggest to colleagues. Finally, we have tried to mention some studies that are still too recent to have been used widely but that have already begun to influence the teaching of Wordsworth's poetry. In no sense, however, should this effort be taken as a thorough review of recent scholarship in the field.

Readers are encouraged to consult more detailed bibliographies and reviews of criticism and to explore the wealth of current Wordsworth studies appearing in such scholarly journals as *PMLA*, *Studies in Romanticism*, *Romanticism: Past and Present*, *ELH*, *Studies in English Literature*, *Criticism*, *New Literary History*, *Modern Language Quarterly*, *Studies in Philology*, and *English Language Notes*. Students and teachers are particularly encouraged to consider the reviews and articles published quarterly in the *Wordsworth Circle*, edited by Marilyn Gaull. The Autumn 1978 issue (9.4), guest edited by John T. Ogden, contains thirty-one short essays on teaching Wordsworth. We recommend that it be consulted in conjunction with the present volume.

The "Readings for Students and Teachers" section below is divided into the following categories: reference works, recommended student readings, Romantic contexts, and studies of Wordsworth. The distinction between "Romantic Contexts" and "Studies of Wordsworth" is largely one of convenience. For instance, we have placed in the former category book-length studies that examine several Romantic poets, including Wordsworth, reserving to the latter full-length studies devoted entirely or primarily to Wordsworth. Readers interested in particular topics or approaches should consult both categories, as well as the titles listed under "Recommended Student Readings."

Reference Works

The vast range of critical, historical, and biographical materials pertaining to Wordsworth has been thoroughly surveyed by scholars in the field. The first two volumes of Donald H. Reiman's nine-volume series, *The Romantics Reviewed: Contemporary Reviews of British Romantic Writers*, reprint nearly "all contemporary British periodical reviews of the first (or other significant early) editions from 1793 to 1824" of works by Wordsworth (1:xxxi). N. S. Bauer's *William Wordsworth: A Reference Guide to British Criticism, 1793–1899* provides an annotated guide to Wordsworth criticism in the nineteenth century. James V. Logan's *Wordsworthian Criticism: A Guide and Bibliography* reviews major tendencies in Wordsworth studies and gives a bibliography of criticism for the period 1850–1944. Elton F. Henley and David H. Stam's *Wordsworthian Criticism 1945–1964* and Stam's *Wordsworthian Criticism 1964–1973* continue Logan's work in a more detailed and comprehensive manner. A more selective bibliography offering a narrative assessment of Wordsworth scholarship (mainly in the twentieth century) is *The English Romantic Poets: A Review of Research and Criticism*, edited by Frank Jordan, Jr. The chapters on the Romantic movement and Wordsworth give useful summaries of modern scholarship and criticism. R. H. Fogle's *Romantic Poets and Prose Writers* is a selective, unannotated bibliography meant for use by students.

Annotated bibliographies of Wordsworth and the Romantic period have appeared annually in *ELH* from 1937 to 1949, in *Philological Quarterly* from 1950 to 1964, in *English Language Notes* from 1965 to 1978, and after 1978 as *The Romantic Movement: A Selective and Critical Bibliography*, edited by David Erdman and others and published as separate volumes in the Garland Reference Library for the Humanities. The annual *MLA International Bibliography* is relatively complete but attempts no annotations, while *The Year's Work in English Studies* provides commentary. Reviews of major Wordsworth and Romantic studies also appear in the Autumn issue of *Studies in English Literature* and in the Summer issue of the *Wordsworth Circle*.

The chronology of events in Wordsworth's life and the dates of composition of his works can be crucial in interpreting and teaching his poetry. It is not surprising, therefore, that several respondents called Mark L. Reed's chronologies "indispensable": *Wordsworth: The Chronology of the Early Years, 1770–1799* and *Wordsworth: The Chronology of the Middle Years, 1800–1815*. Lane Cooper's *A Concordance to the Poems of William Wordsworth* is still in use, although it is keyed to outdated editions of the poetry.

Finally, there are major American library collections of Wordsworth materials at Cornell and Indiana universities. Publications reviewing the holdings of these collections can be consulted as a source of bibliography on the poet.

Recommended Student Readings

According to the survey, many teachers do not require and some may even discourage the use of secondary materials in undergraduate classes. To quote one respondent: "If students wish to do critical reading or undertake term projects on Wordsworth, I help them locate material. For the most part, I hold them responsible for primary reading, and I try to do the critical reading for them." According to another, "the sheer weight of substantive matter to be covered" and "the everpresent problem of simply teaching students to read" make the requirement of critical or background studies impractical. Whether to assign secondary texts at all—not just which ones to assign— would seem an open pedagogical question for a number of undergraduate teachers today.

The secondary work most frequently recommended to students by respondents is Coleridge's *Biographia Literaria*. Chapters 4, 14, 17-20, and 22 discuss and evaluate Wordsworth's poetic theories and style with particular reference to the *Lyrical Ballads*. Whether or not Coleridge's remarks constitute, as has often been claimed, the best introduction to Wordsworth ever written, they raise issues central to the poetry and are particularly stimulating in classroom situations where the Wordsworth-Coleridge "symbiosis" can be studied in some depth. The new one-volume paperback edition of the *Biographia*, edited by James Engell and Walter Jackson Bate, should facilitate such study for students and teachers alike.

Many teachers, it would seem, are more apt to ask undergraduates to read individual articles or collections of essays than full-length critical studies. Two collections of essays edited by M. H. Abrams, *English Romantic Poets* and *Wordsworth*, were mentioned frequently and will be discussed further in later sections. A number of influential essays on Wordsworth and Romantic poetry have been collected in various anthologies of criticism (see the listings of such anthologies at the end of the "Romantic Contexts" and "Studies of Wordsworth" sections). Among the most important categories of essays are those that help place Wordsworth in the literary, historical, and intellectual contexts of Romanticism; those that focus on the poet's responses to nature and his use of nature imagery; and those that explore his concepts of mind and imagination.

Lionel Trilling's "The Immortality Ode" (with which students might compare Helen Vendler's counterstatement "Lionel Trilling and the 'Immortality Ode' ") was the single essay most often mentioned by respondents. Others frequently recommended to students include Frederick A. Pottle's "The Eye and the Object in the Poetry of Wordsworth"; W. K. Wimsatt's "The Structure of Romantic Nature Imagery"; Northrop Frye's "The Drunken Boat: The Revolutionary Element in Romanticism"; Morse Peckham's "Toward a

Theory of Romanticism" and "Toward a Theory of Romanticism: II. Reconsiderations"; Geoffrey Hartman's "Romanticism and Antiself-consciousness" and "A Poet's Progress: Wordsworth and the *Via naturaliter negativa*"; Harold Bloom's "The Internalization of Quest-Romance"; Paul de Man's "Intentional Structure of the Romantic Image" and "Symbolic Landscape in Wordsworth and Yeats"; and M. H. Abrams's "English Romanticism: The Spirit of the Age," "Structure and Style in the Greater Romantic Lyric," and "The Correspondent Breeze: A Romantic Metaphor" (the last three, as well as other seminal essays by Abrams on Wordsworth and Coleridge, are collected in *The Correspondent Breeze: Essays on English Romanticism*).

Of course, many teachers do require or at least strongly recommend that undergraduates consult full-length studies of Wordsworth and the Romantic period. The book most often mentioned in this regard was M. H. Abrams's *Natural Supernaturalism: Tradition and Revolution in Romantic Literature*, which uses Wordsworth as one paradigm for exploring the Romantic investiture of history, literature, and the psychological development of the individual with many of the sacramental values, apocalyptic expectations, and ritual processes associated with biblical tradition. Also mentioned frequently was Harold Bloom's *The Visionary Company: A Reading of English Romantic Poetry*, which is recommended to students for its stimulating, if difficult and sometimes controversial, readings of major Wordsworthian texts.

Numerous book-length studies of Wordsworth's poetry were cited in the survey, some once only, some repeatedly. Those put in students' hands most frequently are Geoffrey Hartman's *Wordsworth's Poetry, 1787–1814*, Mary Moorman's two-volume *William Wordsworth: A Biography*, Carl Woodring's *Wordsworth*, John Danby's *The Simple Wordsworth: Studies in the Poems, 1797–1807*, Herbert Lindenberger's *On Wordsworth's Prelude*, and David Ferry's *The Limits of Mortality*. These works will be considered again in the "Studies of Wordsworth" section. We will note here only that Woodring's *Wordsworth* is a fairly brief, general introduction suitable for the nonspecialist reader. Two other general introductions that might be particularly helpful to beginning students are Helen Darbishire's *The Poet Wordsworth* and Geoffrey Durrant's *William Wordsworth*.

Romantic Contexts

Most teachers would agree that any presentation of Wordsworth, even the discussion of a few poems in one or two sessions of a general survey, should draw on a knowledge of larger Romantic contexts. Accordingly, we list here general studies of Romantic poetry and its backgrounds, as well as more specialized studies of particular trends, topics, and themes that respondents felt were especially relevant to teaching Wordsworth's poetry.

The most frequently cited general study of Romanticism, M. H. Abrams's *Natural Supernaturalism*, has already been noted under "Recommended Student Readings." Another classic work by Abrams, *The Mirror and the Lamp: Romantic Theory and the Critical Tradition*, helps define Wordsworth's pivotal role in English literary history while tracing the shift in eighteenth-century aesthetics, from mimetic and pragmatic to expressive theories of poetry. Four other time-honored studies of eighteenth-century aesthetic, intellectual, and cultural movements associated with the rise of Romanticism also deserve mention here: Samuel H. Monk's *The Sublime: A Study of Critical Theories in Eighteenth-Century England*, A. O. Lovejoy's *The Great Chain of Being*, Basil Willey's *The Eighteenth Century Background*, and Walter Jackson Bate's *From Classic to Romantic: Premises of Taste in Eighteenth-Century England*.

The social background of Romantic poetry, a subject of particular importance to Wordsworth's theory and practice in *Lyrical Ballads* and elsewhere, is explored from differing perspectives in Raymond Williams's *Culture and Society, 1780–1950*, A. D. Harvey's *English Poetry in a Changing Society, 1780–1825*, and Marilyn Butler's *Romantics, Rebels, and Revolutionaries: English Literature and Its Background, 1760–1830*. Among the standard histories of the period, G. M. Trevelyan's *British History of the Nineteenth Century* and *English Social History* are still recommended frequently. More recent general and social histories include two works in Putnam's English Life series—E. Neville Williams's *Life in Georgian England* and R. J. White's *Life in Regency England*—as well as Asa Briggs's *The Age of Improvement, 1783–1867*, E. J. Hobsbawm's *The Age of Revolution 1789–1848*, and Robert K. Webb's *Modern England: From the Eighteenth Century to the Present*.

E. P. Thompson's *The Making of the English Working Class* is extremely valuable for the social background of English Romanticism generally and of Wordsworth's poetry in particular. C. W. Crawley's *War and Peace in an Age of Upheaval, 1793–1830* in the New Cambridge Modern History is a convenient source for students interested in the history of the period, while Carl Woodring's *Politics in English Romantic Poetry* is a thorough survey of the subject that helps clarify both the liberal and the conservative elements in Wordsworth's thought.

Several collections of scholarly essays and primary materials illuminate the historical, social, and literary backgrounds of Romanticism and relate Wordsworth's poetry to its cultural and intellectual milieu. Among them are *Backgrounds of Romanticism*, edited by Leonard Trawick; *Backgrounds to British Romantic Literature*, edited by Karl Kroeber; *The Evidence of the Imagination: Studies of Interactions between Life and Art in English Romantic Literature*, edited by Donald H. Reiman, Michael C. Jaye, and Betty D. Bennett; and *The Romantics: The Context of English Literature*, edited by Stephen Prickett.

Although on one level Wordsworth consciously sought to demythologize contemporary poetry, he participated fully, even centrally, in the myth-making activities so characteristic of the Romantic mode. The use, presence, and nature of myth in Romantic poetry are approached from different angles in Douglas Bush's *Mythology and the Romantic Tradition in English Poetry*, Northrop Frye's *A Study of English Romanticism*, Harold Bloom's *The Visionary Company*, and Abrams's *Natural Supernaturalism*. Closely related to its mythopoeic tendencies are the essential patterns of imagery and symbolism in the poetry of Wordsworth and other Romantic writers. These patterns have been studied closely, with revealing insights into theme and structure, in such works as G. Wilson Knight's *The Starlit Dome: Studies in the Poetry of Vision*, David Perkins's *The Quest for Permanence: The Symbolism of Wordsworth, Shelley, and Keats*, and Albert Gérard's *English Romantic Poetry: Ethos, Structure, and Symbol in Coleridge, Wordsworth, Shelley, and Keats*.

Respondents identified several major topics as particularly important to their teaching of Wordsworth. Foremost among these were the interrelated concepts of nature and imagination. Virtually every critical study of Romantic poetry takes up these ideas in one way or another, but certain works approach them from a historical and philosophical point of view, thus providing a context for teaching and interpretation. Although outdated in some ways, Joseph Warren Beach's *The Concept of Nature in Nineteenth-Century English Poetry* is still referred to frequently, as are H. W. Piper's *The Active Universe: Pantheism and the Concept of Imagination in the English Romantic Poets* and Ernest Tuveson's *The Imagination as a Means of Grace: Locke and the Aesthetics of Romanticism*. Two often-cited recent studies are Thomas Weiskel's *The Romantic Sublime: Studies in the Structure and Psychology of Transcendence* and James Engell's *The Creative Imagination: Enlightenment to Romanticism*.

Two other topics that respondents found crucial were the Romantics' transformation of epic forms (with particular reference, of course, to Milton) and relations between Romantic poetry and modern literature. Karl Kroeber's *Romantic Narrative Art*, Brian Wilkie's *Romantic Poets and Epic Tradition*, Thomas Vogler's *Preludes to Vision: The Epic Venture in Blake, Wordsworth, Keats, and Hart Crane*, and Leslie Brisman's *Milton's Poetry of Choice and Its Romantic Heirs* are especially useful in teaching *The Prelude*.

Among the studies of continuities between Romantic and modern literature that illuminate Wordsworth, viewing him often as the originator of characteristically modern poetic forms, are John Bayley's *The Romantic Survival: A Study of Poetic Evolution*, Robert Langbaum's *The Poetry of Experience: The Dramatic Monologue in Modern Literary Tradition* and *The Modern Spirit: Essays on the Continuity of Nineteenth and Twentieth Cen-*

tury Literature, Frank Kermode's *Romantic Image,* and Harold Bloom's *The Ringers in the Tower: Studies in Romantic Tradition* and *Poetry and Repression: Revisionism from Blake to Stevens.* Two recent works that place Wordsworth in nineteenth- and twentieth-century traditions of literary self-presentation from different theoretical perspectives are Philip Davis's *Memory and Writing: From Wordsworth to Lawrence* and Paul Jay's *Being in the Text: Self-Representation from Wordsworth to Roland Barthes.*

Contemporary literary studies have shown a passionate intensity about theory, and this passion has been evidenced nowhere more intensely than in the field of Romantic literature. Wordsworth's poetry, like that of the other English Romantics, is currently being reexamined through the "terministic screens" of various theoretical perspectives, and this process has obvious pedagogical implications. It would be possible to compile a rather long list of theoretically oriented readings of Wordsworth and Romantic poetry. Instead, we shall mention just two approaches that are gaining acceptance in the undergraduate classroom.

The phenomenon of literary influence, conceived especially as an anxiety about poetic origins and the creation of poetic self-identity, has become a pervasive theme in Romantic studies, in part because of works like Walter Jackson Bate's *The Burden of the Past and the English Poet,* Leslie Brisman's *Romantic Origins,* and Harold Bloom's *The Anxiety of Influence: A Theory of Poetry* and *Poetry and Repression.* Wordsworth himself, of course, is often seen as the major "burden" or source of anxiety for the younger generation of Romantic writers.

Probably the most controversial recent approach to Romantic poetry is that associated with the theory of deconstructionism. While books like Michael Cooke's *The Romantic Will* and *Acts of Inclusion* reaffirm in new ways the engagement with being and the will toward unity in Romantic discourse, others—such as Thomas McFarland's *Romanticism and the Forms of Ruin: Wordsworth, Coleridge, and the Modalities of Fragmentation,* Tilottama Rajan's *Dark Interpreter: The Discourse of Romanticism,* and *Deconstruction and Criticism,* edited by Harold Bloom and others—challenge more familiar "organicist" interpretations. New considerations of the old topic of Romantic irony—Anne Mellor's *English Romantic Irony* and David Simpson's *Irony and Authority in Romantic Poetry,* for example—also bring into question in different ways the values of wholeness and determinacy in Romantic theory and practice.

What has been called by some the current "tyranny of theory" has begun to call forth "antitheoretical" (or at least antipoststructuralist) historical and philosophical reconsiderations of Romantic literature. We can mention in this context John Clubbe and Ernest Lovell's *English Romanticism: The Grounds of Belief,* Jerome McGann's *The Romantic Ideology: A Critical*

Investigation, and Peter Thorslev's *Romantic Contraries: Freedom versus Destiny*.

As one might expect, respondents tended not to recommend the neohumanist and New Critical polemics against Romantic literary and philosophical values that profoundly influenced both criticism and pedagogy earlier in this century. Edward Bostetter's *The Romantic Ventriloquists: Wordsworth, Coleridge, Keats, Shelley, and Byron* was cited, however, more for its insights into Wordsworth's poetry than for its neohumanist point of view.

Finally, students and instructors can turn to a number of critical anthologies devoted to Romantic poetry for interpretation of specific texts, approaches to individual poets, and perspectives on the period as a whole. The anthology recommended most often both for its scope and for its relevance to Wordsworth was M. H. Abrams's *English Romantic Poets: Modern Essays in Criticism*. The collection includes such seminal articles on Romanticism as A. O. Lovejoy's "On the Discrimination of Romanticisms," W. K. Wimsatt's "The Structure of Romantic Nature Imagery," and Abrams's "The Correspondent Breeze: A Romantic Metaphor," as well as a number of important essays on Wordsworth: Basil Willey's "On Wordsworth and the Locke Tradition," Geoffrey Hartman's "Nature and the Humanization of the Self in Wordsworth," Paul Sheats's "The *Lyrical Ballads*," Lionel Trilling's "The Immortality Ode," and Jonathan Wordsworth's "Wordsworth's *Borderers*." Harold Bloom's *Romanticism and Consciousness: Essays in Criticism* was also recommended highly, especially by teachers who see the problem of consciousness and self-consciousness as a determinant concern in Romantic literature. Other cited collections include *Romanticism Reconsidered*, edited by Northrop Frye; *Romanticism: Points of View*, edited by Robert F. Gleckner and Gerald E. Enscoe; *The Major English Romantic Poets*, edited by Clarence Thorpe, Carlos Baker, and Bennett Weaver; *British Romantic Poets: Recent Revaluations*, edited by Shiv K. Kumar; and *From Sensibility to Romanticism*, edited by Frederick Hilles and Harold Bloom. We should also mention here Morse Peckham's and M. H. Abrams's collections of their own wide-ranging essays, *The Triumph of Romanticism* and *The Correspondent Breeze*.

Studies of Wordsworth

We can list here only a few of the many full-length studies of Wordsworth's poetry available to the undergraduate teacher. Our checklist has been guided, as throughout the "Materials" section, by the responses to the questionnaire preceding this volume. According to those responses, the ten critical works that teachers themselves consult most often in preparing classes on Wordsworth and that they recommend most highly to other teachers are Hartman's *Wordsworth's Poetry*, Moorman's two-volume *William Wordsworth*, Lindenberger's *On Wordsworth's* Prelude, Ferry's *The Limits of Mortality*, Woodring's *Wordsworth*, Paul Sheats's *The Making of Wordsworth's Poetry, 1785–1798*, Richard Onorato's *The Character of the Poet: Wordsworth in* The Prelude, David Perkins's *Wordsworth and the Poetry of Sincerity*, Raymond Dexter Havens's two-part *The Mind of a Poet: A Study of Wordsworth's Thought*, and Frances Ferguson's *Wordsworth: Language as Counter-Spirit*. The first five of these works, it will be noted, are also among those most often recommended to students.

Although its arguments and interpretations can be difficult, especially for the nonspecialist, Hartman's *Wordsworth's Poetry* has probably exerted as profound an influence on Wordsworth studies as any work of criticism published in the last quarter century. It explores the poet's epistemology, his problematical relation to nature, and his concept of imagination, defining the latter as "consciousness of self raised to apocalyptic pitch" (17). Ferry's *The Limits of Mortality* has also proved an influential book. It examines, through sensitive readings of *The Prelude* and the shorter lyrics, the conflict between human mortality and nature's seeming permanence and the poet's varied responses to this conflict. The symbolism of death and the "epitaphic mode" in Wordsworth's poetry are also major concerns in Ferguson's *Wordsworth: Language as Counter-Spirit*. Using the "Essays upon Epitaphs" as a basis, Ferguson explores the discontinuities in Wordsworth's theory of language and finds the act of reading itself a primary theme in his work.

Moorman's *William Wordsworth* is a thorough, reliable biography that makes extensive use of *The Prelude*, as well as of the letters and journals of the Wordsworth circle, to reconstruct and to interpret the poet's life and work. Volume 1 covers the period 1770–1803, volume 2 the period 1803–50. Woodring's *Wordsworth* provides an informative general introduction to the poetry and the life, along with careful exegeses of individual texts. Perkins's *Wordsworth and the Poetry of Sincerity* is also an informative and comprehensive study that analyzes major lyrics and *The Prelude* in the light of eighteenth-century and Romantic assumptions about rhetoric, language, and the relation of poet to audience. Paul Sheats's *The Making of Wordsworth's Poetry* examines the poet's early literary attachments and follows the gradual establishment of his poetic voice. Sheats's detailed and serious attention to works such as "Guilt and Sorrow," *The Borderers*, "Descriptive Sketches," and "An Evening Walk " is indicative of a growing interest in Wordsworth's early, pre–*Lyrical Ballads* poetry.

The three studies of *The Prelude* mentioned above differ greatly from one another in critical approach and style. That all three appear among the ten most often cited titles confirms the importance of Wordsworth's masterpiece in the undergraduate classroom. Part 1 of Havens's *The Mind of a Poet*, titled "A Study of Wordsworth's Thought," discusses a number of central philosophical issues applicable to the poetry in general but relating primarily to *The Prelude*. Part 2 is a detailed, book-by-book commentary, including an abundance of now partially outdated biographical and historical annotations, on both the 1805 and 1850 versions of the poem. Onorato's *The Character of the Poet* employs more recent biographical information and a psychoanalytic methodology to trace the largely unconscious processes of character formation revealed in the poem. Unlike many psychoanalytic studies, the book is noteworthy for its sensitive responses to "literary" qualities of tone and style. Lindenberger's innovative and wide-ranging *On Wordsworth's* Prelude takes up the poem from different, sometimes mutually corrective critical perspectives. Principal among these are considerations of *The Prelude*'s language, of its structure and "time-consciousness," of its social values, and of its place in literary history.

Two substantial introductions to Wordsworth's life and poetry, by Danby and Darbishire, were cited in "Recommended Student Readings." Other frequently recommended studies include John Jones's *The Egotistical Sublime: A History of Wordsworth's Imagination*, F. W. Bateson's *Wordsworth: A Reinterpretation*, C. C. Clarke's *Romantic Paradox: An Essay on the Poetry of Wordsworth*, Frederick Garber's *Wordsworth and the Poetry of Encounter*, and Albert Wlecke's *Wordsworth and the Sublime: An Essay on Romantic Self-Consciousness*. These works focus in different ways and from different critical viewpoints on the central problematical interrelations in Wordsworth's poetry between subjective and objective, idea and image, self and other, imagination and nature.

Several recent critical studies deal with these and other topics of interest to the undergraduate teacher. Charles Sherry's *Wordsworth's Poetry of the Imagination* and David Simpson's *Wordsworth and the Figurings of the Real* take up the concept and function of imagination, especially its transformational and figural powers. James Averill's *Wordsworth and the Poetry of Human Suffering* explores the poet's use of pathos both as subject matter and as means to direct reader response, while John Beer's *Wordsworth and the Human Heart* traces the poet's use of the term *heart* and his changing views of sentiment. David Pirie's *William Wordsworth: The Poetry of Grandeur and of Tenderness* focuses on the antithesis between pathos and sublimity in the poetry, and Brian Cosgrove's *Wordsworth and the Poetry of Self-Sufficiency* explores the tension between the poet's desires for both community and isolation. Two specialized recent studies of potential interest to teachers are Lee Johnson's *Wordsworth's Metaphysical Verse: Geometry, Nature, and Form*, which argues for the presence of meaningful mathematical patterns in the poetry, and D. D. Devlin's *Wordsworth and the Poetry of Epitaphs*.

"Biography," to quote one respondent, "is more important in connection with Wordsworth than with most writers," and we need only think of *The Prelude*, not to mention a number of major lyrics, to understand why. Whether teachers stress the biographical context of Wordsworth's art, the implicit patterns of his subconscious life, or his efforts to reshape his experience through poetry and mythmaking, they have frequent recourse to biographical studies. Moorman's standard work has already been mentioned. A once standard biography still frequently consulted is George McLean Harper's *William Wordsworth: His Life, Works, and Influence*. Of supplemental and more specialized interest are Émile Legouis's *The Early Life of William Wordsworth, 1770–1798: A Study of* The Prelude, Willard Sperry's *Wordsworth's Anti-Climax*, T. W. Thompson's *Wordsworth's Hawkshead*, Ben Ross Schneider's *Wordsworth's Cambridge Education*, and H. M. Margoliouth's *Wordsworth and Coleridge, 1795–1834*. F. E. Halliday has compiled a picture biography, *Wordsworth's World*, which some teachers find interesting for classroom use. Ernest de Selincourt's *Dorothy Wordsworth: A Biography* remains the standard study of Dorothy's life.

From the time Coleridge first heralded the philosophical nature of Wordsworth's poetry through the polemics of such figures as Arnold, Mill, and A. C. Bradley and into our own day, Wordsworth's system of thought, the influences that shaped it, and his status as a genuinely philosophical and/or religious poet have been the subjects of sometimes heated debate. Historically, studies seeking to define the philosophical content of his poetry have tended to stress the influence of eighteenth-century associationism (Arthur Beatty's *William Wordsworth: His Doctrine and Art in Their Historical Relations*) or to emphasize its idealist and trancendentalist tendencies (Newton Stallknecht's *Strange Seas of Thought: Studies in William Wordsworth's Philosophy of Man and Nature*, E. D. Hirsch's *Wordsworth and Schelling: A Typological Study of Romanticism*, and Melvin Rader's *Wordsworth: A Philosophical Approach*).

More recent works, such as Alan Grob's *The Philosophic Mind: A Study of Wordsworth's Poetry and Thought, 1797–1805* and John Hodgson's *Wordsworth's Philosophical Poetry*, trace the changes in Wordsworth's philosophical and metaphysical outlook over time and relate them closely to the poetry itself. In *Aspects of Wordsworth and Whitehead*, Alexander Cappon appraises the interest of both men in certain recurring philosophical problems. Wordsworth's central concern with time—its relation to knowledge, identity, growth, death, and transcendence—is explored variously in Stephen Prickett's *Coleridge and Wordsworth: The Poetry of Growth*, John Beer's *Wordsworth in Time*, and Jeffrey Baker's *Time and Mind in Wordsworth's Poetry*.

Two works on Wordsworth as an essentially religious poet that approach this topic from different points of view—the one historical, the other anthropological and mythical—are Richard Brantley's *Wordsworth's "Natural Methodism"* and J. R. Watson's *Wordsworth's Vital Soul: The Sacred and the Profane in Wordsworth's Poetry*. Recent studies of the poet's evolving political and social thought, itself intimately related to his philosophical and ethical ideas, include Michael Friedman's *The Making of a Tory Humanist*, Hermann Wüscher's *Liberty, Equality, and Fraternity in Wordsworth: 1791–1800*, and James Chandler's *Wordsworth's Second Nature: A Study of the Poetry and Politics*.

Another area that many undergraduate teachers emphasize is Wordsworth's use of landscape and his relation to the landscape poetry and painting of the eighteenth century. Recommended studies of these subjects include Russell Noyes's *Wordsworth and the Art of Landscape*, Donald Wesling's *Wordsworth and the Adequacy of Landscape*, Christopher Salvesen's *The Landscape of Memory*, Karl Kroeber's *Romantic Landscape Vision: Constable and Wordsworth*, Peter Bicknell's *The Illustrated Wordsworth's* Guide to the Lakes, and David McCracken's *Wordsworth and the Lake District: A Guide to the Poems*.

For commentary on the *Lyrical Ballads*—their meaning, reception, and relation to literary traditions—teachers were referred to Stephen Parrish's *The Art of the* Lyrical Ballads, Roger Murray's *Wordsworth's Style: Figures and Themes in the* Lyrical Ballads *of 1800*, Mary Jacobus's *Tradition and Experiment in Wordsworth's* Lyrical Ballads, John Jordan's *Why the* Lyrical Ballads? *The Background, Writing, and Character of Wordsworth's 1798* Lyrical Ballads, Stephen Prickett's *Wordsworth and Coleridge: The* Lyrical Ballads, and the essays and excerpted chapters in *Wordsworth:* Lyrical Ballads; A Casebook, edited by Alun Jones and William Tydeman. Heather Glen's *Vision and Disenchantment: Blake's* Songs and Wordsworth's Lyrical Ballads juxtaposes the early lyrics of the two poets, while Don Bialostosky's *Making Tales* examines numerous lyrical ballads and other experimental narratives as examples of a poetics of speech.

For *The Prelude*, teachers may consult, in addition to the books mentioned earlier in this section, Abbie F. Potts's *Wordsworth's* Prelude: A Study of Its Literary Form, Frank McConnell's *The Confessional Imagination: A Reading of Wordsworth's* Prelude, Ted Holt and John Gilroy's *A Commentary on Wordsworth's* Prelude, Books I–V, and the essays edited by W. J. Harvey and Richard Gravil in *Wordsworth:* The Prelude; A Casebook. Jonathan Wordsworth's *William Wordsworth: The Borders of Vision*, although its scope is greater than commentary on just one poem, focuses on the poet's often conflicted writing of *The Prelude* and his emerging conception of "vision." Another important book by Jonathan Wordsworth, *The Music of Humanity*, analyzes the poet's early work, with particular attention to "The Ruined Cottage."

Kenneth R. Johnston, in *Wordsworth and* The Recluse, gives the first sustained interpretation of the poet's projected but never completed masterwork, relating it to *The Prelude* and *The Excursion*, while Jared Curtis studies the poems of 1802 in *Wordsworth's Experiments with Tradition.* Wordsworth's contributions to literary theory, a subject of increasing importance in the undergraduate classroom, are discussed in James Heffernan's *Wordsworth's Theory of Poetry: The Transforming Imagination* and W. J. B. Owen's *Wordsworth as Critic.*

In addition to the anthologies of criticism mentioned in "Romantic Contexts," teachers may wish to consult several valuable collections of essays on Wordsworth that appeared in the 1960s and early 1970s. The most widely used is probably M. H. Abrams's *Wordsworth: A Collection of Critical Essays*, which prints seventeen essays, including Abrams's pedagogically useful introduction, "Two Roads to Wordsworth." The volume contains classic papers by A. C. Bradley and A. N. Whitehead; highly influential critical and theoretical essays by Lionel Trilling, Harold Bloom, Geoffrey Hartman, Paul de Man, and Cleanth Brooks; and important studies of individual topics and texts by Abrams, David Ferry, David Perkins, Robert Mayo, Stephen Parrish, John Danby, Neil Hertz, Jonathan Wordsworth, and John Jones. Jack Davis's widely used *Discussions of William Wordsworth* contains essays by, among others, Coleridge, Arnold, Bradley, Abrams, Basil Willey, F. R. Leavis, Donald Davie, Herbert Read, Trilling, and Hartman.

The most ambitious of these collections is *William Wordsworth: A Critical Anthology*, edited by Graham McMaster. The volume contains nearly 250 pages of commentary and reviews by Wordsworth, his contemporaries, and Victorian critics and over 250 pages of modern views. The latter include essays and selected chapters from books by such scholars and critics as Helen Darbishire, D. G. James, F. W. Bateson, Davie, Jones, Mayo, Ferry, Hartman, and Jonathan Wordsworth. Three other collections that should be mentioned are A. W. Thompson's *Wordsworth's Mind and Art*, Jonathan Wordsworth's *Bicentenary Wordsworth Studies in Memory of John Alban Finch*, and Geoffrey Hartman's *New Perspectives on Coleridge and Wordsworth*, all of which tend to focus on specialized critical, scholarly, and bibliographical concerns. The Spring 1984 issue of *Studies in Romanticism* (23.1) was also devoted to specialized essays on Wordsworth.

Aids to Teaching

Although some respondents considered audiovisual materials "high-school-ish" and a distraction from the written word, many others make use of such aids, and still others said they would if only time permitted. A number of teachers stressed that students, especially urban American students, need to "see" the landscapes described by Wordsworth in order to understand and to appreciate his poetry. To this end, slides, photographs, picture post-cards, and paintings by Beaumont, Constable, Martin, Turner, and others are introduced on a regular basis in many undergraduate classes. Maps of the Lake District are also employed to establish a geographical context for the poetry, especially for *The Prelude*.

While teachers reported making their own slides and photographs of the Lake Country (a few used sabbaticals for this purpose), professionally pro-duced films and sound filmstrips are fairly plentiful. The most elaborate and widely praised of these is Kenneth Clark's program "The Worship of Nature" from his well-known BBC television series *Civilisation*. The program is also available in videocassette. Sixteen-millimeter educational films that might be used in introductory literature classes and that portray Wordsworth in relation to the natural settings that inspired him include *Wordsworth's Lake Country: Image of Man and Nature*, *Romanticism: The Revolt of the Spirit*, *The Wordsworth Country*, and Carl Ketcham's *Wordsworth*. *Coleridge: The Fountain and the Cave* also contains useful material on Wordsworth. Among the thirty-five millimeter sound filmstrips available to college teachers are *Wordsworth*, *The Romantic Age*, *English Romantic Poetry and Painting—A Series*, *The Time, the Life, the Works*, and *Selected Poems of William Wordsworth*, *The Romantic Era*, and *Blake, Wordsworth and Coleridge*. (Bibliographical information on all titles mentioned in this section can be found in the audiovisual aids division of the list of works cited.)

Respondents also suggested books containing illustrations and photographs suitable for use in the classroom. Several have already been mentioned relative to Wordsworth's landscape poetry, most notably Noyes's *Words-worth and the Art of Landscape* and Bicknell's *The Illustrated Wordsworth's Guide to the Lakes*. Two other illustrated editions of Wordsworth's own *Guide through the District of the Lakes* are the 1968 reprint of the original 1822 edition and de Selincourt's paperback *Guide to the Lakes*. F. E. Hal-liday's *Wordsworth and His World*, Peter Quennell's *Romantic England: Writing and Painting, 1717–1851*, and Donald Hayden's *Wordsworth's Walking Tour of 1790* contain photographs, pictures, maps, and drawings of the Lake Country, the West Country, Cambridge, France and the Alps, and other scenes associated with Wordsworth's life and poetry. A convenient source for pictures of the poet is Frances Blanshard's *Portraits of Wordsworth*.

Few teachers reported using recordings of Wordsworth's poetry, and such recordings, fairly numerous in the 1960s and 1970s, are quickly going out of distribution. Of those still available in the United States, Cedric Hardwicke's readings of selected poems in *Poetry of Wordsworth* is the best known. *English Romantic Poetry*, read by Claire Bloom, Anthony Quayle, Frederick Worlock, and Ralph Richardson, includes nine selections from Wordsworth. Two other recordings that include readings of selected poems and passages are Robert Speaight's *Treasury of William Wordsworth* and Bramwell Fletcher's *English Romantic Poets*.

A growing number of audiocassette programs provide critical, historical, and biographical information aimed at the beginning undergraduate student. Currently available cassettes include *Wordsworth: The* Lyrical Ballads and *Wordsworth's* The Prelude by Angus Easson and Terence Wright, *English Romantic Poetry 1780–1820s* by Graham Martin and Mark Storey, *The Romantics* by Christopher Salvesen and William Walsh, *Wordsworth* by Stephen Gill and Mary Jacobus, and the four-part *William Wordsworth* (individual tapes on "Ode: Intimations of Immortality," "Tintern Abbey," *The Prelude*, and the sonnets) by Stephen Prickett.

Finally, for those able to attend, the annual Wordsworth Summer Conference at Dove Cottage provides a memorable opportunity to study the poet in the very heart of Wordsworth country. Groups of students can be accommodated at the conference, and several survey respondents spoke enthusiastically about attending and about the experience of leading student groups from their home institutions. Information is available from Richard Wordsworth, Wordsworth Summer Conference at Dove Cottage, Grasmere, Cumbria LA 22 9SG, United Kingdom.

Part Two

APPROACHES

INTRODUCTION

The thirty essays that follow, written by contributors to the survey preliminary to this volume, reflect a wide range of subjects and concerns identified by teachers of Wordsworth's poetry—historical backgrounds, literary relations, theoretical and critical perspectives, pedagogical strategies, analyses of individual texts, and so on. The collection as a whole attempts to be representative, expressing the interests of a variety of teachers in a variety of teaching situations. It includes essays by well-known scholars who teach Wordsworth primarily on the graduate level and in specialized undergraduate seminars as well as essays by teachers who approach Wordsworth exclusively in lower-division literary surveys. Different institutions with different student populations in different geographical areas are represented. What brings all thirty essayists together here is a common, often passionate, concern for Wordsworth's poetry and a shared commitment to teaching it well.

The essays vary in length, style, and content. Some are overtly pedagogical, focusing on such topics as the choice and arrangement of texts, course development, and teaching methods. Others are more informational, analytical, or theoretical and do not present ready-made classroom models or procedures. Readers will find it necessary to interpret and to adapt the contributor's insights to their own teaching situations. Whether directly or indirectly, however, we are confident that all the essays in the collection, even those (in some ways, especially those) that appear most theoretical, have significant value for the teaching of Wordsworth's poetry on the undergraduate level. At the same time, we hope that specialists in the field, as well as nonspecialists and beginning teachers, will find the collection useful.

The two introductory essays in "On Teaching Wordsworth" are compellingly personal statements about (to borrow a Keatsian term) the "feel" of teaching Wordsworth's poetry. Herbert Lindenberger surveys several decades of changing critical and pedagogical fashions, while Peter Manning identifies the inevitable difficulties—and celebrates the potential rewards—of introducing Wordsworth to undergraduates.

The essays in "Selected Pedagogical Approaches" address a variety of pedagogical concerns. Muriel Mellown and Mark Reynolds discuss strategies for presenting Wordsworth's poetry to particular student audiences, the former at a predominantly black college, the latter at a two-year institution. Their remarks are widely applicable, however, to teaching students with little literary and linguistic training in any educational context. Jared Curtis illustrates with a case history his use of reader-response theory to involve often suspicious or disinterested students with Wordsworth's poetry. Jack

Haeger outlines a comprehensive approach for teaching a crucial, yet difficult, aspect of Wordsworth's poetry, its style, while Nicholas Warner shows how introducing relations between the poet and Romantic landscape painters can enhance classes on Wordsworth. Finally, Anthony Harding and Craig Howes make suggestions concerning course development, Harding proposing a thematic organization for a course on the first-generation English Romantics and Howes describing two honors seminars on Wordsworth and criticism.

The next category, "Teaching Individual Texts," includes essays on teaching some works by Wordsworth that appear most frequently in a variety of undergraduate classes. The *Lyrical Ballads*, the Immortality Ode, and *The Prelude* are emphasized for obvious reasons. Spencer Hall argues that selected sonnets can effectively introduce major topics, themes, and patterns in Wordsworth's poetry and in Romantic poetry generally. Judith Page suggests ways of relating Wordsworth's famous Preface to his practice in *Lyrical Ballads*, while John Ogden approaches the task of teaching the volume as a whole by developing thematic interrelations among individual poems. Perspectives on teaching two of the most influential and often assigned poems in *Lyrical Ballads*, "Tintern Abbey" and "Michael," are advanced by Patricia Skarda and Edward Duffy respectively. John Milstead identifies Wordsworth's conception of "the two selves" as an appropriate and rewarding model for teaching certain post–*Lyrical Ballad* poems. Two essays are devoted to Wordsworth's Immortality Ode: John Mahoney suggests the value of teaching the ode concurrently with Coleridge's "Dejection: An Ode," while Jonathan Ramsey surveys contrasting interpretive approaches to Wordsworth's great poem.

Five other essays round out the "Teaching Individual Texts" category, four of them on various versions of or episodes in *The Prelude*. Lisa Steinman discusses "The Ruined Cottage," a narrative work that, since its appearance in the *Norton Anthology* and elsewhere, has increasingly replaced book 1 of *The Excursion* in undergraduate classes. Jonathan Wordsworth comments on the two-part *Prelude*, the short early version of the poem that, like "The Ruined Cottage," has become a favored text among undergraduate teachers. Anthony Franzese, however, suggests ways of approaching the full-length *Prelude* through the identification and elaboration of thematic and structural patterns. Charles Rzepka, who takes up Wordsworth's formative experience with the French Revolution in books 10-11, and Wayne Glausser, who considers the climactic Mount Snowdon episode, offer ideas about teaching two of the most famous and often discussed "moments" in the poem.

The essays in "Literary and Historical Contexts" assume the importance of teaching Wordsworth's poetry in relation to both literary and social history. Focusing on passages from *The Prelude*, Douglas Kneale uses an intertextualist approach to highlight essential connections between Wordsworth and Milton. F. R. Hart suggests ways of teaching the sociohistorical dimension of Wordsworth's poetry, not as background but as an integral part of the poetry. John Hodgson, exploiting definitive Romantic conceptions of the imagination, structures pedagogically useful comparisons and contrasts between Wordsworth and other major English Romantic poets. Allan Chavkin explores similarly important relations between Wordsworth and such modern poets as Stevens, Roethke, and Yeats.

The final category in the "Approaches" section is "Theoretical Perspectives." The essays in this category outline approaches based on theoretically oriented critical perspectives. Anne Mellor identifies those aspects of Wordsworth's poetry and life of particular interest to the feminist critic and teacher, while Richard Matlak combines the impersonal structures of psychology and the personal revelations of biography in a psychobiographical interpretation of certain frequently taught texts. Don Bialostosky describes a poetics of speech that defines Wordsworth's poetry as "the pleasurable re-creation of utterances" and seeks to characterize the speaker and the utterances in particular ways. Tilottama Rajan applies to Wordsworth's poetry the complex, stimulating, and controversial techniques of deconstructionism. All of these essayists find in Wordsworth an especially suitable subject for their theoretical approaches and consider those approaches viable heuristic methods for the classroom.

ON TEACHING WORDSWORTH

Teaching Wordsworth from the 1950s to the 1980s

Herbert Lindenberger

Since my experience of Wordsworth goes back nearly half a century, I shall preface this introduction with two scenes in which I was the recipient of other people's teaching rather than the disburser of my own. The first took place in 1935, when I was six, in a second-grade classroom in the old T. T. Minor School atop Capitol Hill in Seattle. Anybody passing through the hall would have heard a chorus of children's voices blasting out such lines as "a HOST, of GOLden DAFfoDILS" and "in SUCH a JOcund COMpaNY" with unrelenting devotion to the demands of iambic tetrameter. Between our repeated performances the teacher instructed us that this poem, which she called "Daffodils," could tell us how great poets spend their time—namely, walking about in nature so they may find inspiration to write more poetry. Her key terms were *poem, poetry, inspiration,* and *nature,* all of which became hopelessly implicated with one another either as equivalents or in cause-and-effect relations.

I make no bones about the fact that the regimented reading we were expected to produce, as well as the interpretation to which the teacher subjected the poem, left me with permanently negative feelings—to the extent that I have never cared to read or teach this lyric. Although the options a teacher enjoys for presenting poetry to second graders are obviously limited, the notion that poetic language is recognizable only through obedience to the abstract meter is likely to stifle a child's auditory imagination (I still wince each time I come across the word *jó-cund*). Just as important, the idea that poems derive from poets inspired in and by nature could scarcely seem interesting, let alone inspiring, to a small child. It is likely that this classroom experience planted some seeds of revolt from which my own teaching and writing could later be fed. Certainly this ancient teacher who made a universal poetics out of a characteristically nineteenth-century idea also represented the end of an era during which poetry still counted for something in our culture—counted so much, in fact, that the memorizing and oral performance of canonized works were thought to exercise a civilizing effect on children whose barbaric impulses needed curbing. It scarcely seems accidental that the teacher was about the age of her charges when Matthew Arnold was at the peak of his critical powers.

My second scene took place at Antioch College in early 1948 in a sophomore survey of English literature I was forced to take despite my protests that I was already familiar with everything on the reading list. Most of the time allotted to Wordsworth was spent on a single lyric, "She dwelt among the untrodden ways." Indeed, at least an hour was devoted to two lines, "A violet by a mossy stone / Half hidden from the eye!" Yet this was in no sense a close reading in the New Critical mode. The professor was an old gentleman trained long before in what has variously been called the historical, philological, or positivistic method, an approach that limits what one can properly say about a literary work to publicly verifiable facts—the sort of evidence that would pass muster in a courtroom. Unfortunately, this poem did not offer many opportunities for this kind of analysis. Nobody will be surprised to learn that he raised the question "Who was Lucy?" and reported various speculations that had accumulated in scholarship over the years.

One might wonder how a positivistic mentality could find an hour's worth of data to explain the violet and the mossy stone. Certainly the only historical statement he offered was that before 1800 an obscure flower such as the violet (not to speak of an obscure and simple girl such as Lucy) could not have been deemed significant enough to carry the poetic weight Wordsworth assigned it. Unlike a scholar in our own day, he did not extend his observation to speak of Wordsworth's renewal of the pastoral tradition, for this would have demanded a more theoretically sophisticated argument than he had been trained to develop. Yet he managed to flesh out his class time in a manner I have found common among teachers who thought themselves tough-minded philologists—namely, by alternating historical detail with rhapsodic expostulations ("Isn't it lovely, isn't it moving, to see a slip of a girl compared to a precious little flower!"). Beneath the hard-nosed exterior there lurked enough sentiment to cause acute intellectual embarrassment among his listeners. Like many of his generation who had suppressed their early literary enthusiasm for what passed as scholarly rigor, this teacher was working out of two seemingly incompatible but actually complementary critical paradigms—positivism and appreciationism.

This man's unpersuasive teaching succeeded in knocking this particular Lucy poem out of my canon of readable poems as firmly as had my earlier teacher's presentation of "I wandered lonely as a cloud." Indeed, it made me consider changing my major to a more intellectually vital discipline. Yet two things helped me endure my literature courses—first, the power that I (if not necessarily my teachers) discerned in great literature and, second, my joining a group of undergraduates who, quite on their own, were reading the latest pronouncements of critics such as Cleanth Brooks, R. P. Blackmur, and Kenneth Burke—much as, precisely thirty years later, students would be reading Jameson and de Man as antidotes to what they viewed as the outdated teaching of their New Critical elders.

Certainly the New Critical model served me well throughout my first decade of teaching. The process of reading poems closely, exercising one's wits about their verbal complexities, discovering that the latter also suggested moral complexities with which one could define one's everyday life— all this released an energy in both teacher and student that could never be recaptured in the same way (or with the same poems) in later years. The only trouble, at least from the point of view of the present volume, was that it left little room for Wordsworth. I might add that although I embraced the New Critical paradigm during the '50s, I felt a distinct conflict between my critical commitment and the commitment I had maintained throughout my reading life to Wordsworth and to that other proscribed poet, Milton. Indeed, my book on *The Prelude*, on which I worked from 1956 to 1961, was motivated initially by this conflict, above all by a desire to demonstrate Wordsworth's greatness to those whose critical assumptions could not readily accommodate him.

Unfortunately, not many Wordsworth poems "worked" (to cite a term associated with New Critical teaching) very well in the variety of courses— freshman composition, sophomore world literature, advanced courses in genres and in criticism—that I taught. *The Prelude*, which I once placed in my world literature course during the 1950s, was a conspicuous failure; although I rarely had trouble presenting genres such as the short poem, prose narrative, or verse drama, the students took badly to the rhetoric of a long poem (I had been careful to represent Milton with *Samson Agonistes* rather than *Paradise Lost* in that course). A few Wordsworth lyrics, above all "A slumber did my spirit seal," offered dependable opportunities for successful teaching within the New Critical model; anybody judging Wordsworth by such presentations alone would legitimately have granted him the status of a fine minor poet. The few times I taught the Immortality Ode I did not bother, as Cleanth Brooks had done, to seek out evidences of paradox in its imagery: since this procedure too obviously reduced the ode to triviality, I opted instead to treat it, for better or worse, as a cultural monument and to tell the students they could take it or leave it.

One problem was that those who rejected Wordsworth were usually my brightest students, those whose responses to poetry I was least prepared to inhibit. For several years running I assigned a paper on "Tintern Abbey" in a required junior-level seminar in "practical criticism" (this now-quaint term was once as fashionable as "critical theory" is today). I recognized this assignment as a deliberately perverse act on my part. It invariably resulted in papers far inferior to those I regularly assigned on Donne's "Canonization," Stevens's "Sunday Morning" (Wordsworthian though this poem is), and Joyce's "The Dead." One smart student tried to talk me out of having her write on "Tintern Abbey" on the grounds that the images lacked clarity and that the narrator was unable to distance himself adequately from his material; another challenged me for asking anybody to take seriously a poem containing such sentimental phrases as "little, nameless, unremembered, acts / Of kindness and of love." I admit I had no easy answer, for even if I referred to eighteenth-century notions of benevolence, both the student and I knew that according to New Critical doctrine a historical explanation was no excuse for a poem's failure to follow the rules underlying the paradigm. My most perverse act was probably ramming "Resolution and Independence" down my students' throats: since most of them were aware of my enthusiasm for the poem, they did their best to be tactful about what they viewed as Wordsworth's absurd lapse in poetic tact in the final lines.

By the early 1960s I had come to recognize that my pedagogical technique, which had been shaped by the New Criticism, would have to give way to what I knew, both in my head and in my heart, was intellectually right. The new approach could not come out of the ideology of early literary modernism, as the New Criticism had, but would derive from critical assumptions more compatible with literature written in the early nineteenth century. The approach I developed was suggested by a variety of sources—readings in Continental literature of the period as well as in modern Continental critics such as Poulet, Auerbach, Curtius, and Benjamin; readings in intellectual history of the eighteenth and early nineteenth centuries; the new approaches to Romanticism being worked out in the 1950s by scholars such as Frye, Abrams, Kermode, de Man, and Hartman (the last two in their earlier phenomenological, not their later deconstructive, phase).

Diverse though these sources might seem, they added up to a new way of dealing with the Romantic poets. In my teaching I would no longer need to test Wordsworth's imagery against Donne's or to worry about whether Wordsworth had sufficiently rid himself of the sentimentality that readers associated with Victorian poetry. Although the term *intertextuality* had not yet entered the critical marketplace, my teaching of Wordsworth during the 1960s attempted to confront his poems with earlier poems that he had absorbed and with later texts that were rewriting his own. Thus, to illustrate the problematics of the long poem, I set *The Prelude* next to *Paradise Lost* on one side and Stevens's "Notes toward a Supreme Fiction" on the other. Similarly, I could illustrate the possibilities of *Bildungs* narrative by juxtaposing the poem with Rousseau's *Confessions* and *A Portrait of the Artist as a Young Man*. Even before Abrams's fine essay on the "greater Romantic lyric" came out in 1965 ("Structure and Style"), I had been teaching "Tintern Abbey" and various spots of time as moments in a tradition that stretched back to the seventeenth century and forward to Shelley, Whitman, Arnold, Stevens, and Lowell. I quickly discovered that Wordsworth's greatness emerged for students as soon as he was placed within appropriate contexts. There was no reason, surely, to choose only those contexts in which writers actually possessed knowledge of each other's work. In fact, one of the most intellectually exciting juxtapositions took place in a seminar I gave in 1965 on Wordsworth and Hölderlin, two precisely contemporary poets whose writings mutually illuminated one another in striking ways.

By the early 1970s, however, the new winds blowing from France forced all of us to reconsider the comfortable syntheses we had created. At the very moment that the upper middle class in America turned to Julia Child and the Cuisinart to enhance its culinary skills, the more advanced literary thinkers turned to the French to redirect their critical perspectives. As soon as one had read Derrida and the later Barthes, one began to worry about the tricks authors used to posit metaphysical presences and to make narratives cohere. Not that I stopped confronting Wordsworth's texts with those of other writers. Rather, the confrontations now took on a distinctly antagonistic character, with later texts questioning their predecessors, which in turn were questioning, even subverting, their own predecessors. It was a great game while it lasted; from a pedagogical point of view one might even say it was a dream, for Wordsworth accommodated himself to the method as readily as he had resisted the New Criticism. A bit too readily perhaps: even while toying with what we later came to call deconstruction I never quite lost my own suspiciousness (an attitude I voiced in my book *Saul's Fall*, written in the mid-'70s) toward the suspiciousness at the heart of the method.

Yet I attribute the most exhilarating teaching experience of my life to the power the deconstructive idea exercised in a seminar on romantic long poems that I directed in 1977. The central critical texts through which we viewed works such as *The Prelude* and *Don Juan* were de Man's "Rhetoric of Temporality" and Derrida's "White Mythology." As antitext the students chose Abrams's *Natural Supernaturalism*, a book that I revere but that, in view of the intellectual orientation dominating the seminar, clearly lacked the irony, as well as the concern for irony, that emanated from the other critical texts. Not only was the level of discussion as high as any I have experienced in a classroom, but the seminar papers—many of them built around such predictably deconstructive topics as lost presences, lost girls, lost sheep— achieved a brilliance that can occur only when a group of talented students confront an idea whose moment has come. As one student in the group told me, after six years' retrospect, the skepticism central to the deconstructive texts she was reading at the time seemed a perfect fit for students whose view of the world had been shaped by the late '60s and early '70s.

If I may judge by what this woman and others of her generation are doing now, I see a new paradigm taking shape. I have referred to it as the New History—something quite different from the old historical method, for it is a theoretically informed approach being practiced by a generation trained to think in theoretical terms ("Toward a New History"). Unlike the older method, the New History does not necessarily claim objectivity or disinterestedness; like the feminist research with which it is sometimes associated, it subjects the traditional properties of the field—for example, the canon of standard authors and texts, even the definitions of Romanticism that have reigned for a century—to a fundamental questioning. Let me suggest some questions I hear people asking: How did the scientific and historical writing of the time enter and shape the minds of the Romantic poets? What human and social needs did the viewing of sublime scenery—whether in nature, poetry, or in painting—serve? How did the Romantic poets experience history—the history of ancient civilizations that were just coming to light as well as the events of their own recent history? What ideological assumptions stand behind the poetics of the major poets, and how did their poetics come to triumph over competing ideologies? How did Wordsworth and his contemporaries create their readership, and how did the latter, in turn, create a canon of great Romantic poets to meet its own religious and political needs? In what ways is the canon we teach the result of the institutional arrangements made within departments of English, whose individual members often have sound practical reasons to maintain their allotted parts of the canon even if other arrangements may come to seem intellectually sounder?

Like any incoming critical paradigm, the New History will seek out pedagogical practices in consonance with its underlying ideas. Courses in Romanticism may no longer be built solely out of the so-called major texts but may alternate readings of these texts with the discussion of historical matters for which the preceding paradigms had neither room nor sympathy. We may well, in fact, come to divide our class time between texts traditionally classified as high literature and others drawn from popular literature and from what we have hitherto classified as nonliterary forms of discourse. Popular ballads may share the syllabus with *Lyrical Ballads*; Dorothy Wordsworth's journals may be juxtaposed with her brother's descriptive poetry; essays of the time preaching the virtues of poverty may be read in tandem with Wordsworth's metrical effusions on the poor; travel guides to the regions of the sublime (including Wordsworth's own guidebook to his native places) may compete with the official poetic topographies. Teaching may also prove to be a bit more taxing: whereas the New Critical and the deconstructive modes allowed one to devote the hour to uncovering the ironies and the aporias (respectively) of a single major text, the New History has no ready-made techniques to guarantee easy teaching triumphs.

All this—if it is indeed the direction in which Wordsworth studies are going—should provide a good bit to talk and write about during the present decade. And like all the paradigms I have observed (and embraced with varying degrees of intensity) over the years, this one will doubtless lose its vitality once its most talented practitioners have had their essential say. Critical languages, we now recognize, wear out in much the same way as the languages of poetry. Since recent federal legislation has pushed my retirement age back to 1999, as the '80s draw to a close I expect to be on the lookout for the emerging paradigm of the '90s.

On Failing to Teach Wordsworth

Peter J. Manning

Several years ago a senior colleague and a distinguished Romanticist temporarily eased my discomfort by acknowledging that none of his classes on Wordsworth had ever gone well either. Our experiences were similar: initial sessions that no standard of truth, however lax, would permit one to describe as discussions; hours in which no question, however ingenuous or ingenious, could long disrupt the students' bored silence, that silence which betokens neither resistance nor dislike, either of which is fertile, but merely a collective "so what." But, a few meetings later, if one were lucky, some members of the class would understand, suddenly, their own previous unconcern, and in so doing would understand Wordsworth's ends.

Since success, or that simulacrum of success for which teachers gratefully settle, comes in the end, it may seem inaccurate to call this sequence a failure, but it certainly threatens the pedagogical ambition that each class should be, to appropriate Virginia Woolf's phrase, a little daily miracle. I have endured it often enough, however, at different levels in different universities in different decades, to feel that the rhythm corresponds to a fundamental quality in Wordsworth and that bearing patiently with the doldrums makes possible a deeper understanding than does cannily circumnavigating them.

I teach Wordsworth most frequently at the outset of the second half of a survey of English literature, a prerequisite for the departmental major. Of those enrolled, many are anxious sophomores who have elected to take the ostensibly more familiar modern part before facing the bafflement of Chaucer and Spenser, and others are merely fulfilling general education requirements. Under such circumstances the importance of Wordsworth's place in literary history can be explained but not felt. These students, though scarcely trained in the Augustan decorums Wordsworth combats, nonetheless bring expectations that the *Lyrical Ballads* do not meet. From high school or elsewhere they have acquired the notion that poetry should be poetic, not plain and awkward; Simon Lee's swollen ankles are as disconcerting to them as to Wordsworth's contemporary reviewers.

In other ways, too, the bewilderment of current students repeats the situation Wordsworth described in 1800. Electronic marvels more seductive—and more violent—than the gross stimulants he inveighed against in the preface now compete for attention. In other classes the length of assignments provokes complaints, but it is even harder to exert sustained attention when the object doesn't seem to require it: working through *Our Mutual Friend* gives, if nothing else, the satisfaction of a substantial task accomplished, but who can admit to not understanding something as childish as "We Are Seven" or to being entirely puzzled by the eight lines of "A slumber did my spirit seal"? Few poets are as easy to race over, and miss completely, as Wordsworth: he is done in by his very simplicity.

For the teacher this bareness has a cost. A class confronted by the artifice of a Donne or a Hopkins sonnet knows that it does not know enough to read the poem, and when at the end of the hour information has been imparted, allusions explicated, and image patterns unfolded, everyone is gratified. With Wordsworth one has often rather to show students the inadequacy of understandings with which they have been perfectly happy, to hint that the banality they see reflects their own crude reductions of subtle structures. Few readers, I think, get far into the *Lyrical Ballads* without an uneasy recognition that the edge in Wordsworth's attitude toward his audience is aimed at them. The student who says "so what" to Simon Lee or the Idiot Boy is in a sense responding correctly, or at any rate responding as Wordsworth anticipated. If students are to understand their indifference, they must trust the teacher sufficiently to express it honestly, even while the teacher's task is to retort it on them.

Wordsworth enlarges the sympathies of his readers by disclosing their shallowness, and though this process is founded on the generous assumption that the reader is educable, the teacher who for the moment is its agent takes an uncomfortable stance toward the class. Not every student is glad to learn Wordsworth has deliberately induced frustrations, deliberately left the reader suspended in thought—not even those whose willingness to be teased leads them to appreciate how in "Lucy Gray," for example, through liminal symbols like the bridge and the door Wordsworth carefully mediates the oppositions on which the poem is built and so draws the reader into reconsidering the relation between humanity and nature, life and death. Questions asked not to find answers but instead to suggest precisely, to articulate ambiguities but not resolve them—a form of knowledge that overturns certainties and concisely promotes a "gray" indeterminacy—do not attract pragmatic undergraduates with career plans to pursue. The powers of speculation and surmise that we value as critics of Wordsworth irk as many as they delight in the classroom.

Some are delighted, of course, and discover through Wordsworth's compact lyrics what it means to read intensely, which is to say imaginatively but with discipline. For the present, however, let me continue with those who aren't. The same students who object to Wordsworth's refusal to spell out his message in the *Lyrical Ballads* cry "sellout" when the Immortality Ode elaborates its consolations; the drive of the philosophic mind to summarize and declare often brings students to value retrospectively the enigmatic reserve of the earlier works. The mythic narrative and formal language of that poem also enable students to estimate the experiment of the *Lyrical*

Ballads: to see both Wordsworth's command of traditional literary resources and the audacity of his former determination to do without them.

If the Immortality Ode does not produce that reaction, Keats's "To Autumn" often does, later in the semester. Keats's gorgeousness appeals as Wordsworth does not, but in admiring the rich layering of day, year, and myth in Keats's meditation students will often glance backward respectfully, for the first time, at Wordsworth's comic dialogues and economical understatements. Likewise, students who judge that the speakers of the odes on the Grecian urn and the nightingale agonize a little too exquisitely may do belated justice to the moments of "visionary dreariness" in *The Prelude* and to Wordsworth's effort to root imagination in the ordinary experience of the child. The quarrel with Wordsworth that Keats conducts in his letters reenacts and authorizes student resentment of Wordsworth while testifying to the strength of his introspection. By this point in the syllabus even those once put off by Wordsworth are likely to be engaged by arguments over his development—or decline, as it seems to their youthful faith. The most antagonistic often surprise themselves by extending their instructive debate with Wordsworth into an upper-division Romantics course: intellectual integrity takes many shapes.

This peculiarly delayed effect is characteristic. Wordsworth located the springs of poetry in emotion recollected in tranquillity, and his poems ask of students a similar distance and reflectiveness. All great literature deepens on prolonged acquaintance, but with Wordsworth the contrast between first response and later understanding can be radical; some of his poems, as he acknowledged in the Preface, remain permanently closed, but even the most widely cherished resist immediate comprehension. More than most writers not avowedly hermetic, Wordsworth can be reread, but not read. Hence in practice the two kinds of readers sketched above converge: most good readers of Wordsworth come to him slowly. Pleasure in Wordsworth, if it comes at all, grows in rhythms not readily compatible with the rigidity of a Monday-Wednesday-Friday schedule. Moreover, a poet who works by suggestion frees each reader to read him slightly differently, according to the experience with which that reader answers the poem; reading Wordsworth, we all stand single.

Though such power to call out the individual is Wordsworth's distinguishing quality and saves his poetry from the condescending assumption of superiority in its didactic intent, it also warns the teacher against the honorable performance that tempts the student to substitute a deceptively inclusive lecture for the labor of wrestling with the poetry. The pride one might take in skillfully introducing Wordsworth is tempered by recognition that understanding of him develops largely in the solitude he prized. Disappointed in his confidence that he was a man speaking to men, Wordsworth turned his hopes to posterity, and the posterior understanding in each reader's experience of him that vindicates his faith often lies outside the teacher's ken, as it lay beyond the control of the poet. "I wish either to be considered as a Teacher, or as nothing," Wordsworth wrote in his middle years (de Selincourt, *Letters* 2: 195); the reward and the regret of teaching him is to witness that the truest teaching occurs long after the teacher's voice is heard no more.

SELECTED PEDAGOGICAL APPROACHES

Teaching Wordsworth to Minority Students

Muriel Mellown

The Romantic era is more likely to capture the interest of minority students, especially black students, than is any other period of English literature. Its appeal springs from that revolutionary zeal and enthusiastic idealism which at once arouse a response in students eager to connect poetry with politics and the social order. Of the major Romantic poets Wordsworth offers the greatest scope for discussion since he, more than any previous writer, probes the inner significance of ordinary happenings in ordinary lives. It is, then, Wordsworth the liberal thinker, supporter of the French Revolution, and poet of common humanity and of the common human experience whom I first introduce to students in a historically black college when I teach a survey of English literature course. Later in the unit I proceed to that other Wordsworth whose great themes are the interaction of humanity and nature and the power of the subjective consciousness over the objective world.

In an introductory lecture I emphasize that the Romantic period was preeminently the age of revolution and that, despite the harsh repressiveness of the Tory establishment, the growing radical spirit manifested itself in the movement for parliamentary reform, in the increasing awareness of the conditions of the working classes, and in the antislavery movement. As the students usually know little of this British movement, I describe the concern felt in many segments of English society for the plight of the slave. As instances of this concern I refer to Josiah Wedgwood's designs of the manacled slave and to Blake's engravings for J. G. Stedman's *Narrative of a Five*

Years' Expedition against the Revolted Negroes of Surinam. In addition, I allude to William Wilberforce, who led the political struggle for abolition and whose campaigns aroused the conscience of the English to the point that in 1807, in the midst of the Napoleonic wars, the slave trade was finally abolished in British vessels.

After outlining significant background events, I give a brief biographical sketch, in which I relate Wordsworth to the liberalizing spirit of the age. At Hawkshead he became aware of the nurturing, educative power of nature over the solitary mind, but he also came to know the joys of a simple, stable human society. He shared in the pleasures of a country life, and he lived close to country people—Ann Tyson, the shepherds and cottagers of the vales, and the packman, who figured in the poetry first as the Pedlar of "The Ruined Cottage" and later as the Wanderer of *The Excursion.* Emphasis on this aspect of Wordsworth's life leads naturally to the next important phase of his development, when he espoused the cause of the French Revolution.

The remainder of Wordsworth's life I pass over briefly. I mention, of course, his relation with Coleridge and Dorothy and his residence in the Lake District. I also mention the connection with Thomas and Catherine Clarkson, who until 1804 lived at Pooley Bridge and who were the most intimate friends of the Wordsworths during their time at Dove Cottage. Clarkson, like Wilberforce, devoted himself to the antislavery movement. A leading member of the Society for the Abolition of the Slave Trade, founded in 1787, he supported its efforts by collecting evidence of the horrors of the middle passage. In later years he wrote *The History of the Rise, Progress and Accomplishment of the Abolition of the African Slave Trade*, which the Wordsworths read in manuscript and for which they expressed great admiration. In Clarkson, Wordsworth would recognize one who directed to a single political cause the demand for justice and compassion for the oppressed that had motivated his own early revolutionary sentiments and that still constituted a major element in his poetry.

This initial lecture indicates the essence of my approach. My aim in dwelling on the social and political background is to provide a means by which students can readily respond to the poet. Too often they tend to look at English writers as distant figures whose works have little immediate relation to modern life. I try to counter this impression by showing Wordsworth as a moral poet whose work reflects a passionate belief in human rights and human dignity. While his poems do not speak for a particular political goal, many of them, as Hazlitt perceived, reflect the spirit of the French Revolution and of that democratizing impulse which continues to exercise our minds and imaginations today. Once I have made a connection between Wordsworth and our own time, I attempt to redress the balance by moving to a consideration of Wordsworth as a philosophical poet concerned with nature and with the growth of human consciousness.

After the background lecture most of the unit is taken up with textual analysis. I introduce the *Lyrical Ballads* by referring to the major statements in the Preface about the choice of rustic characters and diction. This literary theory demonstrates the same revolutionary spirit as do the poems, since it is based on a rejection of artificiality and ostentation in both language and life. The first poems we analyze are those that express in stark simplicity Wordsworth's views on nature—"To My Sister," "Expostulation and Reply," and "The Tables Turned." These works then provide a philosophical basis for our reading of the poems focusing on rustic characters, such as "The Thorn," "Simon Lee," "Goody Blake and Harry Gill," and "Michael." Usually I point to the actual objects or incidents from which the poems derived, and then we analyze the way fact has been transformed by the poetic imagination so as to develop universal themes of human suffering, courage, and endurance. While our primary emphasis is on the poems as reflections of Wordsworth's regard for common human beings, we also consider them as dramatic presentations of that sense of kinship between human passion and natural landscape which is the subject of the philosophical poems.

Turning to the 1807 *Poems*, we concentrate on its similarities to the earlier volume. "Alice Fell," based on a story told to Wordsworth by a Quaker friend of Thomas Clarkson, who urged the poet to write it "for the sake of humanity" (Moorman, *William Wordsworth* 1: 523), reveals the sympathy for the poor that was found in "Simon Lee"; "Resolution and Independence" indicates the same reverence for the common human being that appeared in "Michael." Among the "human interest" poems "To Toussaint L'Ouverture" has an obvious appeal. This sonnet, probably more completely than any other short work, presents a fusion of Wordsworth's main themes: his ideals of political and personal liberty, his sense of the union between humanity and nature, and his recognition of the greatness of the human spirit. The Immortality Ode I reserve until last. I treat it as a sequel to "Tintern Abbey," for in it Wordsworth confronts the problem of a diminished response to nature and a discovery that, far from being an unfailing refuge for the human mind, nature is totally separated from the adult consciousness. Yet the poem celebrates the humanizing of the poet's imagination and his reaffirmation of immortality and the unconquerable mind; thus we are able to connect it with our emphasis on Wordsworth as the poet of common humanity.

In most courses I end the unit with a discussion of *The Prelude*, a poem that describes the spiritual and emotional experiences out of which Wordsworth forged the concepts and value systems underlying the works already treated. I concentrate on the sections dealing with childhood and with the French Revolution because my students relate most readily to them. While students sometimes have difficulty in apprehending the subtleties of Wordsworth's philosophy of the relation between the subjective and objective worlds, they are quick to grasp the general depiction of a solitary mind responding to the natural landscape. They also recognize the clash of ideologies and the problems of civil justice and violence presented in the books on the French Revolution. Parallels with the wars and revolutions of our own century are obvious, and students are eager to cite examples of the grim cycle of hope and idealism followed by brutality and repression that so often characterizes the course of human history.

Teaching Wordsworth to minority students may pose one further problem. The students often represent an unusually wide range of competence and levels of preparedness. It is necessary to appeal both to students of outstanding ability and to those who lack adequate preparation for detailed study of literature. In order to meet the needs of this diverse body I employ many different teaching techniques. Often I read passages aloud so that students may get an appreciation of the sound of poetry—for some of them a new experience. I ask questions designed to let them see for themselves the ironies and complexities of apparently simple poems such as "We Are Seven" and "Anecdote for Fathers." I talk about Wordsworth as a poet whose sense of identity is tied up with a keen sense of place. In approaching the philosophical poems I try first to ensure that students have adequate reading comprehension; this effort involves consideration of such mundane but necessary matters as vocabulary and sentence structure. Then I suggest that many ideas in the poems spring from experiences close to our own. After linking the poems with some of their own past feelings, students will eventually confirm the statements about the restorative effects of nature in "Tintern Abbey." Similarly they will respond positively to the sections in *The Prelude* that deal with the child's special perception of the natural universe, and they will quickly comprehend the mixture of wonder and fear with which children view the world around them. I give continuity to the analyses of separate poems by tracing such recurring motifs as the figures of the solitary, the old man, and the child.

The keynote of my approach is flexibility. Pedagogical techniques must vary from poem to poem and from one group of students to another. My one constant factor is the emphasis on Wordsworth as the poet of the human heart. I conclude with an overview of typical characters: Martha Ray, the mad mother who clings to her child, the old Cumberland beggar, the Idiot Boy with his strange visions, the Pedlar who tramps the mountains, the blind beggar seen on a London street, the soldier returning from the war, the patriarchal shepherd, the Leech Gatherer who becomes the embodiment of resolution and independence. These are the inhabitants of Wordsworth's world, a world that testifies to the poet's awareness of the dignity of the common human being and the nobility of the human spirit.

Pre- and Postreading Activities: Teaching Wordsworth at a Two-Year College

Mark Reynolds

Over the past few years I have tried a variety of approaches to teaching Wordsworth in a survey of British literature at a two-year college. To incorporate writing more fully into the course, I require students to keep a reading journal, a spiral notebook in which they respond to course readings, react to class activities, and draft required writing assignments. The journal's major purpose is to serve as an arena for student thought and reaction to course readings. It has enlivened class discussions, and it plays a part in a series of prereading and postreading exercises I use to motivate discussion and to spur reading.

We begin the study of all writers in the course with informal student oral reports that introduce the authors' lives and lay a foundation for studying their works. Because Wordsworth is preceded in our text (*The Norton Anthology of English Literature*) by Robert Burns, whose use of common language and humble subjects in poetry appeals to students, I begin our Wordsworth section with the Preface to *Lyrical Ballads*. I work through it in class with the students, stressing not only the poet's opinions about common language and humble and rustic subjects but also his definition of poetry and his belief that poetry could help keep people human in a technological world. Many students have computer games at home, spend time in video-game parlors, eat in fast-food restaurants, and take computer courses, so they can easily understand the need to maintain humanness in an increasingly complex electronic society. Since most two-year college students assume that poetry is elitist and unfathomable in both words and ideas, the promise of simple language, common subject matter, and human interest is a hopeful one for them.

To demonstrate Wordsworth's accomplishments, I find it essential to read aloud individual poems and work through them in class using related pre- and postreading activities. I often begin with "We Are Seven," where the poet converses with a child who refuses to accept the death of a brother and a sister. The colloquial language of the poet and child, the natural setting, the real incident from everyday life, and the subject of a child's confronting death are all elements that students can see in the poem. As one prereading activity, I sometimes assign a "freewriting" (writing in their journals for ten minutes without stopping or worrying about mechanics) on the following topic: "Reflect on your childhood—when, where, how do you recall first encountering, understanding, accepting the reality of death?" After reading the poem aloud, I then ask how the poem relates to the freewriting. Much of the ensuing discussion can be focused on the poem. Some students have childhood memories of death they are willing to share, but only volunteers are asked to discuss this possibly sensitive subject. For a postreading exercise I ask students to write a stanza-by-stanza prose summary of the poem in their journals.

With the Lucy poems a good prereading activity is to have all students bring to class a favorite love poem. They come with everything from "Roses Are Red" to E. E. Cummings's erotic poems. After students share these works, we turn to Wordsworth's love poems, discussing why they are love poems. Inevitably the question of Lucy's identity arises; students seem genuinely curious. Sometimes we discuss possibilities in class; at other times I ask them to speculate in their journals on Lucy's identity, supporting their speculations with facts from Wordsworth's life they picked up from the oral report and from the text introduction. Another postreading journal activity is to have students compare the love poem they brought to class with one of the Lucy poems.

Several activities have proved successful with "Resolution and Independence." Sometimes I give students this journal-writing assignment the day before the poem is discussed in class: "Who are those people gathering aluminum cans along the roadsides, in the ditches, on the medians?—where do they come from? Why do they do it? How do you feel about them and their activity? Write a brief essay in your journal for the next class meeting." Or: "If you ever see people rummaging through trash bins, garbage dumpsters, or landfills, who are they? What are they looking for? Why are they doing it? How do you feel about them? Write a brief essay in your journal about them."

The next class meeting we may read the poem aloud—each student taking a stanza—and then discuss it. Alternatively, I may assign a separate stanza to individual students at an earlier class meeting and tell them that they are to become experts on their stanza—to read it aloud a minimum of three times, know the meanings of all words, be able to explain any allusions, and be able to relate it to preceding and following stanzas and to the entire poem.

Two elements in "Resolution and Independence" always seem to fascinate students. One is the notion of the often tragic lives and early deaths of creative individuals. Thus I fill in details about Thomas Chatterton's death or have a student give a report on Chatterton. Discussion usually follows with students eager to relate what they know about contemporary personalities who have suffered similar fates. Elvis Presley, Janis Joplin, Jimi Hendrix, and John Belushi are among those usually mentioned. The other area that interests students is the eighteenth-century medical practice of bleeding. Here, again, to capitalize on this interest I either have a student give a report (nursing students often will volunteer), or I supply details. Either way, I always read to the class a brief *Time* article about the recently renewed interest in the medical uses of leeches ("Bloodsuckers").

If I have assigned the prereading journal-writing exercise, class discussion will also include making the connection among can hunters, garbage pickers, and leech gatherers. For a postreading activity, I suggest that students reread "Resolution and Independence" and in their journals try to tie together class discussions and the total content of the poem, paying particular attention to its title.

Similar activities work well with "Michael." The meeting before this poem is covered, I sometimes tell the class the poem's plot up to the point of Luke's leaving home, then ask students to write an ending to the story in their journals. The next meeting I read the poem to the class. Always there is total silence, not so much because students are surprised that Luke disappoints his parents as because of the subtlety with which Wordsworth handles the disappointment. Another time I may simply read the entire poem to the class without comment and then ask students to take out their journals and write whatever thoughts they have for ten minutes. We then have a class discussion, or I form discussion groups, calling for a report from each group after a time. Most often students are full of examples of friends who have let down or disappointed their parents or of parents who have placed enormous responsibilities on children who were unable to handle them.

These before-and-after exercises actively involve students with the world of the poem. They can help make students who are not poetry readers or literature majors more receptive to Wordsworth and enable them to experience, most for the first time, how poetry can make us see anew the common in an uncommon way.

Teaching Wordsworth by Response

Jared Curtis

What a reader wishes to be true strongly shapes the meaning that reader derives from a poem. Both as student and as fledgling teacher I was taught to screen out such wishes in order to reveal the work of art for itself, stripped of any imposed meanings from without. I sensed then and know now that this task is impossible. Gradually I turned my attention to the task of understanding how I understand poetry, examining the process of reading rather than taking what I have read as an end product that exists outside of my own interests and concerns. In teaching Wordsworth's poetry during the last few years I have adapted the principles and procedures of response criticism to the classroom.

Based on the work of David Bleich and others, my approach replaces the term paper with several short responses designed to develop in participants an awareness of their own processes of reading. Initially, I ask students to write their own responses to the chosen poem. Length is not prescribed, but I suggest five to eight hundred words to start with. We duplicate and distribute our response statements—I do one as well. In the discussions that follow we learn the importance of both the style or manner of response and the affective and associative material presented by the reader—how they shape the reader's opinion of the poem, how interpretation seeks to create a desired meaning.

In what follows I present an excerpt from a student's response to Wordsworth's "Anecdote for Fathers, Shewing How the Art of Lying May Be Taught." (The student has kindly granted permission to present the response statement.) While this poem is often regarded (if not dismissed) as a rhymed sermon on the wise child, the responses I received generated far more informative and interesting meanings or interpretations, particularly in the emphasis they place on the "human background" (as one student has put it) of the spare events and thoughts expressed in the poem. Further, the statements confirm Wordsworth's own claim in the Advertisement to *Lyrical Ballads* that the reader's frame of mind is the difference between a stereotypical response to the poems and one that is "pleased" by the "natural delineation of human passions, human characters, human accidents" (Owen and Smyser 1: 116).

This method of teaching Wordsworth's poetry can free students to move from the periphery of the hermeneutic circle, as receivers of approved wisdom, to the center, as the active subjects of their own (and Wordsworth's) experiments in linking ordinary experience with literary experience. In this excerpt from G's response to Wordsworth's poem, she wishes to explain the reason for her "good feeling . . . about the end of the poem."

(1) I think it [the good feeling] may emanate from the boy's delicate lie. I feel there was a kind of sententious, emotional logic behind his lie. Edward's love for his father prevented him from disappointing his father and from saying that he preferred Liswyn farm to Kilve. (Possibly it never occurred to him to make a comparison.) When his father insisted on a reason for his preference, he was trapped. Clearly, he did not have one. To further please his father, Edward could have given an outright but believable, reasonable lie. It is the transparency of his lie that pleases me. Firstly, he resists with silence, then an "I don't know" and finally a transparent lie. I believe it is possible for a five year old to sense what will and will not be believed. If in this instance it is true, then the transparency of his lie suggests that he did not fully acquiesce to his father's pressure. The ridiculousness of his answer could be his way of retaining a little independence and this oblique resistance satisfies me. Clearly, I could be overrating his "emotional intellect" and be manipulating a purely innocent remark into an heroic act. Independence is something I value and so would naturally like to see it in the protagonists.

(2) However, my wish or finding is supportive of Wordsworth's values. That the "child is the father of the man" is a recurring Wordsworthian theme, and this poem seems to be an exemplary statement of it. "Shewing How the Art of Lying May be Taught" is an ambiguous title that suggests at least two possibilities. One, that the poem is an example of the art of lying and with the knowledge gained therein, we may or may not choose to teach this art. Or two, that the art of lying was not taught and therefore implicitly the boy did not lie. I think both interpretations are appropriate to the poem. Wordsworth seems to share my feeling that children are capable of great wisdom. That Edward's lie was a delicate balance between his and his father's needs may have been something that Wordsworth intended us to feel.

(3) Now I am acutely aware of my defensiveness: I have even pulled Wordsworth in for backing. I suppose it is because I need to believe that my interpretation is not solely a product of my emotions. There is nothing concrete in the poem that I can pull out and say "here is the evidence" for my belief in the boy's independence. Rather it is a culminative feeling that took its form from the many hints seeping through the poem. I am suspicious of my belief because I know I want it this way, yet I will not reject it because what I want and what is are

not necessarily mutually exclusive. But I am still unsatisfied because I feel I have not yet been able to find and express the optimal relation between my and the poem's needs.

The high premium G places on independence contributes to her sense of the delicacy of Edward's lie. But more important, Edward's preservation of his personal autonomy is subtly played against his love for his father, so that, in G's view, the boy claims his freedom while at the same time acknowledging his father's authority: "The transparency of his lie suggests that he did not fully acquiesce to his father's pressure." Of the courses she perceives as open to him, Edward chose the one that both "pleases" his father by acknowledging the boy's love and asserts his own independence. It is "this oblique resistance" that "pleases" G (par. 1).

In the two following paragraphs she adopts a strategy similar to the one she perceives Edward to take. First, she seeks confirmation of her reading (actually for her pleasure in the boy's lie—which she cannot therefore regard simply as a lie) in "Wordsworth's values," citing the "recurring" theme of the wise child. But the strength of her pleasure in the boy's independence seems to outdistance the authority and valorization she seeks in Wordsworth's axiom that the child is father of the man. Aware of her defensiveness in pulling the poet in "for backing," she notices that there is "nothing concrete in the poem" that she can confidently point to as "evidence" for her "belief in the boy's independence." The model she uses for her interpretation is the familiar one in which a reading gains the status of objective truth only when convincingly supported by evidence intrinsic to the object under study. Yet though she is "suspicious" of her reading, she refuses to give it up, in the hope that she can find the "optimal relation" between "the poem's needs" and her own. She would like to find the same "delicate balance" that she feels Edward has found between "his and his father's needs."

In our class discussion, though we could not learn from her written response why independence was so important to G, it was evident to all that her own feelings about autonomy—and especially the degree of her own autonomy as an observer and reader in relation to the "authority" of the poem she read—were instrumental in shaping her discussion of "what happens in the poem." Her response paper showed us her struggle—and we all shared this struggle with varying degrees of awareness—between the claims of the "scientific" model for argument about literature and the intersubjective claims made by her experience of the poem.

I have attempted to describe only the beginning of a course in reading Wordsworth's poetry. The direction taken and the distance covered depend a great deal on the willingness of the community to build on and absorb the discoveries we make with this first assignment. On different occasions we have gone on to include a selection of the poems usually studied in a Romantics course—"Tintern Abbey," "Michael," "Resolution and Independence," the two-part *Prelude*, "The Ruined Cottage" and so on. Now alert to the influence of the reader's subjective interests and prepared for a disciplined inquiry into these interests, we discuss our written responses to the poems with a keener sense both of the poet's achievement in creating documents that interest us as they do and of our own interpretive role in forming their meaning.

Teaching Wordsworth's Style: A Cumulative Approach

Jack H. Haeger

Anyone who has encountered Wordsworth's style in its complex variety and has perhaps read some of the article-length and even book-length studies of limited aspects of it can attest to the impracticality of attempting to teach it as a separate or separable unit in a course on the English Romantics. On the other hand, Wordsworth's writing provides such striking proof of the inseparability of style and content that to teach it without addressing style is inconceivable. I deal with this dilemma by incorporating attention to points of style progressively into the various stages of students' study of his poems; this developmental or cumulative approach is useful both for teaching Wordsworth's style and also for representing the full achievement of his oeuvre through analysis of selected works.

I begin coverage of Wordsworth's poetry with selections from the *Lyrical Ballads*, and I purposely confine my initial assignments to poems like "Simon Lee," "Goody Blake and Harry Gill," "The Thorn," "We Are Seven," and "Anecdote for Fathers"—all works involving, as Wordsworth phrased it in his famous Preface of 1800, "incidents and situations from common life" portrayed in "a selection of language really used by men." At this point, however, I do not ask students to read the Preface, for I find it most useful to have them encounter the poetry with a minimum of preparatory theoretical explanation or justification, just as Wordsworth's audience of 1798 did. Yet in a general way, virtually everyone in the class is aware of the fame and controversy associated with that volume of poems. Under these circumstances students' reactions to this first reading assignment are mildly surprising: in effect, they simply do not understand what caused all the fuss over the *Lyrical Ballads*. To them, such poems are about everyday life in the country during Wordsworth's time, described in plain and simple language.

At the outset, then, the teaching challenge involves a combination of historical background, poetic content, and style. I respond to that challenge by reminding students of the principles of literary decorum that shaped readers' expectations in Wordsworth's day and acknowledging that many precedents for poetic descriptions of rustics and nature did exist by 1798, but I suggest that *Lyrical Ballads* conveyed an unprecedented combination of descriptive and narrative directness with calm seriousness and high sense of purpose. I analyze the art of that achievement by first pointing out Wordsworth's skillful use of "simple" diction to establish the tone of folk language without its grammatical and colloquial crudeness. I also borrow from Coleridge's later critique regarding Wordsworth's "matter-of-factness" in relating descriptions and characterizations (*Biographia Literaria: CC* 2.22.126-35), though I emphasize the positive function of this quality as mirroring folk consciousness and expression (later in the term Coleridge will be allowed to speak for himself as to why such qualities are "defects"). But my stongest emphasis falls on Wordsworth's masterful manipulation of voice, point of view, and persona.

I attempt to show that in works like "Goody Blake and Harry Gill" and "The Thorn" Wordsworth draws on ballad convention to evoke a folk consciousness that is somewhat different from the more personal tone of "Simon Lee," "We Are Seven," and "Anecdote for Fathers." This demonstration entails discussion of modulations in his use of the first person. For instance, "I" appears only at the end of "Goody Blake and Harry Gill," and then in direct address to "farmers all" (127); in "The Thorn," moreover, "I" represents a specific character, who is also involved in direct interaction with an audience defined by the poem, as is easily established by noting the pattern of quotation marks in the text. On the other hand, "Simon Lee," "We Are Seven," and "Anecdote for Fathers" feature a narrative voice far less evocative of folk consciousness and far more suggestive of an "I-thou" relation between reader and author.

Students usually grasp the distinction in point of view between the two groups of poems, but with the second group they tend to assume that Wordsworth is speaking to them in his own person. During discussion of these three works, then, I find it important to dwell on the concept of persona. Regarding "Simon Lee," I suggest to the students that just as its "dear reader" is obviously artificial, so too is the "dear author" implied by such a convention. In regard to "We Are Seven" and "Anecdote for Fathers," I acknowledge some biographical veracity in all of Wordsworth's "humble and rustic" poetry, since of course he was a keen observer of local manners and settings, but I also use biographical references to point out discrepancies between Wordsworth and the "I" of these poems (seen easily enough, for instance, in the obviously fictional father-son relationship in "Anecdote"). Such attention to persona establishes the distinction necessary to understand how Wordsworth's art not only reflects the conditions and consciousness of humble and rustic life but also creates the personalized consciousness of a humble and rustic observer.

If poetic voice, point of view, and persona are appropriate initial stylistic topics for the poems of humble and rustic life, then qualified language, syntactic complexity, and—most important—imagery and metaphor become the appropriate stylistic concerns during study of the next assignments. In poems like "Lines Written in Early Spring," "To My Sister," "Expostulation and Reply," "The Tables Turned," and the great "Lines Composed a Few Miles above Tintern Abbey," Wordsworth's genius is that he retains the sense of natural simplicity while weaving ambitious philosophic themes into the fabric of a strongly subjective discourse. Students' previous experience with voice and persona in the first group of poems prepares them to see this intricacy. They readily perceive the more lyrical, contemplative tone and the more unambiguously personal or autobiographical character of the poetic speaker in these poems, and they are therefore disposed to consider the proposition that these works reflect a strong preoccupation with feeling and thought, with the development and movement of personal consciousness.

I find it useful to promote such observations about these poems even before taking up discussion of the ideas they carry, for in the undergraduate classroom few things become more reductive and more subject to misunderstanding than concepts like Lockean epistemology and so-called pantheistic religion discussed apart from the artistic context in which they occur. When we do discuss these ideas, I point out Wordsworth's conceptual tentativeness as seen in his frequent use of litotes and in his even more obvious language of qualification at precisely those points when he offers the highest and most daring notions about the power and beneficence of nature in its relation to the human mind. In "Lines Written in Early Spring," for instance, phrases like " 'tis my faith that . . .," "It seemed . . .," and "I must think, do all I can . . ." signify such tentativeness—as does, of course, the word "may" in probably the most famous quatrain from this group of poems:

> One impulse from a vernal wood
> May teach you more of man,
> Of moral evil and of good,
> Than all the sages can.   ("The Tables Turned")

Despite the high philosophic ambition of these poems, Wordsworth's style reveals that here, as in all of his work that is worthwhile, his strategy is not to reason his readers into acceptance of his views but to make his audience feel them. I point this out in relation to his explicit poetic statements, of course—"We murder to dissect," and so forth—but the truth of such a proposition presents itself most forcefully through Wordsworth's use of imagery and metaphor. I call attention at every turn to the omnipresent visual and auditory images in Wordsworth's descriptions of the mighty world of eye and ear, but I stress especially those more subtle imagistic effects that integrate style and theme—such as imagery of unity and connection, wherein the "thousand *blended* notes" of "Lines Written in Early Spring" and the unifying "one green hue" and cliffs that "*connect* / The landscape with the quiet of the sky" in "Tintern Abbey" (13, 7-8) become far more powerful persuaders of nature's unity and beneficence than any rational discourse could be.

So too with Wordsworthian metaphor. Unlike the artificial use of figure that he deplores in the 1800 Preface (which I do have the class read at about this time), his most successful metaphors are so natural and subtle that I find I must alert students to their presence, as well as indicate their effects. It is true that Wordsworth's poetry includes a share of obvious metaphors—such as the natural calendar opposed to the "joyless" mechanical one in "To My Sister" (17), or as in the line "Let Nature be your Teacher" in "The Tables Turned" and the like—but these examples are comparatively incidental, and I use them by way of entry into more complex figural concerns. In fact, at this early juncture I seize the opportunity to introduce the Wordsworthian version of that metaphorical phenomenon most familiarly known as Romantic "displacement."

Displacement—the stylistic device by means of which Romantic poets exploit material familiar to their culture by evoking it in order to substitute their own more idiosyncratic terms and beliefs for its original details and ideas—takes two forms in these early Wordsworth poems. One will soon fade from his style, while the other will characterize his mysticism and his sense of poetic mission until it transposes back to its original nonmetaphorical terms in his later career. In the first, Wordsworth—never a whole-hearted adherent of either Locke's epistemology or Hartley's associationist psychology—nevertheless exploits the recognizable terminology of their teachings to promote his own doctrine of nature. Accordingly, I call attention in class not only to the all-important second verse paragraph in "Tintern Abbey" but also to the semantic charge imparted to Wordsworth's language by words like "impress," "feeling," "sensation," "impulse" whenever he is either counseling or giving testimony regarding "wise passiveness" in his early meditative nature poetry.

The second form of displacement is, of course, that which Wordsworth achieves through his use of religious language. During class discussion I focus not only on such obvious lines as "There is a blessing in the air" (which will be echoed in the opening of *The Prelude*) but also on Wordsworth's use of "feed" and "drink" as naturalistic allusions to the sacrament, including even such playfully ghoulish punning as "drink the spirit breathed / From dead men to their kind" in "Expostulation and Reply." Besides their direct application to interpretation of this early group of poems, such observations help prepare students for Wordsworth's later donning of "priestly robe" as he pursues his poetic destiny, a "renovated spirit" (*Prelude* 1. 53, 54) whose Romantic natural-supernatural quest M. H. Abrams and others have documented so thoroughly.

A large stylistic concern most appropriately taken up in conjunction with study of *The Prelude* is Wordsworth's blank verse, especially his long period. I say something about the history of the blank-verse form, its special character and effect, but my comments do not suffice to overcome reading problems for students not used to syntactic complexity or to Wordsworth's deliberate strategy of parenthesis and qualification—a strategy intended to produce that sense of mental exploration and tentative conclusion immediately modified and revised by further thought that characterizes his own ruminative poetic mind. I have found that the most effective means of teaching this feature of his style is simply to select several important but syntactically difficult passages for reading aloud in class. This device may seem elementary, but it serves the twin purposes of, first, applying the intonations, emphases, and pauses of the human voice to the problem and, second, demonstrating that individual students have indeed solved that problem for themselves.

Another broad feature of Wordsworth's style that I find of crucial importance in teaching his works is his use of allusion. Wordsworth's allusiveness takes at least two forms—conventional and personal. As with all allusion it creates special problems for the undergraduate, whose reading background often is in relatively early stages of development. I therefore find it necessary to rehearse some rather elementary matters—for instance, the conventions of classical epic invocation when we discuss the Prospectus to *The Recluse*— and simply to identify any literary references students are not likely to recognize on their own. Of course, allusions to specific writers call for more careful attention. I supply special background on Wordsworth's relation to Milton, and I go so far as to read directly to the class such passages as that from book 12 of *Paradise Lost* (no longer, alas, quite obvious and well known to college students) which Wordsworth so carefully and so self-consciously recasts in the first nineteen lines of *The Prelude*.

Wordsworth's personal allusions—that is, references to his own earlier attitudes and, sometimes, even to the words of his earlier poems—present an interesting means of assessing thematic development and change in the course of his writing. Such allusiveness can be subtle, as in later books of *The Prelude*, where the earlier dominance of sensory experience gives place to the mind and imagination and where we find the mind characterized as "lord and master—outward sense / The obedient servant . . ." (12. 222-23) in a perhaps unconscious modifying of the earlier marriage metaphor in the Prospectus. Or it may appear more obviously, as in "Resolution and Independence," "Ode to Duty," and "Peele Castle." In the last, for example, the line referring to a former illusory sense of "A steadfast peace that might not be *betrayed*" (32) clearly echoes—and in so doing qualifies—the famous early conviction that "Nature never did *betray* / The heart that loved her" ("Tintern Abbey" 122-23).

In this brief discussion I have been able only to touch upon the many points of style to be addressed during the teaching of any fully representative unit on Wordsworth, but I hope I have given some substance to my contention that style must be included in discussion of his works from first to last and that one can treat it in a cumulative fashion, beginning with elementary and limited stylistic principles and building up an increasingly complex and flexible awareness of style as students progressively encounter Wordsworth's variety.

Wordsworth and the Sister Arts

Nicholas O. Warner

Throughout his career, Wordsworth revealed a deep interest in the relation between the sister arts of painting and poetry, and my own experience indicates several pedagogical advantages in comparing his poetry to visual art. They include the vivid illumination of key Wordsworthian passages and Romantic concepts; the stimulation of student interest through slides and other visual material; a change of pace in classroom teaching methods; and the communication to students of a richer sense of the cultural and artistic context of Wordsworth's poetic theory and practice.

Because I use the visual arts to supplement rather than to replace student study of the poetry, I spend my first few class sessions on Wordsworth examining texts alone, such as the Preface to the *Lyrical Ballads* and various poems that introduce Wordsworth's main concerns. Once students have read and discussed these works, we move on to the poetry's relation to eighteenth- and early nineteenth-century English painting. (By this time, the class will also have seen Kenneth Clark's film "The Worship of Nature," which gets students thinking about Romanticism in interdisciplinary terms and is a charming general introduction to Wordsworth's era.)

For organizational clarity, I divide my comparatist approach to Wordsworth into two sections: the first is based on those poems where Wordsworth's subject matter and attitudes reveal an affinity with the works of English landscape painters, notably Gainsborough, Wilson, Constable, and Turner; the second section is based on those poems where Wordsworth describes actual works of art (what Jean Hagstrum in *The Sister Arts* calls "iconic" poetry), by such painters as Raphael, Rubens, Leonardo da Vinci, Haydon, and Beaumont. I introduce the topic of literary-artistic relations in a lecture that begins by distinguishing landscape painting from history painting and portraiture; I then move on to trace the parallel development of eighteenth-century landscape poetry and painting toward those qualities we call "Romantic" (Kroeber, *Landscape* and "Constable," is of great value here, as are Clark, *Landscape*, and Tinker). While I refer to Wordsworth's connections to the picturesque and show a few slides of the works of Girtin, Gilpin, and Wilson, the first painter I compare in detail to Wordsworth is his closest visual forerunner, Gainsborough.

At the very root of Wordsworth's affinity with Gainsborough is, of course, the humble subject matter often chosen by both. Dying just a decade before the appearance of the *Lyrical Ballads*, Gainsborough left behind him (with the exception of such works as portraits and mythological scenes) a body of painting that treats "low and rustic life" and that, as Tinker says of Gainsborough's *The Woodman*, "is in truth a prelude to the work of that poet who was to make Michael, Simon Lee, and the Old Cumberland Beggar familiar names in the history of poetry" (98). Even the titles of paintings like *Shepherd-Boy in a Storm*, *The Cottage Door*, *The Old Horse*, *Landscape with Bridge*, and *The Market-Wagon* resonate with true Wordsworthian rusticity. As we look in class at these and other pictures, I depart from lecturing to invite student commentary on specific parallels between these scenes and Wordsworth's poems. Out of this discussion grows a consideration of broader issues: to what extent are Wordsworth's and Gainsborough's works dissimilar? Do students find either or both of these men's attitudes sentimental? Are there any patterns to their portrayal of women? How are children depicted in their works? Such questions generate lively exchanges and stimulate greater student interest in Wordsworth's poetry and even, mirabile dictu, in his poetic theory.

After Gainsborough's paintings, I introduce students to those of Turner, John Crome, and, especially, Constable. Using a lecture-discussion format, I explore the striking similarities between Constable's vision and that of Wordsworth—for example, their fascination with the interplay of sky and landscape; their loving presentation of ordinary things in an unusual light; their revolution against the "established artistic hierarchy" (Paulson 108); their emphasis on the union of imagination with nature. Our main study of Wordsworth's relation to Constable comes later, however, after students have reached the "spots of time" passage in *The Prelude*. I begin by lecturing briefly on analogues to Wordsworth's "spots of time" in Constable's work (Kroeber, *Landscape*, and Swingle are particularly helpful here). Following this lecture, we discuss (with healthy skepticism, I might add) the extent to which certain Constable paintings (*The View on the Stour*, *The Hay Wain*, *The White Horse*, *The Cornfield*, *The Leaping Horse*, and the various views of Salisbury Cathedral) do or do not qualify as parallels to the "visual set-pieces" (Swingle 82) and "spots of time" found in *The Prelude* and elsewhere in Wordsworth's poetry. Especially useful for this discussion, as well as for the general study of Wordsworth's poetry in relation to art, are "Descriptive Sketches," "Tintern Abbey," "I Wandered Lonely as a Cloud," "The Solitary Reaper," *The Prelude*, *The Excursion*, and "Home at Grasmere."

At this point in the course I generally assign a short paper on one of several interdisciplinary topics: a comparison-contrast study of a painting and a poem; a limited research exercise in late eighteenth-century aesthetic theory; a discussion of painterly images in Wordsworth's poetry. One such topic that has had considerable success requires students to choose a painting by Gainsborough or Constable that they would like to have described by Wordsworth, as well as a passage by Wordsworth they would like to have depicted by the same artist, and to explain the reasons for their choices. Students also have the option of writing on an interdisciplinary topic for their term papers.

I conclude my segment on Wordsworth and the sister arts with one session devoted to his "iconic" poems, particularly to the most famous of them, "Elegiac Stanzas." After lecturing on the poem, I show students a slide of Beaumont's *Peele Castle*, and we discuss in detail the connections between Wordsworth's poem and Beaumont's painting. This discussion in turn leads to questions on the general relation between visual artifacts and literary descriptions of them and on various specific issues such as the relation between Wordsworth's view of "This sea in anger, and that dismal shore" (line 44) and other Romantic poets' images of the sea. Discussions of this last topic, in fact, have led to some fine student papers on storm and ship-wreck imagery in Romantic poetry and art. Such papers, as well as student enthusiasm for the approach outlined here, amply testify to the values and pleasures of teaching Wordsworth's poetry in relation to visual art.

A Thematic Arrangement of the Major Texts

Anthony John Harding

For those students, a majority at my university, who come to a second- or third-year class on the Romantic period with little or no previous experience of poetry, an author-by-author approach (doing all the Wordsworth before reading any Coleridge) seems rather forbidding, and an approach by way of either poetic kinds or literary history (the discrimination of romanticisms) seems too technical. My preferred approach, therefore, is thematic. The initial aim is to reach students where they are, in their suspicion and distrust of poetic utterance, rather than to impress them with the mysteries of the poet's vocation or of poetic influence. These things come later, but not too much later, and almost always emerge from the students' own questions. I follow chronology only in that I cover the first-generation Romantics in the first of two thirteen-week terms and the second-generation Romantics (with a few further Blake and Coleridge texts) in the second term. The dominant figures are Wordsworth in the first term and Shelley in the second.

There are several advantages to abandoning a strictly chronological and author-by-author arrangement. The first section of the course, Literature of Protest and Compassion, on the social dislocations of the 1790s, treats Blake's *Songs* alongside Wordsworth's "Simon Lee," "Old Man Travelling," "We Are Seven," "The Last of the Flock," and—eventually—"Michael." Wordsworth and Blake are both aware that merely to describe the mind and emotion of a subject would be in some way to belittle him or her. The chimney-sweeper, shepherd, and retired huntsman have different consciousnesses; each is formed by and sometimes threatened by his experience of the world. Simple as this assertion sounds, it posts an effective warning against the automatic reading of every poem as the expression of the poet's feelings or point of view. We also explore the resemblances and differences between Wordsworth's treatment of the rural and urban dispossessed and Thomson's and Goldsmith's descriptions of similar figures. The section ends with more overtly political material: Blake's *Visions of the Daughters of Albion*, Wollstonecraft's *The Wrongs of Woman*, and Wordsworth's account of his revolutionary enthusiasms in books 6 and 10-11 of *The Prelude*.

Having learned from both Blake and certain of the lyrical ballads that "the eye altering alters all," we enter the second section (on Coleridge's and Wordsworth's vision of landscape) with rather different preoccupations than we would have if we had begun the study of Wordsworth with "An Evening Walk" and "Descriptive Sketches." The main business of this section is the close study of Coleridge's conversation poems and Wordsworth's "Tintern Abbey," "A Night-Piece," "Nutting," "Michael" again, and several selections from *The Prelude*—principally books 1 (the ravens'-nesting and boat-stealing passages) and 12 (the "spots of time" passage). Students also read parts of Dorothy Wordsworth's journals. The poets' use of the term "sublime" in its psychological as well as in its aesthetic sense invites discussion of why the Romantics had to pass beyond the aesthetic categories offered by Gilpin, Price, and other writers on the picturesque.

Wordsworth's claim, astonishing to most students (and rightly so), that in certain kinds of experience the mind is "lord and master" (*Prelude* 12.222) propels us vigorously into a section on nightmare, madness, and imagination, with "The Rime of the Ancient Mariner," "Christabel," "The Pains of Sleep," the Lucy poems, "Resolution and Independence," and "Elegiac Stanzas" as key texts. (The class is also encouraged to read some John Clare, particularly "Decay" and "I Am.")

By this time most students have seen that one aim of the first three sections of the course is to stimulate inquiry into the Romantic understanding of perception: how perception is not uniform but is affected by the nature and experience of the onlooker. Had this proposition been presented at the beginning of the course, it would have been dismissed as either improbable or self-evident, but since it emerges now from careful examination of certain poems and certain realized moments of perceptual awareness, it stimulates rather than predetermines discussion. Since Blake's Oothoon and Wollstone-craft's Mary are still fresh in students' minds, the use of female figures—Christabel, Lucy, Geraldine, Abyssinian maid—to invoke what Shelley calls the unchangeable forms of human nature often leads students to investigate the Romantics' sense of a crippling antinomy in our notions of gender.

The first half of the course reaches its climax in the section Poetic Failure and Poetic Rebirth, which examines those great affirmations of the possibility of a different kind of perception: "Kubla Khan," "Ode: Intimations of Immortality," "Dejection: An Ode," "Home at Grasmere," and books 1, 4, and 14 of *The Prelude*. The abandonment of chronology once more brings considerable benefits. Students who have already read "Resolution and Independence" and "Elegiac Stanzas" are less likely to interpret the Immortality Ode as facilely optimistic or as self-indulgently nostalgic, and they tend not to seize on the paradise themes in "Kubla Khan," *The Prelude*, and "Home at Grasmere" as evidence of Romantic longing for the unattainable but to give these themes due recognition as evidence of a faith upheld amid difficulty and pain. Lastly, by confronting the first three hundred lines of *The Prelude* only after wide acquaintance with the resources of Wordsworth's language, students are better prepared to see that Wordsworth is interested not in Rousseauvian "confessions," recording his autobiographical highs and lows, but in transforming altogether the way we think about individual lives and moments.

A thematic rather than chronological arrangement helps conquer students'
suspicions about poetry in general and Romantic poetry in particular. It
stimulates critical discussion through juxtaposition of poems on related themes
by two or more authors. The symbiosis between Wordsworth and Coleridge
emerges much more clearly. The principal pedagogical advantage, however,
is that each section of the course, while possessing its own intrinsic interest,
builds on what has gone before and prepares for what comes afterward.
Students feel no sense of anticlimax, as they might if, for example, *The
Prelude* were taught early in a section on Wordsworth. Moreover—for me
one of the most significant benefits—when the students propose their topics
for the major paper in the second term, they invariably avoid the well-
trodden path of the single-author topic and devise original and inventive
comparative topics that open new perspectives on the achievement of the
first-generation Romantic poets.

The First-Generation Romantic Writers: A Sample Syllabus

1. Literature of Protest and Compassion
Thomson: *The Seasons*, "Winter" (1746 version) 276-321
Blake: *Songs of Innocence and of Experience*
Wordsworth: "Old Man Travelling," "The Reverie of Poor Susan," "We Are Seven,"
  "Simon Lee," "The Last of the Flock," "Michael"; *Prelude* (1850) 4.370-460 (the
  discharged soldier), 6.323-74, 10.48-299, 11.52-152 (France and Revolution); 1800
  Preface to *Lyrical Ballads*
Blake: *Visions of the Daughters of Albion*
Wollstonecraft: *The Wrongs of Woman*

2. Picturesque and Sublime Landscape
Thomson: *The Seasons*, "Spring" (1746 version) 67-78, 498-525
Goldsmith: *The Deserted Village* 1-34, 287-309
Coleridge: "Reflections on Having Left a Place of Retirement," "The Eolian Harp,"
  "This Lime-Tree Bower My Prison," "Frost at Midnight"
Dorothy Wordsworth: journal for 25, 27, 31 January 1798, 24 March 1798
Wordsworth: "A Night-Piece," "Nutting," "Lines Written in Early Spring," "Mi-
  chael"; 1850 *Prelude* 12.208-86 (spots of time), 1.301-498 (ravens'-nesting, boat-
  stealing); "Tintern Abbey"

3. Nightmare, Madness, and Imagination
Coleridge: "The Rime of the Ancient Mariner," "Christabel"
Dorothy Wordsworth: journal for 7 March 1798, 3 October 1800
Wordsworth: "Strange fits of passion," "She dwelt among the untrodden ways,"
  "Three years she grew," "A slumber did my spirit seal," "Resolution and Inde-
  pendence," "Elegiac Stanzas"
Coleridge: "The Pains of Sleep," "Limbo"
John Clare: "I Am," "Decay"

4. Poetic Failure, Poetic Rebirth
Coleridge: "Kubla Khan"
Wordsworth: "Ode: Intimations of Immortality"
Coleridge: "Dejection: An Ode"
Wordsworth: "Home at Grasmere"; 1850 *Prelude* 1.1-300 (glad preamble; poet seeks
    his task), 4.297-338 (vocation), 14.130-232 (river of Imagination)

(Blake's *The Marriage of Heaven and Hell*, parts of Coleridge's *Biographia Literaria*,
    Austen's *Northanger Abbey*, Mary Shelley's *Frankenstein*, and the poetry of Byron,
    Shelley and Keats are covered in the second term of this two-semester course.)

Two Honors Courses on Wordsworth and Criticism

Craig Howes

Wordsworth wrote his criticism of life and art simultaneously, and most successfully in his poetry. I will outline two courses that suggest the range of possibilities Wordsworth's brooding presence allows for in a class whose central concern is critical.

Critical methods courses often have a "Thirteen Ways of Looking at a Poem" quality that emphasizes how many things you can do rather than how suitable an approach might be for reading a specific work. I have tried to avoid this problem in my first honors seminar, Critical Approaches to Literature, by choosing four masterworks as test cases for studying the strengths and limitations of various critical methods. Wordsworth's poetry is one of these texts, sharing the semester with *King Lear, Paradise Lost*, and *A Portrait of the Artist as a Young Man*. Although most of the critical perspectives I introduce could apply to any of my texts, in the ten class sessions on Wordsworth I stress those perspectives that concentrate on the writer's relation to and status within the text.

Though *Lear* or the two major versions of *Portrait* would be excellent examples for teaching textual criticism, facing-page editions make *The Prelude* ideal for examining the stages a text can pass through before "completion." Wordsworth's canon also helps students see the advantages of biographical approaches to literature. I draw on firsthand accounts—Dorothy's journal entry on the daffodils always excites and confuses students about the nature of poetic inspiration—and I distribute a chapter from Moorman's biography, especially since she makes a concerted effort to integrate *The Prelude* into the life. Wordsworth's critical prose also raises questions of voice and poetic calling, but it demonstrates as well the insights gained and difficulties encountered when reading poets about themselves. The Preface to *Lyrical Ballads* is perhaps the best text I know for testing Lawrence's "Don't trust the teller; trust the tale"; trying to reconcile Wordsworth's theories about poetic diction with the Miltonic *Prelude* leads easily into discussion of "Simon Lee," or even "We Are Seven."

One rich topic for debate is Wordsworth's claim that "the feeling [in his poetry] gives importance to the action and situation, and not the action and the situation to the feeling" (Preface to *Lyrical Ballads*, Stillinger 448). The Lucy poems show how this principle operates but also challenge it, since the students soon see that the diction and imagery may block access to—or even erase—a prior moment that might have provoked the emotion expressed. And, of course, the Preface's claims about true poets and their place in literary tradition become particularly important when the students have already read Milton and Shakespeare. I finish the Wordsworth section with those chapters from Coleridge's *Biographia Literaria* that tie the poet, the critical assumptions, and the poetry together. In short, Wordsworth helps the class explore a number of problems that any introduction to critical theory must confront.

In my second honors seminar, Literature and Society: Changing Perspectives on the Artist, Wordsworth becomes the pivotal figure in a study of literary and aesthetic tradition. Starting with the *Ion* and the *Poetics* and moving through Sidney, Shakespeare, Dryden, and Pope into early modernism, the course focuses on the history of critical and creative writing about literary artists—their sources of inspiration, their special qualities, their social roles, and their activity's relation to other human endeavors. The Preface and *The Prelude* follow Boswell's *Life of Johnson*, and the classes center on how Wordsworth responds to the cultural changes that Johnson recognizes and relates to the writer's calling. The greater dissemination of literature to a growing audience, the transformation of the English landscape and work force, and the conceptual realignment of the various mental faculties—most notably, the new primacy of the creative imagination—are all subjects that make Wordsworth crucial to the course.

One particularly rich session examines the artist's response to innovation and revolution. By this point, we have read many arguments for poets as the apologists or panegyrists for existing secular and sacred institutions. *The Prelude* explores in detail the conflicts that declaring for or against the status quo entails. The French Revolution becomes Wordsworth's trial by fire, forcing choices among ideologies, national allegiances, and versions of history. Wordsworth, then, is the course's Janus figure, since he shows why the Romantic artist has always been linked to philosophical, political, and aesthetic upheavals but also why the movement from one perception of the artist to another is not an absolute break but a new configuration. He provides a fresh rhetoric that becomes fully significant as the course moves to Shelley and Arnold. Thus, Wordsworth provides the text for two major issues. As historical fulcrum, he represents the innovations associated with Romanticism; as figure within a tradition, he provides a revitalized rhetoric for understanding how the world perceives artists and how artists perceive themselves.

Wordsworth is an excellent focus for a critical theory course. First, his poetry makes students address the question of speaking voice, whether as biological figure, as contemplative and social subject, or as occupant of a moment in literary history. Narrative, generic, and linguistic concerns all become subordinate to Wordsworth's problematic assertion of self. Second, the easy move from Wordsworth's prose to the equally significant criticism found in his poetry forces the student to recognize the difficulty of separating the critical from the creative. Finally, Wordsworth's suitability as a test case for so many different critical perspectives suggests that his canon is a virtually inexhaustible ground for contemplation and learning. Though these courses surround him with different texts, Wordsworth remains the focus, a point of departure and return.

TEACHING INDIVIDUAL TEXTS

Scorn Not the Sonnet

Spencer Hall

It is probably not common knowledge that Wordsworth wrote over five hundred sonnets or that his stature as a writer of sonnets figured significantly in contemporary appraisals of his place in literary history. I suspect, however, that many teachers rely heavily on the sonnets in the classroom, particularly nonspecialists teaching introductory literary surveys. My own experience is that selected sonnets make a useful introduction, both to Wordsworth's poetry and to English Romanticism.

One might begin with a brief (and necessarily superficial) glance at literary backgrounds. I tell my students that, after almost a hundred years of neglect, the second half of the eighteenth century saw a virtual renaissance of sonnet writing, which the major Romantic poets, with Wordsworth and Keats preeminent among them, exploited, advanced, and passed on to the later nineteenth century. I ask students to consider these questions: Why would the sonnet, as a poetic form, appeal to the Romantics? What historical associations of the form would be most important to them? In what ways would you expect them—and especially Wordsworth—to adapt the form given their characteristic views about poetry and the imagination? Even beginning students see fairly quickly that the vogue of the sonnet was related to the prominence of lyric modes in Romantic poetry and to the sonnet's valuation of feeling, sincerity, and personal experience. They require a little more direction to see the connection between the sonnet and Romantic attempts to identify with Renaissance poetic traditions while rejecting Neoclassical literary standards, which included a general denigration of the sonnet as a serious poetic form.

Wordsworth's late "Scorn not the sonnet" is both a fair example of his use of the form and a clear statement of the associations with which he invested it. (See also his other famous sonnet on writing sonnets, "Nuns fret not at their convent's narrow room.") He calls the sonnet the "key" with which "Shakspeare unlocked his heart" and the "glow-worm lamp" that "cheered mild Spenser, called from Faery-land / To struggle through dark ways." Characteristically, however, his interest is less in the form's gentler, largely amorous associations than in its adoption by Milton for more serious purposes:

> . . . and when a damp
> Fell round the path of Milton, in his hand
> The Thing became a trumpet; whence he
>   blew
> Soul-animating strains—alas, too few!

Wordsworth's self-conscious measuring of his poetic identity and historical mission against those of Milton is an important topic to raise with undergraduates, either as an "anxiety of influence" or in a less antithetical context. A number of the powerful political and ethical sonnets written in 1802 show Wordsworth taking to his own lips Milton's prophetic "trumpet." He admonishes his compatriots for having "forfeited their ancient English dower / Of inward happiness" ("London, 1802"), exhorts them to return to "the good old cause" of freedom and morality ("Written in London, September, 1802"), reminds them that "Great men have been among us," and cautions that "We must be free or die, who speak the tongue / That Shakspeare spake; the faith and morals hold / Which Milton held" ("It is not to be thought of that the flood").

In his important and pedagogically useful letter to Lady Beaumont (21 May 1807), Wordsworth claims that the various sonnets in his *Poems, in Two Volumes* "collectively make a [single] Poem on the subject of civil Liberty and national independence, which either for its simplicity of style or grandeur of moral sentiment, is, alas! likely to have few parallels in the Poetry of the present day" (Zall 79-80). (This claim, by the way, can provide students with topics for research and analytical papers.) Many of us emphasize in our teaching Wordsworth's boast, in the Prospectus to *The Recluse*, that he will "pass . . . unalarmed" Milton's Christian mythology to proclaim his own myths of nature and of mind. We may neglect, however, the extent to which he dons Milton's prophetic mantle and practices Milton's sonnet form to express an increasingly conservative and nationalistic response to Napoleonic France and to the moral condition of his own country. We are speaking here of the "reactionary" element in English Romanticism, which is often undervalued in our legitimate fascination, in undergraduate classes, with the "revolutionary."

The letter to Lady Beaumont also contains a revealing exegesis of Wordsworth's own sonnet "With ships the sea was sprinkled far and nigh." This analysis, studied in conjunction with the poem, is one of the best introductions I know to certain essential aspects, both stylistic and psychological, of Wordsworth's poetry. It clarifies for students his intention to trace in his poems "some general principle, or law of thought, or of our intellectual constitution" (Zall 81)—a claim first made in the Preface to *Lyrical Ballads*—and warns them that in Wordsworth's poetry description is always a kind of creation, that external images are always referable to the mind that perceives them and gives them significance.

The Norton Anthology of World Masterpieces (ed. Mack), the required text for the Western literature survey at my school, prints two sonnets by Wordsworth: "Composed upon Westminster Bridge" and "The world is too much with us." Taken together, they provide a point of entry both into Wordsworth's major poetry and into salient features of Romantic literature. I ask students to contrast the two poems, paying particular attention to speaker and tone. The resulting class discussion will formulate certain basic distinctions. "Westminster Bridge" illustrates the concept of Romantic vision, as the poet, dramatizing a privileged moment of imaginative perception, asserts a quasi-mystical insight into the heart of things: "Ne'er saw I, never felt, a calm so deep!" In "The world is too much with us," we have the typical other side of the Romantic coin: the lament for vision lost ("Little we see in Nature that is ours"), the cry of alienation that almost always haunts the Romantic assertion of oneness.

Oneness with what? Alienation from what? I introduce here the great Wordsworthian theme of nature, or, more precisely, the relation between humanity and nature. In the first sonnet, human-made London, so problematically portrayed in book 7 of *The Prelude*, is redeemed, made beautiful and vital (note the overtones of Genesis in the poem), by "opening" itself to and becoming an organic part of its natural surroundings. In the second, human life is polluted by the socioeconomic "world" of "getting and spending," which stands in stark opposition to organic "Nature" and thus estranges us from our deepest natural selves, from "our powers," "our hearts," our intrinsic humanity. A third widely printed sonnet, "It is a beauteous evening," adds the characteristic figure of the child (in this case, his own daughter Caroline) to Wordsworth's myth of natural piety. These sonnets provide an easily taught conceptual and symbolic framework for approaching such major texts as "Tintern Abbey," the Immortality Ode, and *The Prelude*.

The "narrow room" of the sonnet is a useful vehicle for getting students to think about matters of form, style, and interpretation. "Westminster Bridge" has become a favorite of mine in introductions to poetry as well as in general education and Romantic surveys. (In addition to its inherent riches, the poem can be compared with Dorothy's description of the same scene in her journal for 30 July 1802. Students enjoy these comparisons, which often lead to deepened insights into Wordsworth's style and which can make interesting paper topics.) After making sure that students see the "organic" nature of the imagery, especially the manner in which human-made particulars— "Ships, towers, domes, theatres, and temples"—are subsumed in the larger natural scene, I ask them if they find anything paradoxical, unexpected, or unusual in the poem's language. As Cleanth Brooks has argued, the entire situation is, in one sense, paradoxical since the poem turns on the poet's visionary apperception of "this City" as alive and beautiful when he had expected it to be otherwise (5-7). The mild paradox of "touching in its majesty" perhaps enforces the unaccustomed wholeness of this visionary moment.

I emphasize, however, the only overt simile in the sonnet—"This City now doth, like a garment, wear / The beauty of the morning"—in order to bring up the topic of poetic figuration, which moves us beyond Brooks's New Critical formalism and toward a tentatively deconstructive or antithetical reading of the "garment" image. (Garment imagery, as Geoffrey Hartman has suggested, is frequently problematical in Wordsworth's poetry, [*Unmediated Vision* 11-12].) Wordsworth's obvious intention is to picture London as "bare" and "open" to nature, yet the image is one of covering; the fissure between these two meanings opens the possibility that the city, beneath its vestment of natural beauty, remains unredeemed. (Wordsworth records that Mrs. John Kenyon pointed out the apparent incongruity to him. "The contradiction," he replied, "is in the words only." See Woodring, *Wordsworth* 166-69.) Also, I have always found a few students in every class who respond to the last line—"And all that mighty heart is lying still"—as an image of death, an image that casts a pall (to continue the garment image) over the sonnet's apparent idealism. We might even entertain the possibility that "lying still" betrays a thematically relevant pun.

Heuristic ingenuity is really not the point here. In the first place, Wordsworth's poetry is pervaded by complex emotional, psychological, and textual oppositions—turbulence and calm, energy and restraint, will and passivity— that often coalesce around the confrontation with mortality. (The Lucy poems are probably the most obvious examples on the usual undergraduate reading

list.) "Westminster Bridge" provides for the beginning student a comparatively accessible entry into these poetic complexes and also into the concept
of skeptical subtexts in Wordsworth's poetry and in Romanticism generally—
that is, the concept of implicit levels of discourse that deny or qualify the
poet's overtly intended meanings. More important, close study of the sonnets
may help students attend to the often deceptively nonfigurative texture of
Wordsworth's poetry and respond to the equally deceptive resonance of his
language. Perhaps more important still, students can be led to consider,
consciously and critically, the process of interpretation itself and their own
acts of reading. Such critical self-awareness was, after all, one of Wordsworth's major goals both as literary theorist and as poet.

The Preface in Relation to the *Lyrical Ballads*

Judith W. Page

When I teach the Preface to *Lyrical Ballads* in my undergraduate course in Romanticism, I spend the first class placing it in its literary-historical context and the second relating it to the lyrical ballads themselves. I try to show that the ideas in the Preface grew naturally out of Wordsworth's experiments with the poems in the 1798 and 1800 editions of *Lyrical Ballads*, that the theory of the Preface is directly related to Wordsworth's discoveries as he composed poetry. My main emphasis is on its psychological orientation. I isolate three major areas for discussion: (1) associationism: the purpose and definition of poetry; (2) style: poetic diction and meter; (3) subject matter: the elevation of the commonplace and ordinary.

Most students have little difficulty understanding the association of ideas, although they usually have no background in the British empirical tradition on which Wordsworth's theory is based. After outlining this tradition, I discuss the importance of the ideas of the Preface for Wordsworth's poetry and poetics. Wordsworth's theory of associationism is based on a whole concept of the human mind and its development over time, a theory that Wordsworth developed through his experiences and worked out in his poetry. Wordsworth's major poems are mimetic not of action in the Aristotelian sense but of mental processes. I point out that this theory was adopted by a poet who, in 1798, was beginning to construct his major long poem as the story of the growth of his own mind.

The poems in the *Lyrical Ballads* often represent Wordsworth's attempts to understand the workings of the human mind during intense moments or states of excitement. When Wordsworth proclaims his interest in the way we associate feelings and ideas in a state of excitement, he means that he is interested in mental properties that all people or particular groups share. In "The Idiot Boy" he traces the "maternal passion" through its various stages; in "The Thorn" he demonstrates the way a superstitious mind works on a scene and half creates it through imagination.

I draw a distinction between Wordsworth's creation of such characters as Betty Foy and the retired sea captain of "The Thorn" and his creation of the autobiographical persona in "Tintern Abbey." Here it is easy to see that he is showing the way his own mind associates ideas in a state of excitement, half creating and half receiving the landscape before him. I use "Tintern Abbey" to illustrate that Wordsworth's train of thought moves from the immediate scene of 13 July 1798 back to his memory of earlier times. Thus, his associationism involves recollection of an original experience or feeling and leads to a recognition of how the passage of time has changed his being.

I also point out the technical devices that Wordsworth develops for representing mental processes. For instance, he says in the note to "The Thorn" that repetition is the mark of conversational speech. In a poem like "The Thorn" this repetition seems forced and self-conscious, but Wordsworth wants it to represent the fluxes and refluxes of his superstitious sea captain's mind. In "Tintern Abbey" the repetition strikes us as much more natural and un-self-conscious, although it is every bit as artful. Students can see how the repetition in "hedgerows, hardly hedgerows, little lines / Of sportive wood run wild" traces the speaker's mental processes as he looks out on the Wye Valley and re-creates the scene before him, correcting and revising his vision as he goes along. Working carefully through the repetition in the first verse paragraph of "Tintern Abbey" impresses the concept of associationism on students and provides the perfect blending of the immediate and concrete (the present scene) and the abstract or imaginary (what the present scene conjures up in the mind). It also shows the relation between poetic language and thought processes.

This topic brings up the concept of style in the Preface and in the poems. Wordsworth's theory of language and meter is colored by his psychological orientation. For him, diction is appropriate only if it has psychological propriety, and meter is justified on the grounds that it helps to express emotional and mental attitudes. Students are quick to assume that when Wordsworth claims to adopt "the very language of men" (Owen and Smyser 1: 130) he means that he will adopt the language of Lake District rustics; but the poems, they notice, do not bear this claim out. Now is the moment to ask whether Wordsworth's definition of "the very language of men" implies not so much a cultural as a psychological reality.

I use the examples that Wordsworth supplies in the Preface, such as Gray's "Elegy on the Death of Mr. Richard West," to illustrate his principle and to contrast his practice with that of previous poets. Wordsworth's reading of Gray's poem is suggestive; he does not object to obviously poetic syntactic inversions such as "A different object do these eyes require" or "And in my breast the perfect joys expire," which he considers part of that "very language," the language of prose. What he does object to are expressions like "reddening Phoebus," used for the sun. I ask the students why he objects and suggest that he does so because such an expression is merely conventional and therefore has no psychological reality. (No one gets up in the morning and sees the sun as reddening Phoebus—not even in eighteenth-century England.) I contrast this expression with Wordsworth's personification in "Tintern Abbey" of the Wye River as "Thou wanderer through the woods"; here the expression grows out of the poet's deepest feelings and thoughts about a particular natural object and the processes of the natural world.

It might also be helpful to contrast Gray's "Elegy on the Death of Richard West" with the Lucy poems, which are certainly elegiac if not elegies proper. "A slumber did my spirit seal" is about loss, death, total absence of the loved one, but there is no reference to the "amorous descant" of birds, "smiling mornings," or "cheerful fields" oblivious to human grief. Instead we get the stark contrast between the speaker's past feeling ("She seemed a thing that could not feel / The touch of earthly years") and his realization that Lucy is gone forever ("No motion has she now, no force"). The primarily monosyllabic and bisyllabic language comes not from the conventions of poetic diction but from the mind of the speaker who has lost so much that he feels numb.

When students see that Wordsworth relies not on conventional ornaments of style associated with eighteenth-century poetry but on psychological reality, they will be ready to understand his comments on meter. Meter, which in the hands of a skillful poet is directly related to emotional tone, is one way that Wordsworth either subdues or intensifies ordinary language. A close reading of the paragraphs on meter in the Preface will reveal Wordsworth's understanding of this relation, just as a close analysis of any number of poems will show that he manipulates metrical patterns to enhance psychological power. In the *Lyrical Ballads* Wordsworth often uses a literary variation of ballad meter based on syllables and stress, setting up expectations with a light and airy meter only to disappoint those expectations with the content of the ballad. The Matthew poems, "Two April Mornings" and "The Conversation," provide excellent examples of the way Wordsworth ironically juxtaposes a light and jaunty measure with a sobering revelation about human life. Frequent instances also appear in the Lucy poems, many of which contrast the simple and pleasurable ballad rhythms with a complicated and disturbing insight into the human mind. Finally, Wordsworth's blank verse in "Tintern Abbey," "Michael," and "The Brothers" reveals his skill in that form; the metrical style of each supports the feelings and thoughts of the speakers.

"Michael" is an especially important poem because it illustrates how the plainness and austerity of the language and the blank verse match the stark dignity of Michael and enhance the value that Wordsworth places on humble domestic affections. Telling a class that "Michael" was originally conceived as a jocular, mocking ballad always jars them into thinking about the power of form to transform the meaning and tone. "Michael" also demonstrates Wordsworth's rejection of traditional heroic ideals in favor of the homely life of peasants, shepherds, and country poets. In writing domestic, rural poems like "Michael" and "The Brothers" he is breaking the traditional hierarchy that calls for elevated forms (such as blank verse, which until Cowper's *The Task* had been associated with Milton's *Paradise Lost*) to celebrate elevated subjects. Students can then easily see that Wordsworth's choice of metrical form is a kind of political statement about the proper subject matter for poetry.

The rural emphasis of the *Lyrical Ballads* supports Wordsworth's contention in the Preface that technological and popular trends were blunting "the discriminating powers of the mind." Wordsworth blamed the "encreasing accumulation of men in cities, where the uniformity of their occupations produces a craving for extraordinary incident" for this disintegration (Owen and Smyser 1: 128). In the *Lyrical Ballads* he places the humble pleasures and occupations of the country above the "outrageous stimulation" and technological developments associated with the city (130). The poems make dramatically clear Wordsworth's emphasis on basic human passions of forsaken women, betrayed fathers, and idiot boys, elemental emotions that transcend the historical moment Wordsworth understood so well.

After reviewing and relating these three basic categories—associationism, style, and subject matter—students should be prepared to see why Wordsworth felt uneasy with the traditional contract between poet and reader. Wordsworth knew that in order to enjoy the *Lyrical Ballads*, late eighteenth-century readers would have to change their literary taste for works that featured external actions and situations, conventional poetic diction, and conventionally heroic characters and classes. By choosing the basic ballad form, which had folk rather than literary origins and was therefore not governed by traditional rules of decorum, Wordsworth initiated his program for poetry and laid the foundations on which the poems of his great decade would be written. The Preface to *Lyrical Ballads* is his attempt to prepare eighteenth-century readers for this initiation. Almost two hundred years later, it is still the best introduction to his poetry.

What Wordsworth Has Made of Man: Teaching the *Lyrical Ballads*

John T. Ogden

"What man has made of man"—a subject of meditation for both Wordsworth and Coleridge—provides a unifying theme for studying *Lyrical Ballads*. These twenty-three poems are especially well suited as a unit for teaching, whether in an introductory class or in a more advanced seminar: instead of having a selection made by twentieth-century editors for twentieth-century readers, students can read the poems as they were put together by Wordsworth and Coleridge in 1798. (A more extensive study could well include the forty-one poems added to the second edition of 1800, but I shall limit my discussion to the first edition.) No other collection of verse has had such an impact on the course of English literature. The volume deserves to be studied as a whole, as James Averill has so well argued ("Teaching").

Separate editions of *Lyrical Ballads*, such as those edited by W. J. B. Owen and by Brett and Jones, have the advantage of presenting the poems in their original form and arrangement. (Page references in this essay are to Owen's edition.) The teacher who is already using a larger collection of Wordsworth's poetry (such as Stillinger's) or an anthology of Romantic poetry (such as Perkins's) may give the student the 1798 table of contents and supply a few of the lyrical ballads these collections lack. (Larger anthologies, such as the Norton, contain too few to convey an adequate impression of the original.) Showing students a facsimile of the 1798 edition will make them give more thought to how these varied poems, separated in most modern editions, originally composed a single entity.

Lyrical Ballads invites a wide variety of approaches. Here I shall limit my observations to some of the many interrelations among the poems—comparisons, recurring themes and motifs, juxtapositions, and groupings—that lend themselves to class discussion. Much has been written about these matters, so that the advanced student has ample opportunity for research (see especially the books by Danby, Parrish, John Jordan, Jacobus, and Sheats, and the collection edited by Jones and Tydemen); however, all these interrelations can be pursued without relying on extensive background information. I find these relations valuable not as an end in themselves but as a means to encourage a careful reading of the poems, to draw attention to style and technique, and to assist in an accurate understanding of tone and sensibility (insofar as one age can understand another). Each poem takes on a fuller, richer meaning from its context in the volume as a whole.

Before pursuing interrelations, students should gain sufficient familiarity with the individual poems. For class discussion, I like to use questions that the poems themselves imply or prompt. What is it that ails young Harry Gill? While the initial answer is simple, and in that respect good for getting a quick response, the full answer involves an exploration of justice and psychology as they are represented in the poem. Why does the Ancient Mariner stop the Wedding Guest? To tell his tale, of course, but why the Wedding Guest, and why so compulsively? What tale are we to make of the incident in "Simon Lee"? What should a simple child know of death? What does the poet learn from his dearest boy? Why does William sit alone on that old gray stone? Why does poor Martha Ray go to the dreary mountaintop at all times of night and day? What has man made of man?

"What man has made of man" is often misquoted as "man's inhumanity to man." Thoughtful students will be able to distinguish between the two phrasings. Of course "Lines Written in Early Spring" nowhere directly states to what the phrase refers: students should figure out how Wordsworth controls it and gives it a specific meaning by implication—how the contrast between the poet's grief and his pleasure indicates that "what man has made of man" is just the opposite of the blended notes, intermingling growth, excited activity, and lively interaction of the grove.

Other lyrical ballads do give explicit examples. The openness of the phrase "what man has made of man," so characteristic of Wordsworth's style, lets it apply to different poems and acquire different meanings. What has society made of the Female Vagrant? In "Lines Left upon a Seat in a Yew Tree," what has the man made of himself? In the companion poems "Anecdote for Fathers" and "We Are Seven," we see adults trying to make something of children that the children resist. On the other hand, what does Betty Foy make of her Idiot Boy? What does the Ancient Mariner make of the Wedding Guest? Or what does the poet make of his dear sister in "Tintern Abbey"?

In a discussion of "The Thorn," the question may be played out in all its variations to expose the levels of the poem. What has Stephen Hill made of Martha Ray? What has Martha Ray made of herself, or of her baby (if she indeed had a baby)? What have the villagers made of Martha Ray? And what has the narrator made of her? This last question becomes the most important because it addresses the poem itself; the first three questions after all depend on hearsay. Finally, what are we the readers to make of Martha Ray?

Martha Ray is typical in her isolation, loneliness, and alienation. Because of crime, pride, sickness, age, poverty, guilt, or even self-consciousness, most characters in *Lyrical Ballads* have no one to help them and frequently lack the emotional resources to cope with their suffering. Is the isolation and misery the fault of the character or of the human community, or are these simply the conditions of being human? Each poem provides a somewhat different answer, none of them simple. All of them together show "what man has made of man"—largely a cause for grief, but a grief that can be transmuted into "the still sad music of humanity."

Dialogue in *Lyrical Ballads* may be seen, then, not just as literary form but as a means of overcoming alienation and establishing in a most rudimentary way a sense of human community. (On another level the role of dialogue indicates the importance of Wordsworth's deceptively simple definition of the poet, in the Preface to *Lyrical Ballads*, as "a man speaking to men" [Owen 165]). In some poems the dialogue fails or only serves to accentuate differences, but even there it may represent the need to make contact with another human being and to gain a sympathetic understanding. Where the dialogue succeeds, it joins speaker and listener in a communion that, in varying degrees, gives relief from suffering, strength to bear misery, and—when it achieves its fullest form—a sense of the joy and dignity of being human.

What one human being makes of another begins in the acts of perception and response. For example, consider whether the response in any given poem is open or prejudiced, respectful or disdainful, energetic or lethargic. The eye and ear that can half create our perceptions can create distortions and perversions or can simply refuse to see and hear. Many of the lyrical ballads show how one's response to the natural environment may correlate with one's response to other people—hence the moral impact of viewing scenery. Such perceiving and responding involve workings of the imagination, "the faculty which produces impressive effects out of simple elements," as Wordsworth first defines it in his note to "The Thorn" (Owen 139). Martha Ray, for example, may be seen as witch, martyr, or perhaps even saint as she becomes separated from the human community and associated with extraordinary natural and supernatural powers. Trying to identify as specifically as possible what the impressive effects are and how they are produced is one of the best ways to get at the heart of each lyrical ballad.

My original theme has branched out to encompass half a dozen significant themes in the volume. There are still many more, but I leave them for readers to pursue on their own so that I can briefly mention other considerations of form, style, and organization.

The title *Lyrical Ballads* raises questions of genre. The varying mixtures of lyric and narrative in the poems show that "the feeling therein developed gives importance to the action and situation and not the action and situation to the feeling," as Wordsworth explains in the 1800 Preface (Owen 159). Narrative form is fully developed in "The Ancyent Marinere" but then is variously reduced to anecdote or incident, retarded by uncertainty or digression, and in other ways subordinated to a lyric impulse. Dramatic form should also be examined to see how it helps establish character and point of view. The mixture of genres suggests the Romantic resistance to formal and conventional restrictions and willingness to include whatever elements the organic unity of a poem can absorb.

Style varies among the poems in ways that are instructive. How does the effect of the pentameter line differ from that of the tetrameter? Both ballad stanza and blank verse are used for narration and for meditative verse, but each form shows different possibilities and limitations. How do the poems display "the language of conversation in the middle and lower classes of society," as Wordsworth announces in the Advertisement (Owen 3)? Students might contrast the simplicity of diction in "Lines Written in Early Spring" with the more elevated diction of "Lines Left upon a Seat in a Yew-Tree," the loquaciousness of "The Thorn" with the conversational rambling in "The Nightingale," or the archaic diction of "The Ancyent Marinere" with the colloquialism of "The Idiot Boy." A more sophisticated examination might consider how Wordsworth's style compares with Coleridge's.

The collaboration represented in *Lyrical Ballads* can be explored not only through the interesting historical circumstances of the two poets but also through ways in which the poems complement one another. How do Coleridge's poems fit in thematically? Compare the ways in which the two poets address the same issues—for example, how Wordsworth's moralizing conclusion to "Lines Left upon a Seat in a Yew-Tree" applies to "The Ancyent Marinere." Coleridge later explained that his "endeavours should be directed to persons and characters supernatural, or at least romantic," while Wordsworth would stay within the natural world (Engell and Bate 2: 6): how does the supernatural imagery of "The Ancyent Marinere" compare with the natural imagery of "Lines Written in Early Spring"? or the Mariner's supernatural curse with Harry Gill's natural curse? (Coleridge's retrospective claim to this division of labor, though not borne out fully, helps students focus on some important issues.) In what different ways do Coleridge and Wordsworth modify the ballad stanza? Does the blank verse of "The Nightingale" differ from that of "Tintern Abbey"? If students are overly eager to draw distinctions on the basis of their knowledge of authorship, they should be told that the original reviewers of the anonymous *Lyrical Ballads* understood the poems to be the work of one author (see Donald Reiman's collection *The Romantics Reviewed*). In 1798 "The Ancyent Marinere" and "Tintern Abbey" were read as the work of a single poet.

Finally, the order and arrangement of the poems may be taken into account. Wordsworth took the trouble to rearrange them for the second edition: Was the rearrangement an improvement? Does it significantly change the effect? What is the difference between beginning the collection with "The Ancyent Marinere" and beginning it with "Expostulation and Reply"? In 1798 "Anecdote for Fathers" precedes "We Are Seven," but in 1800 the order is reversed. In 1798 "The Nightingale" follows "Lines Left upon a Seat in a Yew-Tree," providing a second chastisement of melancholy; in 1800 it follows "Lines Written in Early Spring," showing a different response to nature's music. Both editions conclude with "Tintern Abbey": how well it serves as conclusion may be seen from the way it echoes, reflects, and fulfills many themes and intentions of the lyrical ballads that lead up to it. Though highly personal and even idiosyncratic, these lines represent what the poet can make of humankind.

Verbal Repetitions in "Tintern Abbey"

Patricia L. Skarda

Throughout "Tintern Abbey" Wordsworth repeats particular words in new contexts, sometimes with new inflections and often with new meaning, in a quasi-religious ritual that celebrates the unity of humanity and nature and exalts human intuition through themes of loss, memory, and interfusion. Students note at once the weariness through time implied in repetitions of "five" and "long/length" (lines 1-2) and "again" (2, 4, 9, 14) in the almost elegiac first verse paragraph. They must be carefully shown the hope and promise in the optative tone and the language of blessing in the last verse paragraph, where "lofty thoughts" (128) in "this green pastoral landscape" (158) echo the "lofty cliffs" (5) and "green" (13, 17) of the beginning. By looking at such verbal repetitions, students see that "Tintern Abbey" anticipates the "ennobling interchange" (13.375) between the human mind and the natural world celebrated in *The Prelude* more surely than it completes the experiments of *Lyrical Ballads*, to which it was added in press.

The most telling repetition in the poem is the use of "all" in the fourth verse paragraph. Here the poet-speaker indexes the stages of his development as a lover of nature. For the youth in the past, nature was "all in all" (75), all things altogether, an inclusive, delightful whole, requiring no thought for pleasure. "All" avoids precise definition but suggests the uncertainty of what he has lost. Every simple youthful happiness—"all" the oxymoronic "aching joys" (84) and "all the dizzy raptures" (85)—has passed. For the man in the present, nature has become an equally vague and inclusive "presence" (94), evoking elevated thoughts of "a sense sublime / Of something far more deeply interfused" (95–96). Just what is "interfused" remains ambiguous, for the comparison remains incomplete, as William Empson has said (153). What is clear is that "something" joins suns, ocean, air, sky, and the human mind. This godlike, mystical presence "disturbs" (94) the poet and "impels / all thinking things, all objects of all thought, / And rolls through *all* things" (101-02), without regard for time or space.

Emblematically, the imagining poet becomes an archetype of humankind, as "we" replaces "I" in the poet's restatement of his love of "all that we behold / From this green earth; of all the mighty world / Of eye and ear" (104-06). All nature and all human perceptions suggest the unity of objects and thoughts, the communion of humanity and nature both in thoughtless youth and in thoughtful maturity. The extraordinary repetition of "all" (sixteen times in the poem) dynamically links humanity and nature, self and other, past and present, gain and loss, as the poet-speaker conceives and senses, half creates and perceives intangible ideas in the tangible world.

"All" so powerfully encapsulates the relationship between humanity and nature that this interfusion successfully counters all oppositions to unity and concord. The burdens of "all this unintelligible world" (40) and "all / The dreary intercourse of daily life" (130-31) can be and are ameliorated by the active "faith that all which we behold / Is full of blessings" (133-34). The poet, whom the thought of something fusing all things "disturbs" (94), firmly states that the "solitude, or fear, or pain, or grief" (143) of past, present, or future experience cannot "disturb" (132) his and his sister's faith. Wordsworth creates more specific images for human trials than for human triumphs because even he knows life's difficulties better than he knows the healing powers of harmony and joy. Still, no example of disharmony or disappointment contains the patterns of language repetition found in the passages describing unity or interfusion.

The "indistinguishable unity" (Ferry 107) presented in the opening landscape, from which the poet has been excluded for "the length / of five long winters" (1-2), may imply more consciousness of loss than of gain in the present. But gradually the "unremembered" feelings and acts (31, 34) are remembered. Then nature's quiet and beauty "impress" (6, 126) the mind and lead to repeated "joy" (48, 94, 125, 145) that can "feed" (64, 127) the poet and his sister now and in time to come. Through memory, intuition, and the sharing of his vision with others, the poet-speaker will go on seeing "into the life of things" (49). The poet's loss turns to gain; debts "owed" (26, 36) are repaid; blessings received are returned in the final prayer. From beginning to end, Wordsworth demonstrates by verbal repetitions and language patterns the interfusion he remembers, then re-experiences, and finally shares in this dramatic lyric, almost an ode, before the epic "consummation" (Prospectus to *The Recluse* 58) he describes more fully in *The Prelude*.

That the Center Hold: "Michael" and the "Spots of Time"

Edward Duffy

"Michael" is a narrative that may be quickly summarized in a classroom. A native of Grasmere at some unspecified time before Wordsworth's own childhood in the region, Michael is an elderly but still vigorous shepherd. Moved by family ties rather than investment opportunities, he has mortgaged part of his land to finance some enterprise in the "industrious life" of a nephew. When this far-off capitalist venture fails, Michael can avoid the loss of his land only by sending his only son and heir off to an urban world of getting and spending. In anxious anticipation of this impending rupture, the shepherd urges Luke to remain attached to the land and life of his fathers—an admonition ritualized into biblical dignity when, at his father's direction, Luke lays the cornerstone for a sheepfold to be completed by Michael.

In this explicitly named covenant between generations, the father prays that, no matter how far Luke may range, he will still center himself on this moment, will still return in spirit to the cornerstone of his life: "Luke, I pray that thou / May'st bear in mind the life thy Fathers lived" (409-10). The son soon turns prodigal, however, "slackens" in his duty, gives himself over to "evil courses," and flies off "to seek a hiding place beyond the seas" (442-47). The desired center manifestly does not hold, and mere dispersal is loosed on the world, with the estate sold "into a stranger's hand" (475), the cottage gone, the land plowed up, and little of Michael's ethos left but "a struggling heap of unhewn stones" (17).

A classroom summary of the poem will have to be more diffuse than a written synopsis, but in my experience it can just as efficiently establish the two competing motions of "Michael": a prayed-for centering versus the actual and devastating dispersal. In fact, one gesture here may be worth several hundred words. With the scene of the covenant, for example, I have found it effective to extend my arms and then slowly contract both arms and hands into a spot of symbolic space, where the class is to imagine the cornerstone and its would-be centering power.

After a summary of the poem's action, the next order of business is Michael's portrayal (40-77) as someone "prompt / And watchful more than ordinary men," someone who has "learned the meaning of all winds," someone whose everyday surroundings are "like a book," speaking to him of the accumulated pastoral acts of a lifetime and laying "strong hold on his affections." Wanting to bequeath this plenitude of meaningfulness to his son, Michael prays that the stone of the covenant mean as much to Luke as it does to him. It does not, and that is what the story is about—a pastor/father who is centered on his land and all it means, and a lost sheep/son who, because he is not similarly attached, does not stand fast, is dispersed and scattered.

This plot summary and characterization, which takes no more than twenty minutes, is all prelude to the central business of the hour: the directing of the students' attention to what in their private readings they may have skimmed over—the first thirty-nine lines of introductory framework, and especially these climactically placed lines:

> It is in truth an utter solitude;
> Nor should I have made mention of this Dell
> But for *one object which you might pass by,*
> *Might see and notice not.* Beside the brook
> Appears a straggling heap of unhewn stones!
> And to that simple object appertains
> A story.   (13-19; emphasis added)

A retrospective reading of this passage should make clear that the teller of the tale is confronting an explicitly imagined reader with an apparently random sprawl, which the teller can make significantly coherent only if this reader stops and notices, only if this reader becomes more than commonly attentive to the details of scene and story through which the poem will imagine such a reader as moving.

All this close communal reading leads up to another kind of summary to the effect that we have (1) a story in which the cornerstone of the covenant is bindingly significant to Michael but not so to his son and (2) a rhetorical framework for this story in which the teller of the tale addresses his reader as potentially one of the dull of soul who might pass and notice not. With this parallel between the tale and its rhetorical framework made manifest, one can more fully appreciate why Wordsworth should be offering this tale "with yet fonder feeling, for the sake / Of youthful Poets, who among these hills / Will be my *second self* when I am gone" (37-39; emphasis added). For such replication is what Michael wants of Luke. In trying to make the stone of the covenant the holding center of Luke's affections, Michael is performing a would-be pastoral act. He is praying that his son stay in the fold, and the straggle of stones is the sign of his failure. Meanwhile, however, the poet is shepherding this very straggle into a symbolic value of sufficient substance and gravity to take hold of a reader's affections. A pastor of the imagination, Wordsworth takes a scene that is apparently a semiotic zero and makes it into the coherently summarizing sign for the loss of all that Michael so nobly and tragically stands for. Even if Luke has not borne in mind the life his fathers led, the reader of his story is still asked to give heed to the poet as he confronts this scattering of human life and takes on himself, right now, the pastoral duty of making his reader stop and be more fully responsive to it.

This insight makes a class on "Michael" that, because it illuminates Wordsworth's sense of poetic mission, may also serve as a cornerstone for all the major poetry, especially the "spots of time" in *The Prelude*. Throughout several classes on Wordsworth's autobiographical epic, I assert that the poet struggles against the fragmentation of modern life by centering himself on those moments in childhood when the world of eye and ear opened itself to him in significant shapes not to be put by. Then (with appropriate gestures) I refer back to the prayer for centering that is itself at the center of "Michael." As Luke relates through space to the stone of the covenant, so Wordsworth relates through his life to the anchor of a spot of time. That Wordsworth might well have become the moral equivalent of a Luke dispersed beyond the seas is the fear that *The Prelude* seeks either to surmount or to keep at bay. (Moreover, distinctions between the spots of time and "Michael" can be mutually illuminating. Essential to a spot of time, for example, is that it comes to Wordsworth as a given, a peculiar grace: he makes no vows and forces no meanings; instead, these vows and meanings are made for him. By contrast, Luke's father is a spirit on the stretch, trying for salvation by works. He is trying to manufacture a significant spot of time—and for someone else.)

Not-to-be-evaded spots of time, holding centers of love, focused cynosures of attention—they all speak from Wordsworth's profoundest urgency that neither he nor his fellows become any more slackly dull of soul but that, instead, they be attentive, that they be "on." Hence the central importance of "Michael" as a story about failed response, whose introductory framework subtly but explicitly challenges the reader to be more alert, to look again and more closely. By close retrospective reading of the text, I try to pass this challenge on to my students—to look again and to look intently this time.

The Two Selves in Wordsworth's Middle Lyrics

John Milstead

M. H. Abrams says that *The Prelude* evokes "the former self which co-exists with the altered present self in a multiple awareness that Wordsworth calls 'two consciousnesses.' There is a wide 'vacancy' between the I now and the I then" (*Natural Supernaturalism* 75). Instead of trying to deal with this psychological structure initially in *The Prelude* itself, I have found it better for undergraduates to meet this self-transformation as it is demonstrated in a few of Wordsworth's shorter poems of the years 1800-05.

Three poems of this middle period make a convenient package for student analysis of the confrontation between the two selves: "Resolution and Independence" (1802), "I wandered lonely as a cloud" (1804), and "Elegiac Stanzas Suggested by a Picture of Peele Castle" (1805). Each poem describes a mental state, then recounts or alludes to an incident, and finally describes an altered mental state. The altered states draw forth powerful responses in the will, the memory, and the imagination. The power of the transformation is so great that by the end of the poem we feel the presence of a self different in one or more ways from the self with which the poem begins. That is, we cannot conceive of the later self feeling and acting in the same way as the earlier self did if for some reason the poem were to be rewritten. And since the later self in each of the three poems is different from the later self in the other two, students see that it is not precisely equivalent to the biological entity William Wordsworth or, for that matter, to the authorial voice that exercises final control over the composing process.

"I wandered lonely as a cloud" is the best poem of the three to begin with. It illustrates simply and clearly the structure of opposing selves: the earlier self is governed largely by a physical stimulus-and-response mechanism; the later has gained mental self-sufficiency. The first self responds almost automatically in Wordsworthian joy to the daffodils. His intellectual faculties are suspended: "I gazed—and gazed—but little thought. . . ." His will is captured by the sight: "A poet could not but be gay, / In such a jocund company." Where the first self is an external person, as the stimulus-response event attests, the self of the last stanza is an internal person, not dependent on a physical stimulus for pleasurable sensations. Rather, the daffodil companions are emblems of mental activity, which relieves vacant loneliness by bringing before the inward eye ("Which is the bliss of solitude") permanent forms of beauty and joy. Thus a poem that might be read as a contrast between an external and an internal aspect of the same self in reality describes a transitional event in the progress from a passive to an active self, from a consciousness defined by nature to one defined by imagination.

In "Resolution and Independence," as later in "Elegiac Stanzas," the poet describes the earlier self as illusioned: "My whole life I have lived in pleasant thought / As if life's business were a summer mood . . ." (36-37). This earlier self is reprehensibly complacent in contrast to the later, chastened self that recognizes the need for effort in the face of hard circumstance. The rest of the poem accounts for this change by describing the encounter with the Leech Gatherer. The burden the old man bears and his power of endurance are in sharp contrast to the poet's emotional roller coaster. The old man is bent over, as though bearing "a more than human weight" (70). His condition makes the occasion for the poet's depression seem trivial by comparison. The Leech Gatherer also teaches the poet a lesson in the proper use of one's intelligence. Whereas the writer has read poets, the old man reads the pond: " . . . [he] fixedly did look / Upon the muddy water, which he conned / As if he had been reading in a book" (79-81). Humbled by the old man's noble application of his critical faculties, the poet determines that the Leech Gatherer's virtues will inspire him. The power of memory, which "I wandered lonely as a cloud" celebrates as spontaneous, here unites with the power of the will to bring about self-development.

"Elegiac Stanzas Suggested by a Picture of Peele Castle" presents the starkest confrontation between the two selves to be found in this group of poems.

> Not for a moment could I now behold
> A smiling sea, and be what I have been:
> The feeling of my loss will ne'er be old;
> This, which I know, I speak with mind serene.   (37-40)

With only a brief reference to a death, the poem passes from a description of the illusioned self to the self that has gained an insight into the powerfully ambiguous relation between suffering and hope. Serenity, perhaps even joy, is suspect to this later self. Instead, hope has been added to will and memory in Wordsworth's exploration of psychological values. The serenity of the castle by a calm sea, as the earlier self would have painted it, is replaced as an image of truth by Beaumont's "passionate Work" (45). The earlier self addresses the castle in the second person, apostrophizing it as an agent of divine power: "Thou shouldst have seemed . . . a chronicle of heaven . . ." (21-22). But the more disciplined later self commends Beaumont's painting as a symbol of the humanized soul.

I try to impress on my students the psychological universality in Wordsworth's presentation of the various selves: pleasurable memories, the need and desire for "resolution and independence," despair eventually chastened and transformed into a more realistic view of the world and one's position in it. When we view these poems as a single group we see highly suggestive archetypal patterns. As a collective entity, the earlier self is emotionally unstable, subject to whims and chance events. He is complacent and rather self-centered in his view of himself and the world. Consequently, he lives in an illusioned state of mind. The collective later self, on the other hand, comes through as humanized force: his mental self-sufficiency; his determination to attach himself to his own personal models of stoic endurance; his dedication to his humanized vision of truth, purpose, and compassion—these qualities are impressive. On consideration, however, we would probably not care to be either of these archetypal selves. That is to say, they perform a vital function of literary figures: they project the basic passions and aspirations that we all share but that we conceal under the masks of our daily lives.

Teaching the Immortality Ode with Coleridge's "Dejection: An Ode"

John L. Mahoney

There is no need for elaborate biographical documentation of the relation between the two great odes; one simply tells students that Coleridge wrote "Dejection: An Ode," originally a long verse letter to Sara Hutchinson, in response to hearing Wordsworth read aloud the crucial first four stanzas of the Immortality Ode. Studied in conjunction, the two poems illuminate each other. Particularly important pedagogically is the extent to which the tragic quality of Coleridge's poem contrasts with and thus helps to clarify the complex affirmation contained in Wordsworth's.

It is best to begin by setting down for consideration a central premise articulated recently by Edward Proffitt. The Immortality Ode, he says, far from being "a dirge sung over . . . departing powers," is a work celebrating "gain," a work that finds in memory and in its resources an occasion for joy in the face of loss (75). As early as 1802, if not earlier, Wordsworth expressed anxiety concerning his power to sustain the youthful vision and passionate involvement in natural processes that he cherished. The first four stanzas of the ode, which were written in 1802 and which form a minidrama within the poem, convey this anxiety, but in so doing they set the stage for the affirmation that will follow. (Stanzas 5-11 were written two years later, in 1804).

It is helpful to focus sharply on this four-stanza minidrama as the class begins. Reading the stanzas aloud helps students see the dialectic of time past and time present. Stanzas 1 and 2 celebrate a past time when "The earth and every common sight" seemed to radiate "The glory and the freshness of a dream," while they lament that "The things which I have seen I now can see no more." Stanzas 3 and 4 further reveal the unfolding tension, matching moments of ecstasy with present reminders of that ecstasy slipping away. Still, even as the ecstasy departs, the speaker catches himself and, as if by an act of will, refuses to allow the joy to fade. As the four stanzas end, what had been dialectic gives way to question, the central question of the poem and, although dealt with in remarkably different ways, of Coleridge's poem also: "Whither is fled the visionary gleam? / Where is it now, the glory and the dream?" By focusing on these climactic questions and by encouraging students to think about Coleridge's responses to them in "Dejection," one can approach the special character of Wordsworth's problem and ultimate affirmation.

With the Immortality Ode opening still fresh in our minds, we proceed directly to Coleridge's poem, especially to the first five stanzas. How different its speaker's joyless voice, its dark shadings, its mysterious language and imagery, but especially its facing of similar questions. A wide range of possibilities for paper topics or oral reports can be found in contrasting these specific sections of the two poems. Where Wordsworth's opening stanzas raise the problem of advancing age and the toll it takes on the capacity for sensuous response, Coleridge's condition seems already complete. Stanzas 2 and 3 of "Dejection" dramatize a psychological predicament, a sense of deadness within that seems to defy all remedy. These express no Wordsworthian confidence in the possibility of growth, of compensation—only definite assurance that "I may not hope from outward forms to win / The passion and life, whose fountains are within." Both Wordsworth and Coleridge share a faith in the active, creative power of the imagination, in the power of the mind to find meaning and hope in experience. Yet Coleridge's speaker cannot cling to the affirmation of Wordsworth's. He cannot know a "Joy" given only to the "pure," a force "Which wedding nature to us gives in dower / A new Earth and new Heaven."

Moving forward in teaching the Immortality Ode, we note in the remaining seven stanzas a fascinating two-pronged structure. There is first (stanzas 5-8) a starkly beautiful series of ruminations, of interior monologue matched by the erratic and uneven rhythms of the Pindaric ode, in which the speaker answers, however reluctantly, the question of the first movement of the poem. We want our students to have at least a general grasp of the Platonic quality of imagery, although Platonism is not the central issue. What emerges clearly is the image, almost archetypal, of despiritualization, of a journey of loss. It is a journey in which "Our birth is but a sleep and a forgetting"; in which, although the child still sees the "light" of infinity, all too soon "Shades of the prison house" of age begin to cloud that light until finally only the dimness of "common day" can be seen.

The last movement of the Immortality Ode (stanzas 9-11) reveals a troubled speaker's shock at the image of loss he has just created and his need to find a new fire in the ashes. Reading aloud continues to be a useful device—and it can involve not just the teacher but any good reader in class—in revealing a certain artificial tightness and sing-song rhythm that characterizes the almost too neat opening of stanza 9. There is something formulaic or trance-like about:

> O joy! that in our embers
> Is something that doth live,
> That nature yet remembers
> What was so fugitive!

Still, in spite of everything, memory will breed "perpetual benediction."

How strikingly the speaker turns earlier images to new purposes. Now "inland," the Soul can "have sight of that immortal sea / Which brought us hither," can "see the Children" and "hear the mighty waters rolling evermore." He has found a new faith that will not tolerate grief for the loss of youthful intensity. It is a faith in the "philosophic mind," a mind not capable of being in doubts, almost stridently confident that the love of nature can be deeper and richer than it once was, if not so intense.

Again, directing students to the appropriate stanzas of "Dejection" helps them to understand Wordsworth's hard-won affirmation. They are consistently struck by the way stanza 6 of Coleridge's poem sharply echoes, for the purpose of contrast, the first stanza of the Immortality Ode.

> There was a time when, though my path was rough,
>   This joy within me dallied with distress,
> And all misfortunes were but as the stuff
>   Whence Fancy made me dreams of happiness.

Coleridge once had the gift of "hope" and could appreciate the Wordsworthian sense that some gain was possible in spite of eroding youthful blessings. Now there is a finality, a firmness of tone in his convictions about the present: "But now afflictions bow me down to earth" and "each visitation / Suspends what nature gave me at my birth, / My shaping spirit of imagination."

In the following long, irregular stanza a flow of grotesque, nightmarish imagery graphically reveals the differences in tone and theme between the two odes. Students not only enjoy but find valuable an assignment to write about such differences and how they strengthen an understanding of both poems. The speaker of "Dejection" finds no "joy" in the "embers," no gatherings with children, no union with nature. The "Joyous song" of the "young lambs," the "gladness of the May" in the Wordsworthian ode give way to "the wind, / Which long has raved unnoticed." The lute, so unlike the melodious Aeolian harp of Coleridge's earlier poem of that name, sends forth "a scream / Of agony by torture lengthened out." The wind is not a Wordsworthian "correspondent breeze" but a "mad Lutanist." The story it tells is not one of triumph over loss but a darkly ironic version of the drama of Wordsworth's "Lucy Gray." Students will already have read the latter poem and will be struck by the contrast between Wordsworth's serene narrative of the charmed girl's story and Coleridge's ready identification with her plight:

> 'Tis of a little child
> Upon a lonesome wild,
> Not far from home, but she hath lost her way:

And now moans low in bitter grief and fear,
And now screams loud, and hopes to make her mother hear.

The concluding stanza of "Dejection" has a special beauty in itself and a special significance in the way it illuminates the contrast between the two odes. Questions that invariably stir lively classroom response or trigger interesting short papers involve speakers and listeners in the poems. How would you describe the speakers and what kinds of listeners do they seek? What are their concerns? Do those concerns tell us anything about Wordsworth and Coleridge as Romantic poets? about the variety of Romantic poetry?

Wordsworth's poem ends confidently, firmly focused on the speaker and on his faith that age brings gifts that are greater than the losses, that memory can bring thoughts that are "too deep for tears." Coleridge's concluding stanza begins on a similarly self-centered note, but it is a self centered on sadness, not on recompense: "'Tis midnight, but small thoughts have I of sleep." Yet quickly the self-centeredness gives way to blessing, to an imaginative concern for the other, to a gentle good wish for the "Lady." His strongest prayer is for her inner strength, for the capacity to feel, to imagine, to know joy, to internalize the vitality of nature's processes:

> Joy lift her spirit, joy attune her voice;
> To her may all things live, from pole to pole,
> Their life the eddying of her living soul!

The lines are a prayer for experience the speaker can no longer know but would nonetheless bestow. Coleridge defers to another the joy and imagination that Wordsworth had kept for himself.

The affirmation of Wordsworth, the joyous confidence in the fundamental bond between mind and nature, the images of light, the brilliant rhythms—these elements stand as values in themselves, and we want our teaching of the poem to reveal them. Yet tracing the responses in "Dejection"—the joyless voice, the brilliant capturing of macabre loneliness, the images of darkness, the speaker's despair for himself but hope for others—adds a special dimension to the study of the Immortality Ode. Classes will differ considerably on many of the issues and questions raised, but the comparative approach may help students understand both poems more fully.

Contexts for Teaching the Immortality Ode

Jonathan Ramsey

Not only is the "Ode: Intimations of Immortality" the most widely quoted, misquoted, praised, and parodied of Wordsworth's poems, for many readers it has also come to characterize poetry in general. Such poetic touchstones as "splendor in the grass," "The Child is father of the Man," "the visionary gleam," "trailing clouds of glory," and other half-remembered parts of the poem have served its friends as well as its detractors. The Immortality Ode thus presents unusual challenges to undergraduate students, for the poem's distorted reputation compounds its inherent difficulties. Even apart from the preconceptions that work against a clear-minded reading, the work's overall structural complexities, its several obscure passages and images, and its sometimes ornate diction make it tough for students to appreciate.

I believe that teachers of the Immortality Ode should face these extrinsic and internal difficulties head-on, even place the apparent problems at the center of class discussion. One can, for example, organize interpretations around the touchstone lines themselves, thus working to defamiliarize certain commonplaces while paying homage to their place in students' memories. The line "trailing clouds of glory," for example, may stimulate discussion of the literal and metaphoric "splendor" of childhood experiences in stanzas 1-4, their significance as a kind of "immortality," and the more "sober coloring" of the closing stanzas. Or one can raise at the outset the traditional complaints, including Coleridge's, against the poem's philosophic wobbles, seeming contradictions in tone and imagery, or version of developmental psychology. One advantage of this approach is that the poem becomes an occasion for debate and for problem solving; a disadvantage may be a student tendency to treat it as a complex document rather than an artistic construction of remarkable beauty and insight. The documentary and discursive temptations can be used productively, however, if the teacher guides students toward the evidence of tone, metaphor, prosody, and elegiac conventions, all of which lend substance and context to the poem's more overt statements of its meaning (including Wordsworth's own 1843 note to Isabella Fenwick, which is often printed as a headpiece to the poem and which has acquired too much authority over it).

The whole issue of preconceptions and the centrality of the Immortality Ode suggest even more significant classroom strategies. Since the poem's meaning and form trace the evolution of Wordsworth's visual perceptions and moral and imaginative responses at different stages in his life, the work seems to invite an excursion into our own underlying assumptions as readers and students of literature. I would not propose anything too theoretical for most undergraduate settings (except perhaps for a senior seminar or honors course), but aesthetic principles and modes of knowing are close to Wordsworth's heart and to the Romantic enterprise in general, and I have found that a reading of the Immortality Ode that exposes our interpretive premises enhances student appreciation for the poem.

I have made successful use of Lionel Trilling's essay on the ode and Helen Vendler's response to Trilling. Other contrasting interpretations might be employed instead (e.g., from Brooks, Abrams, Hartman, and Bloom), but Trilling and Vendler offer special advantages for classroom use. Both of these excellent essays use language accessible to students, present fairly mainstream critical positions (indeed, Trilling established the frame of reference for most subsequent readings of the Immortality Ode), relate Wordsworth to "real world" issues of thinking and feeling, and deal directly with the critical presuppositions that make the activities of understanding possible. If classroom time is limited, it is best to use dittoed excerpts from the two essays or a few summary statements about them and to weave Trilling and Vendler into the main order of business, which is Wordsworth's poem and student response to it.

Among the more logical places to start are the epigraph to the Immortality Ode, especially the line "The child is father of the Man," the expression "natural piety," and the "obstinate questionings / Of sense and outward things" of stanza 9 and the Fenwick note. These sections help introduce us to the sensory, psychological, imaginative, and sacramental continuities that either survive through the changes explored in the poem or are supplanted by other, more or less satisfying powers of feeling and knowing. They also bring us squarely to questions about the poem's autonomy or its intertextual relations and raise the more fundamental issue of its structural, thematic, and metaphoric claims to overall unity. One can ask students whether they believe Wordsworth's epigraph urges us to read "My heart leaps up" in some relation to the Immortality Ode or whether his reference in stanza 3 to a "timely utterance" invites us to bring in our experience with such works as "Resolution and Independence" (as Trilling suggests), other early Wordsworth poems on childhood (for example, "We Are Seven," "Anecdote for Fathers," "The Idiot Boy," "Tintern Abbey," and perhaps the two-part *Prelude* of 1798–99) or even Coleridge's "Dejection: An Ode" (occasioned in part by stanzas 1-4 of the Immortality Ode).

If my experience is representative, most students will maintain that the Immortality Ode must stand by itself and that we should not "read in" other works. Curiously, though, the same students are likely to admit into evidence Wordsworth's prose explanation made forty years after the Immortality Ode was completed. Their general skepticism toward an expanded context invites quick references from the teacher to the poetic dialogue Wordsworth held with himself throughout a long lifetime of retrospective revisions and re-shapings (seen most clearly in the complex evolution of *The Prelude* from at least 1798 to 1839); to his likening of all his "minor Pieces" to "the little cells, oratories, and sepulchral recesses" of "a gothic church" constituted of his major and minor works (Preface to *The Excursion*, Stillinger 470); and to the apparent responsory relation among "Frost at Midnight," early parts of the 1799 *Prelude*, the Immortality Ode (in which stanzas 5-11 emerge two years later and in response to stanzas 1-4), "Dejection: An Ode," and "To William Wordsworth" (which responds both to the completed Immortality Ode and to the 1805 version of *The Prelude*).

This set of references does not begin to exhaust the potential intercon-nections for expanding the reading of Wordsworth and Coleridge through several class sessions, retaining the Immortality Ode as the organizing cen-ter, nor does it even touch on the poem's relation to conventions of the elegy and the Pindaric ode. Students get the point, however, and some may be intrigued enough to modify their premise of the self-enclosed work of art whose internal unity and completeness we can take for granted as we read it closely.

The next direction for discussion moves easily toward Wordsworth's sac-ramental and sensory vocabulary of "gleams," "vision," "splendor," "glory," and "light," which runs throughout the poem as one of several aesthetically rewarding image patterns—a pattern that also helps us appreciate the child's adventures amid "the light of common day" in stanzas 6-8. Helen Vendler is sensitive to these variations in "the visionary gleam," and at the same time her focus on the poem's metaphoric progressions contrasts sharply with Trilling's more discursive, philosophic, and psychoanalytic reading of the poem. Vendler characterizes Trilling's approach as a subordination of art—particularly of the significance of metaphor as an agent of knowledge and artistic expressions—to life and moral instruction. Trilling, she says, fails to separate Wordsworth's stated philosophic intentions in the poem from his actual accomplishments in poetic language; in focusing on the poem's as-sertions and explicit questions he slights the language patterns that not only comprise the work's aesthetic appeal but also generate its central "mean-ings."

And yet Trilling's more "naturalistic" and psychological approach to the poem and his confidence that Wordsworth is describing phenomena of per-ception and states of mind known to all of us, not just to special people who are poets, will appeal more immediately to students than does Vendler's much closer attention to tone, imagery, and the epistemological supremacy of metaphor. Trilling, students will note, was making his own way in 1942 against the biographical criticisms of the Immortality Ode, which argued both for the uniqueness of Wordsworth's experience as man and poet and for the explanatory power of certain events in Wordsworth's life. In this context Trilling was not only returning to look closely at the poem in its own right but also championing the relevance of Wordsworth's art to the lives of modern readers. This was a worthy aim, and if Trilling tends to treat the poem as a psychological and moral essay, he also makes an insightful case for Wordsworth's humanistic significance to all of us.

That both Trilling's and Vendler's critical assumptions bring forth and obscure different aspects of the poem leads nicely into a discussion of the evidences of survival and recompense that dominate the last three stanzas of the Immortality Ode. Whether persuaded more by Trilling's humanistic or by Vendler's metaphoric interpretation of the concluding celebration of "the philosophic mind," students should be asked whether they are satisfied by the vigor of Wordsworth's concluding imagery, tone, and philosophic stance. I like to remind them during these final moments of discussion that the Immortality Ode centers on how people respond to and make sense of their experiences as they move through different periods of their lives. Our critical activities as readers require a similar flexibility of mind and a conscious effort to gauge the power of our assumptions to reshape the objects of our study. Unity of being is perhaps the most compelling of our assumptions as readers, and students might be led to consider whether too many other delights and abilities are sacrificed, either by Wordsworth or by his interpreters, in order to bring about closure and completeness in the Immortality Ode.

"A Power to Virtue Friendly": On Teaching "The Ruined Cottage"

Lisa Steinman

When teaching the 1799 version of "The Ruined Cottage," I generally begin by having my students read James Thomson's "Summer" (lines 432-61), from the last version of *The Seasons*, and by comparing Thomson's poem with the strikingly similar opening of Wordsworth's. Placing Thomson in line with eighteenth-century poets such as Collins, whose anxiety over their poetic power is explicit, I can describe Thomson's shifts of scene as, in part, a series of falls into self-consciousness about the derivative nature of his poetic vision, described in language authorized not by divine inspiration or by the natural world he claims merely to describe but rather by his literary predecessors, especially Milton and Spenser.

Both Thomson and Wordsworth are concerned with perception, with the limits of physical vision, and, most strikingly, with poetic vision. Thomson's defense of poetry "from Moses down to Milton" in the early preface to "Winter" invokes an uneasy marriage of divine and natural inspiration; his implicit wish to be counted with those who write "the peculiar language of heaven" and who "awake . . . moral sentiment" by describing nature is, however, accompanied by a tacit recognition that he does not have access to the authority he desires (Thomson 239-41). Claiming nature as his muse, Thomson is unable to locate himself within the line of sublime poets whose authority he admires.

Wordsworth begins with a description of a dreamer that recalls Thomson's figure in retirement. As in *The Seasons*, the figure is clearly imagined, an emblem of the poet in nature; Wordsworth goes on, however, to include a story of human suffering and to suggest that poetry helps call forth human sympathy. His emphasis on storytelling also suggests that the poem is concerned not only with sympathy and suffering but also with the source and ends of poetic power. Armytage opens part 2 claiming that a "power to virtue friendly" (229) must inform his tale, without which his act of narration would be "a wantonness" (221). Having read Thomson, students can easily see that the complex narrative structure of "The Ruined Cottage" shifts them from an image of the poet as one who sees to an image of the poet as storyteller. They can also see, however, that both the content of Armytage's story and the inclusion of a narrator who listens to his story problematize the moral authority claimed for poetry.

In "The Ruined Cottage" Wordsworth explores poetic authority in the terms set for him by predecessors such as Thomson, but he ultimately uses his major characters—Margaret, Armytage, and the poet-narrator—to re-define the issues that plagued the eighteenth-century poets of vision. To demonstrate this contention, I ask students to compare Margaret and Ar-mytage. All Wordsworth's major characters are distinguished by their ties to nature, although Margaret's response to the losses nature and society have visited on her is diametrically opposed to the acceptance of loss that Armytage preaches and seems to exemplify (Parker 103, 110). By asking students to discuss how the vision of different characters is portrayed (focusing on images of the eye), I can usually elicit a comment on how similar Margaret and Armytage seem at first. Specifically, as Paul Sheats notes (*Making* 157), Margaret is marked as a Wordsworthian figure of imagination not only by her restlessness but also by her fixed gaze: we last hear of her with her eye "busy in the distance, shaping things" (456). Like Margaret's, Armytage's eye shapes things: "I see around me here / Things which you cannot see" (67-68). However, he also chastises the poet-narrator for reading the "forms of things with an unworthy eye" (511) when the latter contrasts the "secret spirit of humanity" with nature's "oblivious tendencies" (503-04). Armytage implies elsewhere, too, that he knows how to read nature properly; his reports of Margaret, for instance, are drawn in part from a reading of the landscape. Underlining one important way in which he differs from Mar-garet, Armytage claims to draw comfort from nature, as his first and last readings of landscapes illustrate. Margaret, on the other hand, misuses imag-ination by refusing to accept what the natural world can offer her: "About the fields I wander, knowing this / Only, that what I seek I cannot find" (350-51).

But the line between proper and improper uses of the eye and of imag-inative vision is not as clear-cut as first appears (*Making* 206-07; Parker 111). It is difficult to avoid asking whether the comfort Armytage finds is natural, virtuous, or convincing. Certainly, his communion with Margaret's spring is peculiar: he says that he and the spring waters "*seemed* to feel / One sadness" (83-84, emphasis added) and then says that for the waters "a bond / Of brotherhood is broken" (84-85); they no longer minister to "human comfort" (88). The shared sadness, it appears, is over the fact that nature does *not* minister to humanity. As when the "blighting seasons" (134) help lead to Margaret's loss, as when we read of those whose "place knew them not" (144), nature and humanity do not seem to have an easy relationship.

Instead, nature seems to offer Armytage emblems of its own inadequacy. Geoffrey Hartman argues that—unlike Thomson, who would have nature point to God—Wordsworth usually insists that nature "suffices imagination," but in an odd way, telling us only that it will not sustain us (*Wordsworth's Poetry* 298, 140). "The Ruined Cottage" may even suggest that nature teaches us not to care. Students reading the poem often complain that Armytage

does not stay and help Margaret, that his later moralizing is thus uncon-
vincing. This contradiction is in part a result of the most disconcerting aspect
of Armytage's apparent lesson: what he learns from nature is to be detached,
to have no home (which presumably accounts for the end of the 1799 poem,
where the two travelers move on to an inn, a mere "evening resting place"
[538]). Early Wordsworth uses cottages as emblems of peace, love, and hope
(*Making* 138); thus the very title of "The Ruined Cottage" calls into question
whether the natural world can be, as Armytage seems to suggest, a comfort
or home to human beings.

Finally, however, the questionable status of Armytage's view of nature
discredits neither him nor the poem. Having noted Margaret's fixity of vision
and imagination and questioned the comfort Armytage seems to say comes
from viewing nature, the class can return to the question with which it
began, namely, what—if anything—the poem claims as the source of poetic
power. Looking at images of idleness and power in the poem, students see
that Armytage is instructing the poet-narrator (and ultimately the reader)
on how to avoid "the impotence of grief" (500) but that his final instructions
are as much in how he tells us as in what he says. Impotence is what
distinguishes Margaret from Armytage: Margaret's futile attempt to recap-
ture the past is associated with idleness (383, 431, 451), while Armytage's
claim to power in the present shows that, unlike the Thomsonian figure with
which the poem opens, he is not an "idle dreamer" (231; Parker 94-95).

But what of the power Armytage claims? And in what way can Wordsworth's figure claim the authority Thomson's could not? After all, Armytage
was impotent when face to face with Margaret and her grief: "I had little
power / To give her comfort" (275-76). It seems that the poem desires the
power to offer comfort, and it can lay claim to such power, not in the time
about which we are told, but in the present act of storytelling. That is, the
power Armytage can claim is in what Neil Hertz calls the narrative present
(20-21), which includes the fictionalization of his otherwise powerless past
self. In short, the sources of power in "The Ruined Cottage" are finally not
so much in nature as in narration. What replaces the idle or impotent dream
of "what we feel of sorrow and despair" (520) is "meditation" (524) or the
present narration of the past rather than nature or powerless nostalgia for
what is lost or irremediable. Armytage's exemplary lesson for the narrator-
poet (and for the reader) is finally in the use of his voice, not of his eye.

The poem takes on yet another dimension when seen as a critique of poets
such as Thomson. In "Lines Left upon a Seat in a Yew-Tree," Wordsworth
cautions the reader against being one "whose eye / Is ever on himself" (55-
56), but he celebrates those who in "inward thought, / Can still suspect, and
still revere [themselves]" (62-63). Thomson, trying to place himself in history, falls into self-consciousness as he tries to see himself claiming authority

for his vision. Wordsworth inverts Thomson's self-conscious gaze and shows us that claiming the power to narrate one's self (or to create the self in a fiction) is a form of authority, a way of turning a closed past into presence and of opening a place—in the telling of the poem—where humanity can dwell, temporarily.

Teaching the Two-Part (1799) *Prelude*

Jonathan Wordsworth

From a teaching point of view *The Prelude* in its established versions of 1805 and 1850 is too long. Only those students with time to specialize can get a sense of the whole work, and selections give a false impression by going (understandably) straight to the visionary moments. Until ten years ago only a handful of scholars knew that there was also a compact early version of the poem still in manuscript—a version in two parts, as against the thirteen books of 1805 (or fourteen of 1850). Since its appearance in the *Norton Anthology* in 1974, the two-part *Prelude* has been recognized by teachers both as a natural introduction to the later versions and as a great poem in its own right. Students who come to it for the first time are struck at once by its immediacy. "Was it for this?" Wordsworth begins, asking himself strange compulsive questions and arresting the students' attention from the start.

Was what for what? Answers will take teachers, if they choose, to Milton and *Samson Agonistes*; to *The Recluse* and Wordsworth's own sense of a divinely appointed mission; to Coleridge, who fostered this sense and for whom above all the poem is being written. At line 8 comes the affectionate quotation from "Frost at Midnight," pointing to a relation with the Coleridge conversation poem and behind that with Cowper. By line 27, students—now aware of some different contexts of the poetry—find themselves started on a sequence of boyhood episodes that seldom fail to stir the imagination. It is unlikely that they will have encountered writing of anything like this kind before, yet the poetry has an uncanny power:

> Oh, when I have hung
> Above the raven's nest, by knots of grass
> Or half-inch fissures in the slipp'ry rock
> But ill sustained . . .
>
> . . . .
> With what strange utterance did the loud dry wind
> Blow through my ears; the sky seemed not a sky
> Of earth, and with what motion moved the clouds!
> (1799 *Prelude* 1.57-60,64-66)

Urban students who know nothing of what it might be like to be taking eggs from a rock face in the English Lake District respond to the writing because it has the power to evoke primal experience. And this extraordinary—and very teachable—poem evokes such responses again and again. To Wordsworth himself the episodes have

> Such self-presence in my heart
> That sometimes when I think of them I seem
> Two consciousnesses—conscious of myself
> And of some other being.   (2.28-31)

It is this ability of the poet to enter into the mind of his former self, and yet at the same time to stand back from it and watch, that makes the two-part *Prelude* an especially attractive text. Students who are themselves beginning to look back on childhood and adolescence with a certain curiosity are intrigued by an adult writer who values these periods as the sources of his creative power. And the more they read, the more they find that Wordsworth has been before them, asking questions, providing tentative answers:

> Who knows the individual hour in which
> His habits were first sown even as a seed?
> Who that shall point as with a wand, and say
> "This portion of the river of my mind
> Came from yon fountain"?   (2.245-49)

Who indeed! But Wordsworth in this poem is prepared to have a try.

Certain key passages need to be dwelt upon in the classroom. In part 1, for instance, it is important to notice that the claims put forward become more complex as the poet moves from the relatively straightforward account of the child's imaginative response (in the woodcock-snaring, birds-nesting, and boat-stealing episodes) to consider the creative implication of memory. In my experience only the most accomplished students follow without prompting Wordsworth's associationist reference to

>   tragic facts
> Of rural history, that impressed my mind
> With images to which in following years
> Far other feelings were attached. . . .   (1.282-85)

And if they have grasped the passage thus far, they may still not be too confident about the final lines:

>   —with forms
> That yet exist with independent life,
> And, like their archetypes, know no decay.   (1.285-87).

Wordsworth's assertion of an independent life of the mind in which natural forms "know no decay" is not in itself difficult to accept. It is the wistful further implication—that mind can have the permanence of mountains—

that leads to difficulties among a generation of students for whom hyperbole (in Donne, for instance) no longer seems easy to gauge. As teacher one does well to pause, not because the lines are in themselves especially impressive but because if their overstatement is properly understood, they take one close to the center of Wordsworthian Romanticism.

Classroom experience suggests that the "spots of time" that follow—and that develop Wordsworth's discussion of mental "archetypes"—never fail as poetry. The woman on the hill especially, with her pitcher of water on her head and her garments "vexed and tossed" by the wind, lives on in the memory of countless students, just as she lived on in the mind of Wordsworth himself. Without guidance, however, students are not likely to see how carefully the poet has worked to create the hold that she has over their imagination. Much cannot be explained, but one can at least draw attention to the associative links by which the terror of the child in the preceding lines (lost alone on a moor where a murderer has been hanged) is transmuted into the "visionary dreariness" with which Wordsworth invests the details of the landscape. And one can point as well to the parallel process that has gone on in the student's own mind, as the poet's evoking of murder and mystery creates the heightened consciousness in which the woman comes to be viewed:

> down the rough and stony moor
> I led my horse, and stumbling on, at length
> Came to a bottom where in former times
> A man, the murderer of his wife, was hung
> In irons. Mouldered was the gibbet-mast;
> The bones were gone, the iron and the wood;
> Only a long green ridge of turf remained
> Whose shape was like a grave. I left the spot,
> And reascending the bare slope I saw
> A naked pool that lay beneath the hills,
> The beacon on the summit, and more near
> A girl who bore a pitcher on her head
> And seemed with difficult steps to force her way
> Against the blowing wind.   (1.306-19)

"It was in truth," Wordsworth continues—and both the effect of his pro-testations and the artfulness of his repetition may well be lost on students who do not expect to find themselves played on by a poet so famous for his simplicity:

                             It was in truth
An ordinary sight, but I should need
Colours and words that are unknown to man
To paint the visionary dreariness
Which, while I looked all around for my lost guide,
Did at that time invest the naked pool,
The beacon on the lonely eminence,
The woman and her garments vexed and tossed
By the strong wind.   (1.319-27)

From the teacher's point of view the "spots of time" are a godsend because their account of the imaginative process is offered in poetry that is itself vividly imaginative. The same cannot be said for the centerpiece of part 2, in which the poet traces the river of his mind back to the fountain of maternal love. Without guidance students easily skip over the infant babe (2.267-310), put off by the expository tones and the distance of the writing from personal experience. In a post-Freudian world they are no longer surprised by Wordsworth's intuition of the formative value of the child's relationship with the mother. And few will make anything of the more exalted lines in which the baby becomes, for all his tender years, a type of the poet himself:

            powerful in all sentiments of grief,
Of exultation, fear and joy, his mind—
Even as an agent of the one great mind—
Creates, creator and receiver both. . . .   (2.300-03)

Once again the nearness to hyperbole is disconcerting. Expecting an ordinary baby, the student is bound to ask—as Coleridge did of the "Mighty Prophet! Seer blest!" of the Immortality Ode—what gives this child such extraordinary powers. It is not an easy question, of course, but, as with the mental landscapes that "like their archetypes, know no decay" (1.287), it is a case in which the teacher does well to pause and grapple with the difficulties. The lines contain after all the earliest definition in either Coleridge or Wordsworth of the primary imagination. Wordsworth is not just talking of a period when he held mute dialogues with his mother's heart.

Teaching the 1850 *Prelude*

Anthony J. Franzese

Whether I can allot to *The Prelude* four class meetings with a group of undergraduates or six and more with graduate students, I attempt to rally a study of the whole poem around three points: (1) an identification of the poem's "vital principle" of composition; (2) the projection of a spatial design through which students may grasp the poem's form; (3) the application of (1) to (2), whereby the students may understand their act of reading as the imaginative reenactment of the growth of the poet's mind.

At the outset, I name the "prime and vital principle" (14.215) as the shaping power of the imagination. The point at issue is whether the name corresponds substantively to the poetic development. We turn to book 1, where our task is theoretically simple: Does the poet display a characteristic behavior of mind from which we may infer the power that shapes its growth (or, at least, its activity)? Does the poet act in a recognizable way? At this point, of course, I pray for the arrival of the delightfully demonic student: "Yes. He talks and doesn't get anywhere." "He's confused." "He's boring." "He doesn't know what he's talking about." Excellent! The poet "begins" and continues for two hundred and sixty-nine lines and has yet to come up with a topic, much less a theme! So, these early lines are prethematic; they should bear the character of the poet's "pure" mind, before it engages a theme. What characterizes this prethematic mental activity? It aspires and withdraws. It dares to try and gives up, waxes and wanes, advances and retreats, leaving the poet "Baffled and plagued" (1.257) to pass his days in "contradiction" (1.238). The shaping power is evidently a sort of dynamo, an energy expressed in polarities. (No need to stumble on the dynamo metaphor; the most acculturated solid-state student will at least recognize that certain gadgets burn out on direct current and run on alternating current. Moreover, I welcome such a digression as an opportunity to distinguish, at least, mechanical from vital metaphors: dynamos; alternating current; the tick-tock rhythm of a conventional timepiece versus inspiration and expression, as in the activity of the lungs; concentration and expansion, as in the systole and diastole of the chambered heart.)

In addition to alternating impulses, the poem's early and dis-contented lines reveal the strong working of a mind that is nevertheless best pleased

> While she as duteous as the mother dove
> Sits brooding . . . [with] goadings on
> That drive her as in trouble through the groves. (1.140-43)

The point I mean to emphasize is that the baffled mind is nevertheless driven; the power that shapes the alternating impulses of the disengaged mind also purposively directs that mind. Both behaviors, I point out, are captured in the ambiguous metaphor of "brooding." Students will recognize this shift from idling activity to purposive development of mind on the strong evidence that book 1 concludes after all with the poet's choice of "a theme / Single and of determined bounds" (1.641-42). There is, evidently, a

> something far more deeply interfused,
> .   .   .   .
> A motion and a spirit, that impels
> All thinking things, all objects of all thought,
> And rolls through all things.   ("Tintern Abbey" 96, 100-02)

I ask my students now to apply this conceptual identification of the vital principle to book 1. Here are some sample instances of their applications with consequences that I attempt to draw out: (1) The power is evident in the alternation between the poet's active and anxious grasping for a theme (1.1-269) and his passive and relaxed "recollection" procedure (beginning 1.270-339). Composition of poetry and composure of mind are evidently alternate states as well as gestures of creativity. (2) Immediate experience and mediated discourse alternate, as in the stolen-boat episode followed by the "Wisdom and Spirit of the universe" discourse (1.401). The poem is moving through experience and reflection toward a knowledge that must be both affective and cognitive. (3) The boy spins and sets the world to spinning (1.452-60). More, he does both simultaneously, being the internally "reeling" but externally still center of his turning universe. This collapse of customary subject-object dualisms foreshadows the conflation of imitative mind with creative mind, as being "truly from the Deity" (14.112). (4) The inspirational breeze brings joy from the "green fields" and from the "azure sky" (1.4). The natural world provides a model for the intimacy of immanence and transcendence. (5) The power is expressed in the poet's primal verbal influences: the river Derwent and the nurse (1.271; cf. 14.194-96). Schematically, "his murmurs . . . / That flowed along my dreams" and "[her] song" that flowed in verbal discourse identify a primary system of alternating correspondences: male/female, natural/human, spontaneous/mediated. This instance of the vital principle, however, clearly states the "blending" of the river's murmur with the nurse's song.

The point of emphasis here for a useful understanding of the vital principle is that the alternating terms of the power, in every instance, are dynamically bound together; the terms indicate a single but polarized power like the "poles" in an attitudinally clear magnetic field. In fact, like the terms in polarities such as left/right, parent/child, perception/creation, each term is bound by definition to the other. The power is dialectical. Students with a grasp of this vital principle can read the poem; I have found that a heavy investment of class time here is ultimately both efficient and rewarding.

With the sense of a shaping vital principle in hand, I sketch for my students a spatial diagram for the whole poem:

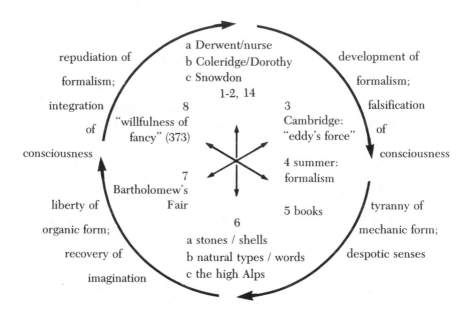

I use the diagram for theoretic purposes to remark on two ways of viewing narrative structure: (1) The progress of the poem follows the circumference of our model from book 1 to the "beginning" in book 14 (i.e., to the thematic and experiential self-realization of the poet, who is then first prepared, in reality, to visit his place of childhood and to recollect the story of his growth). (2) The architectonic design of the poem centers on the pairings of opposed books and groupings of books. I use the diagram for pedagogic purposes to tease meaning out of and purpose into my students' readings. A general application of the diagram suffices for the sake of orientation. I then clarify and verify readings by applying the vital principle to the diagrammatic patterns.

With regard to the first view (plot as development), the diagram indicates that books 1-6 mark the buildup of language skills, of formal craft, and of a correspondent and inevitable false consciousness. Books 7-11, in contrast, trace a literary letdown, perhaps, but also a vitally exciting and important phenomenology of conscience; this section returns from the social to the personal and redeems both after the expansion from the personal to the social and the failure of both in books 1-6. With regard to architectonic design, I use the diagram to indicate that the poem cleaves at its center along any diameter. The Snowdon-Alpine axis rightfully commands our primary attention, and this pair of opposed experiences certainly should be studied together. Still, I direct attention elsewhere as well: for example, to the intellectual confusion at Cambridge (book 3) resolved through recourse to abstract formalism (see below) versus the existential confusion in London (book 7) resolved through recourse to the experiential vitalism of lines 740-71. This contrast, of course, reflects both the poet's development (following the directional circumference) and the system of dynamic polarities (established in the diametrics of the circle).

A brief tracing of the circle, mindful of both progress and dialectic process, will show the errant progress of "a Pilgrim resolute" (1.91). Action develops from a post-Edenic phenomenology of natural influencings (books 1-2) to a polarized discourse on the "surfaces of artificial life" (3-562) at Cambridge where "Imagination slept, / And yet not utterly" (3.260-61) amid a host of "Majestic edifices" (3.384) and abstractions (3.598-611) as the poet is sucked "in with an eddy's force" (3.14) "through strange seas of Thought" (3.63). Thus, books 1-2 and book 3 represent an amplified dynamic unit of the poem's shaping principle: natural/artificial, home/school, concrete/abstract ideation—all in a dialectic moment of "eddy."

The tension here between "books" and the "lovely forms" (3.362) of nature is resolved into a lovely literary formalism through books 4 and 5. There, our young formalist perceptually reintegrates the edifice of "the snow-white church" (4.21) into his beloved vale, though generally "Of that external scene which round [him] lay, / Little, in this abstraction, did [he] see" (4.160-61). Naturally, he links Euclid and Cervantes, geometry and poetry, the one "a stone, the other a shell" (5.112), though "both were books" (5.113). The fruit of the young poet's labor, however, is neither slight nor merely natural. In the interiority of his dream life, the poet assimilates "sea" and "book" (5.139-40), the visions of poetry and science, the "consecrated works of Bard and Sage, / Sensuous or intellectual, wrought by men" (5.42-43). Thus, by analogy, the works of humankind and nature correspond and reflect "Powers / For ever to be hallowed" (5.218-19) that illuminate "all the host / Of shadowy things" "through the turnings intricate of verse" (5.598-99, 603).

Book 6 marks the ultimate achievement (and failure) for the young formalist bound on his line of errant progress. There, like the shipwrecked wretch taking consolation from "a single volume," a "treatise of Geometry" (6.145-46), the poet asserts:

> So was it then with me, and so will be
> With Poets ever. Mighty is the charm
> Of those abstractions to a mind beset
> With images, and haunted by herself,
> And specially delightful unto me
> Was that clear synthesis built up aloft
> So gracefully.   (6.157-63)

Thus, Mont Blanc, both stone and shell, is a "book" (6.543) that the poet "could not choose but read" (6.544). The "soulless image on the eye" (6.526) corresponds to the poet's own "unripe state / Of intellect and heart" (6.542-43). Later, the "stern mood" of another "sadness" in the immediacy of the poet's existential discovery of loss on the Simplon Pass issues from a "source" that is "Mixed" with the "soft luxuries" of the Mont Blanc formalism (6.557-61). Whatever one might say about the positive aspects of the poet's experiences on Mont Blanc and the Simplon Pass, the maturing poet will travel some distance again before the living and joyful truth of his active imagination comes home to seek "no trophies" but to "fertilise" his own beloved vale (6.610-16). In the high Alps, Wordsworth was "lost" (6.596) amid "Winds thwarting winds" (6.628); only much later, at home, recollected, and to his "conscious soul," can he "say— / 'I recognise thy glory' " (6.598-99). As the shaping principle of imagination operates from moment to moment in book 1 and more amply in the movement embracing books 1-2 and book 3, so it operates most amply in the movement embracing books 1-6 and 7-11, the movement from formalism to vitalism.

Finally, books 12-14 describe the recovery of the imagination: form wedded to content in a relation of generative "spiritual Love" (14.188). This "absolute power" is the fullest "amplitude of mind" (14.190-91) and a power that is nevertheless "thine / In the recesses of thy nature" (14.215-16). The formal processes of the poem embody its spirit and meaning. The whole poem is as organically whole as any other living thing; it can be identified and analyzed genetically at any level, but it can be known only wholly.

Books 10 and 11 of *The Prelude*: The French Revolution and the Poet's Vocation

Charles Rzepka

Books 10 and 11 of *The Prelude*, describing Wordsworth's experiences during the latter part of the French Revolution, provide a much more important commentary on his greatest poetry, and on his conception of the poet, than is usually assumed. In addition, they can be made particularly appealing to undergraduates, for they represent the poet making his choice of life in the crucial passage from adolescence to manhood. This choice confronts all college students—deciding how best to establish a real sense of oneself as a participant in the adult world, how best to fit one's own "story" into the larger chronicle of history, with the conditions and opportunities for self-fulfillment that one finds there. Books 10 and 11 describe Wordsworth's failure in that first choice, as an "active partisan" (11.153), and help us understand his final choice, as a poet of "wise passiveness."

Before discussing *The Prelude* with my students, I turn to the Preface to *Lyrical Ballads* and point out two curious things: First, an argument about poetry soon comes to focus on the nature of the poet—his inner disposition, sensibility, and point of view—rather than on his formal practice or profession ("poetry" per se). Wordsworth's emphasis is mostly on internal qualities, not outward abilities (Stillinger 453). Second, Wordsworth feels it necessary to tell his readers that he has, in *Lyrical Ballads*, annulled the tacit historical "contract" between poet and reader in favor of proposing to himself what he is to perform. Thus, in line with his emphasis on the inner rather than the outer person, Wordsworth delegitimizes the expectations of poetic performance historically imposed on poets by their readers. If readers feel disappointed, that is due to their lack of imaginative identification with the private aims and feelings of the poet, not to the poet's professional incompetence. The Preface, then, is Wordsworth's attempt to gain public confirmation of a private poetic identity that is apparently at odds with society and history.

Wordsworth's attempt in the Preface to strike a contract with himself and to stress the poet's inner nature is motivated in part by the failure of the tacit contract he struck with the leaders and participants of the Revolution as an "active partisan" on behalf of their cause, a young man "led to take an eager part / In arguments of civil polity" (11.76-77). Wordsworth felt he had entered upon "a work of honour": "from all doubt / Or trepidation for the end of things / Far was I, far as angels are from guilt" (10.142-45). But guilt arose. The English declaration of war on France split Wordsworth's identity

113

into two incompatible parts, a son of England and a Son of Liberty: "Not in my single self alone I found, / But in the minds of all ingenuous youth, / Change and subversion from that hour" (10.266-68). Wordsworth is forced to submerge his sympathies with the Revolution and to leave off his public enthusiasm for it. For the first time, he feels that he is not the person others take him for: his inner self becomes a thing apart from his apparent identity.

The Reign of Terror brought further confusion to Wordsworth's already ambivalent feelings by betraying the real self, the partisan that had been submerged and secretly nurtured. Wordsworth's depiction of his nightmares at this time, his "ghastly visions" of "despair / And tyranny, and implements of death . . ." (10.402-03), suggests that he felt not just wronged but indicted for his role in earlier advocating measures that had led to this outcome.

> suddenly the scene
> Changed, and the unbroken dream entangled me
> In long orations, which I strove to plead
> Before unjust tribunals,—with a voice
> Labouring, a brain confounded, and a sense,
> Deathlike, of treacherous desertion, felt
> In the last place of refuge—my own soul.   (10.409-15)

Wordsworth suspects that the self he had so jealously protected and preserved inviolate in its commitment was, perhaps, not worth saving after all.

But with the death of Robespierre, these doubts were momentarily put aside. Wordsworth began to hope that he could vindicate his inner self in the eyes of the world. This hope gradually took on such an edge of fanaticism, however, that even the French invasion of Spain and Italy, instead of disillusioning him, only made him more desperate in defense of his commitment to the Revolution. Refusing to accept "the shame / Of a false prophet," Wordsworth strove "to hide, what nought could heal, the wounds / Of mortified presumption" (11.213-16). Through sophistries, cant, and sterile rationalizations he sought to maintain a definite sense of himself in society.

Ultimately, however, Wordsworth came to feel that he had been betrayed, by an assumed understanding with history, into being false to himself. In response he withdrew from active partisanship into a "nightmare subjectivism," as David Perkins puts it (*Quest* 5), a process described in 11.292-333. Out of this radical withdrawal grew a new hope for self-realization: to find himself under the name of "Poet" and to make that his "office upon earth." Significantly, it is Dorothy who facilitates this new emergence of the "true self" and who keeps Wordsworth in touch with reality.

> Then it was—
> Thanks to the bounteous Giver of all good!—
> That the beloved Sister in whose sight
> Those days were passed, now speaking in a voice
> Of sudden admonition— . . .
>
> . . . .
>
> Maintained for me a saving intercourse
> With my true self; for, though bedimmed and changed
> Much, as it seemed, I was not further changed
> Than as a clouded and a waning moon:
> She whispered still that brightness would return,
> She, in the midst of all, preserved me still
> A Poet, made me seek beneath that name,
> And that alone, my office upon earth.
> (11.333-37, 341-48)

In the end, Wordsworth becomes (1) a man primarily of feeling, not of action; (2) a man of nature and impulse, not of society and rationale; and (3) a man seeking an audience of intimates, like Dorothy and Coleridge, a captive audience whose expectations he can count on as coinciding with his own, rather than an audience of strangers. The Preface appears, then, as an attempt to make Wordsworth's audience share his expectations of himself. That sense of a captive audience is easy to spot in the *Lyrical Ballads*— "Expostulation and Reply," "The Tables Turned," "To My Sister," "Simon Lee," and of course "Tintern Abbey," where Dorothy, who had earlier confirmed him in his new "office upon earth," reappears to confirm him still "a lover of the meadows and the woods," a "worshipper of Nature" (103, 152). The emphases in these poems on feeling over intellect, passivity over action, impulse over intentionality, and nature over society are all compatible with Wordsworth's new enthusiasm for the ahistorical self, the self of a poet, not that of a partisan. Books 10 and 11 of *The Prelude* give students an important insight not only into the impact on Wordsworth of the definitive historical event of the age but also into the character of the poet and the nature of his poetry.

Mount Snowdon and the Wordsworthian Sublime

Wayne Glausser

When Wordsworth on Mount Snowdon sees the ground in front of him suddenly brighten, he has no time to form explanatory thoughts: "Nor was time given to ask or learn the cause" (14.37). The vision of a moonlit mist startles his mind into activity, and having taken away his first chance to answer a question, it sets him a compensating challenge—to decipher the meaning of what he has just seen. Wordsworth proceeds to do just that, and he finds in the scene an emblem of the mind's power to perceive or create such sublime visions.

This climactic episode of *The Prelude* earns the title "sublime" from Wordsworth as well as his interpreters. The designation is appropriate but not simple to understand or teach. As Thomas Weiskel has pointed out, two versions of sublimity enter Wordsworth's poetry: a negative or Kantian sublime in which outer, usually natural power overmatches inner or imaginative power, leaving the imagination overextended, halted, perplexed; and a positive or egotistical sublime, in which the imagination recognizes itself in nature and celebrates the merging of inner and outer into a single creative presence (34–62). If the first stage of the Mount Snowdon passage, the narration of the vision, belongs to the negative sublime, the second or interpretive stage deserves to be called a climax of the egotistical sublime. Wordsworth grants the imagination ultimate authority—"Such minds are truly from the Deity, / For they are Powers" (14.112–13)—but only as, married to the external world through the image of the mist, it belongs to or coincides with the identical power of nature.

Students may find both stages of the Snowdon passage difficult to interpret—the first because it gives them too few clues, the second because it gives them too many. The first or narrative stage can be taught effectively through comparisons with other *Prelude* spots, particularly those concerning the Simplon Pass (book 6), the gibbet and girl (book 12), and the death of Wordsworth's father (also book 12). The second or interpretative stage of Snowdon, which may be a little more difficult for students to discuss, can also be approached through comparison. Since Wordsworth draws on imagery associated with creative power in the primal texts of Genesis and *Paradise Lost*, I give students excerpts from both, as well as a passage from the 1805 *Prelude* that differs interestingly from its 1850 counterpart. Focusing on just a few lines from the 1850 Snowdon episode, we consider how Wordsworth has followed and revised the earlier texts:

There I beheld the emblem of a mind
That feeds upon infinity, that broods
Over the dark abyss, intent to hear
Its voices issuing forth to silent light
In one continuous stream;   (1850 *Prelude* 14.70-74)

                               . . .Thou from the first
Wast present, and with mighty wings outspread
Dove-like sat'st brooding on the vast abyss
And mad'st it pregnant: What in me is dark
Illumine, what is low raise and support;   (*PL* 1.19-23)

In the beginning God created the heaven and the earth. And the earth
was without form and void; and darkness was upon the face of the
deep. And the spirit of God moved upon the face of the waters. . . .
And God said, "let us make man in our image, after our like-
ness." (Gen. 1.1–2, 26)

But there went up a mist from the earth, and watered the whole face
of the ground—and the Lord God formed man of the dust of the
ground. . . . (Gen. 2.6–7)

The perfect image of a mighty mind,
Of one that feeds upon infinity,
That is exalted by an underpresence,
The sense of God, or whatso'er is dim
Or vast in its own being, . . .   (1805 *Prelude* 13.69–73)

In comparing Wordsworth with Milton, students see right away that
Wordsworth refers to the human mind rather than to the Holy Spirit as the
brooding power. They may also remark how Milton's Holy Spirit, a combination of female and male, makes the abyss pregnant; whereas Wordsworth
wants to discover and appreciate the abyss as abyss. Such a contrast seems
more obvious in the 1805 *Prelude*, where the abyss remains dim and vast,
than in the 1850, where Wordsworth draws more form and clarity out of
that abyss. We then move backward to Milton's source, Genesis, in its two
versions. In the "priestly" chapter 1, the spirit of God hovers or broods like
Milton's Holy Spirit and Wordsworth's mind, and it ultimately improves the
abyss by creating a Godlike man. In the "Yahwistic" chapter 2, where man
at first seems more earthly than divine, students will recognize Wordsworth's
mist and note how it accompanies God as a creative presence. It springs up

out of the earth, rather like an "unfathered vapour"—Wordsworth's Simplon Pass simile describing the imagination.

Finally comes the 1805 *Prelude*. Besides hiding the Miltonic allusion (for whatever reasons, anxious or innocent), this earlier version also differs in its treatment of the abyss. In 1850, the abyss is equated with "infinity"; thus the mind broods over infinity. In 1805, a series of variations gives us a different perspective on the abyss: from "underpresence" to a "sense of God" to "whatso'er is dim / Or vast in its own being." Students profit from discussing the whole series, and they usually bring up the connotations of "underpresence" as well as the difference between "sense of God" and "God." But especially in the last term of the series, the 1805 Snowdon passage associates the abyss with the mind itself: the mind broods over the mind. The image fits well with the already mentioned passage from the Simplon episode, where imagination "rose from the mind's abyss / Like an unfathered vapour . . ." (5.594–95). It would seem, then, that in his 1805 even more than his 1850 Snowdon passage, Wordsworth brings the negative and positive sublime together: he imagines a mind in awe of itself as an unfathomable but not unprecedented creative power.

LITERARY AND HISTORICAL CONTEXTS

Wordsworth and Milton

J. Douglas Kneale

Wordsworth's involvement with Milton began early and lasted most of his life. We know from Christopher Wordsworth's *Memoirs* that "at an early age [Wordsworth] could repeat large portions of Shakespeare, Milton, and Spenser" (1: 34), and the poem "At Vallombrosa," written only ten years before his death, shows signs of an intertextual relation between the two poets that grew rather than diminished with time. The achievement of Milton, of course, was felt by all the Romantic poets, and each responded to that achievement, or to its limitations, in his own way. But Wordsworth's response, characterized dialectically by his tropes of usurpation and collaboration, stands as the longest and arguably the most complex intertextual affair in Romantic literary history. It was not just a response to Milton's thought, to his views on religious, civil, and domestic liberty; nor was it concerned simply with Milton's success with specific genres of literature—the epic, the pastoral elegy, the masque, the drama, the sonnet—though these examples provided challenges enough to any poet who hoped to emulate them. It was an involvement acted out, essentially, on the level of language, in a word, a phrase, an image, a cadence, and the level of structure, in the turns and counterturns of a text's rhetorical organization.

The teaching of Wordsworth's relation to Milton should begin by distinguishing between the concepts of *influence* and *intertextuality*. It is an important distinction to make these days, since the former term refers to authors, biographies, and a history of ideas, while the latter, as its name implies, refers to texts and their techniques of quotation, reference, allusion, and echo. The clearest definition would be that intertextuality is the expression of influence, whether we are speaking of literary or other texts. The study of literary influence is author-oriented and implies a heuristic belief in authorial intention; intertextuality is text-oriented and does not depend on historical or psychological reconstructions of an author's biography. In either case, biographical parallels between Milton and Wordsworth—for example, each was Protestant, lived through a failed political revolution, suffered eye problems, and dictated his poetry to female amanuenses—may be of incidental interest but do not help explain either the effect of one person on another or the relation of one text to another.

Though some critics (Bloom, *Map*, esp. 17–21, and *Anxiety*; Culler 100–18) deny any connection between intertextuality and allusion, verbal echoes remain the teacher's most straightforward key to helping students see how one text is shaped partly in response to another. On this level of language, then, the student perceives that poems are written with a sense not just of the pastness of the past but also of its presentness in the form of a text. Milton the man died almost a century before Wordsworth was born, but Milton's poetry lived into Wordsworth's moment of composition.

The best examples of such allusive responsiveness are to be found in *The Prelude*'s reminiscences of *Paradise Lost*. In a sense, *Paradise Lost* should be prerequisite reading for an undergraduate course in the Romantics, for Wordsworth's poem has so thoroughly appropriated Milton's on both the lexical and structural levels that our interpretation of *The Prelude* often depends on our reading of the rhetorical pattern of *Paradise Lost*. This entire dimension of Romanticism is lost to the student who does not have a background in Milton, not to mention in Shakespeare and Spenser. Let us take a few instances of echo—some old, some new—to show how Wordsworth adapts his Miltonic background.

Our first example appears in line 14 of the 1850 *Prelude*: "The earth is all before me." The echo is of the closing lines of *Paradise Lost*, in which Adam and Eve leave the Garden of Eden with the prospect that "the World was all before them." Readers usually notice this echo, but they often overlook its reappearance in a different form at the end of book 1 of Wordsworth's poem: "The road lies plain before me" (640). The imagistic shrinking from all the earth to a road gives the poet a focus that is "single and of determined bounds" (641); at the same time the rhetorical transition from "the earth is all before me" to "the road lies plain before me" shows, perhaps more clearly than any other echoic shift in *The Prelude*, Wordsworth creating his own poetic voice above the sound of Milton's.

What Adam and Eve are leaving, strictly speaking, is not Paradise—at least not the *locus amoenus* of the earlier books of *Paradise Lost*. W. J. B. Owen has reminded us that at the end of the poem the garden turns into a desert, a place uninhabitable, a demonic parody of the pleasance ("Annotating"). What does Wordsworth do with this detail? He characterizes his entry into the earth as a release from a similarly uncomfortable place: in the earlier versions he leaves "a house / Of bondage" (1805 *Prelude* 1.6–7), an image that alludes not only to the Exodus of the Hebrews (Exod. 13.3) but to Milton's Samson, who makes his first appearance in *Samson Agonistes* coming from such a house of bondage. In the 1850 edition Wordsworth revises his language to embody another strong echo of *Paradise Lost*: he says that he has "escaped / From the vast city, where [he] long had pined / A discontented sojourner" (1.608). The lines come directly from book 3 of Milton's poem, where the narrator invokes the "holy Light" (3.1) of heaven after being confined for the first two books to the darkness of hell; he has "escap't the *Stygian* Pool, though long detain'd / In that obscure sojourn" (3.14–15). Wordsworth's rhetoric of allusion indicates that he is leaving not a specific, referential city—neither London nor Goslar nor Bristol—but a place closely identified with Milton's hell.

My purpose in this essay is not to give extended interpretations of specific Miltonic allusions but to outline in a more general way how these intertextual tropes can be used in the classroom to illustrate Wordsworth's appropriation of Milton. Before proceeding far in this line, however, the teacher will be forced to consider the nature and function of allusion in general, and what part it plays in Wordsworth's style in particular. Miltonic allusiveness is usually recognized as being far more serious than mere lexical gesturing; it often serves a structural function in his poetry, and it can involve a complex system of ironies reaching forward and backward within a given text. Wordsworthian allusiveness, partly derived from Milton's example, is often equally far-reaching in its structural implications, but frequently the verbal keys are so radically submerged or displaced that the Miltonic background is hidden. It should be noted that allusion performs a structural function not only within texts but between them: a single verbal echo of *Paradise Lost* comes into a text silently trailing the entire rhetorical structure of Milton's poem; hence echo's proper tropological status is that of synecdoche, the trope in which the part (echo) stands for the whole (source text) (see Ben-Porat).

Let us consider an example of this type of structural allusion. Wordsworth begins book 7 of *The Prelude* with a backward glance toward his "glad preamble" (7.4)—that is, the opening lines of the poem as a whole—and a forward view of the "tamer argument, / That lies before us, needful to be told" (7.50–51). The narrator's looking before and after recalls Milton's exactly similar actions in the opening paragraph of book 7 of *Paradise Lost*, where the speaker reviews his progress through the first six books and states: "Half yet remains unsung, but narrower bound / Within the visible Diurnal Sphere" (7.21–22). The thematic similarity between Wordsworth's "tamer argument" and the more narrowly bound argument of Milton is clear enough, but more interesting in terms of these poems' structures is how their narrative pauses create a strategic fulcrum between two halves of a self-balanced whole. The balance in Wordsworth is inexact, as the poem's shifting organization from thirteen to fourteen books might lead us to expect, but its intertextual rhetoric invites alignment with Milton's poem—an alignment that is further supported by similar metaphors suggesting the problematics of composition (Milton fears to go "hoarse or mute" [7.25]; Wordsworth's song has been "not audible" [7.11]) and by images of ascent and descent, from heaven to earth and from the Alps to London.

In addition to specific allusions on lexical and structural levels, Wordsworth's intertextuality takes the form of engagements in terms of genre. His adaptation of the Miltonic sonnet is a case in point. Both Dorothy's diary of 21 May 1802 and Wordsworth's note to Isabella Fenwick attest to the effect a reading of Milton's sonnets had on Wordsworth one afternoon, when he "took fire" and composed three sonnets after being inspired by Milton's. Years later, in a letter to Alexander Dyce in 1833, Wordsworth shows that he had thought long and deeply about the Miltonic sonnet and its relation to the Italian model. Formal comparisons between Wordsworth's and Milton's use of the sonnet can lead to thematic considerations in the classroom— the various public and private voices that Wordsworth, like Milton, uses to express social, political, religious, meditative, or autobiographical sentiments. Or they can lead to even larger formalist questions, of the type raised by Donald H. Reiman, who has suggested that *The Prelude*'s entire fourteen-book structure is meant to be read as a macrosonnet, with the first eight books as the octave (ending with a modified *volta* in "Retrospect") and the final six books as the sestet, with the books on France as one tercet and the restoration of imagination in the last three books as a final tercet ("Poetry" 176–77, n. 35, and "Beauty"). Here is an instance of intertextuality on a new level insofar as *The Prelude*, that great Romantic lyrical epic, accommodates its epic scope to a lyrical shape that owes something to Milton's experiments with the sonnet form. The shift from thirteen to fourteen books in *The Prelude* reveals a lyrical structure that was there all along, even as the change from ten to twelve books in *Paradise Lost* perfects a dramatic structure whose emphasis, as Arthur E. Barker once showed, had been originally misplaced.

If we wish to extract a teaching method from the examples of interpretation I have given so far, the procedure would involve the students' first recognizing and identifying the source of an allusion to Milton's poetry, then explicating the function of the source passage in Milton, and finally explicating the function of the allusion in the Wordsworth text under discussion. Does the echo suggest a similarity between the two texts, or does it point up contrasts in the handling of theme or character? Does the presence of a Miltonic voice, or its echo, confer authority on the alluding text, or does it actually work as a destabilizing linguistic element by denying closure to its foster poem and by introducing unavoidable ironies? These questions are as relevant to echo and allusion as they are to the more foregrounded tropes of quotation and reference; they all repeat a tale of two texts.

The detective work of tracking down Wordsworth's allusions to Milton and other writers—and, by extension, of following up echoes of Wordsworth in later poetry of the nineteenth and twentieth centuries—is still worthwhile for students, as it allows them to build up their own sense of a literary history from the basics of literature: language. The point of such findings, however, should not be simply to show that Wordsworth had read Milton or to enumerate echoes for their own sake but to elucidate Wordsworth's developing response to Milton, the shifting rhetorical strategies of approach and involvement that engage Wordsworth not merely with a distant historical person but with an ever-present text.

In larger terms, Wordsworth's relation to Milton may be described by the dialectical movements of what Wordsworth calls usurpation and collaboration. The first movement is most clearly seen in the Prospectus to *The Recluse*, in which Wordsworth pictures himself as passing "unalarmed" the "strength" and "terror" of Milton's achievement —his muse, his God, his heaven, his hell. Though this usurpation can be read and taught as a discontinuity in literary history, Wordsworth's dialectic of response also offers a hope of continuity through a trope of collaboration in which Wordsworth and Milton are figured as "joint laborers" in a common task. The statement of this cooperative faith is found at the end of book 13 of *The Prelude*, where Wordsworth affirms "that Poets, even as Prophets, [are] each with each / Connected in a mighty scheme of truth" (13.301–02). Yet one need not accept the notion of a transcendental "scheme of truth" in order to see Milton as an imaginative collaborator with Wordsworth; from an intertextualist perspective, Milton is a joint laborer to the extent that his texts are appropriated by Wordsworth's and become crucial to their interpretation. The real interaction takes place always on the level of language, in the rhythms and cadences, the images and tropes, the phrasing and syntax of a rhetorical structure whose assimilation of Milton is complete. That assimilation, if it involved anxieties and embarrassments, dealt with those burdens in a profoundly creative way: Wordsworth's poetry dared to become the thing that it beheld, and then it created itself anew.

After *The Prelude*: The Historicity
of Wordsworth's Ideas

Francis Russell Hart

In "The Sense of the Past," which I ask my students to read, Lionel Trilling tells us the literary text is "ineluctably a historical fact," we are "creatures of the historical sense," the text's historicity is "a fact in our aesthetic experience" (179–83). How so? My task is to approach the teaching of the mature Wordsworth in historical context. The approach is valuable as long as we realize history as a context of meaning instead of slipping back into a pedagogy that "taught" context extrinsically and left the text to be "appreciated" for itself. Wordsworth's biography and the history of his times are not our concerns here. Our goals are (1) to understand works more fully, (2) to discover the special insight literature provides into a "past," (3) to discover the role literature can play in historical process. To pursue them, we can focus on four interrelated thematic terms: *power*, the poetic *vocation* as a cultural force, the return to *nature*, and the figure of the *child*. Our students bring their own urgent meanings to such terms. Our task is to help them discover that such meanings have histories.

Early admirers viewed Wordsworth's impact as a cultural force. Arnold's "Memorial Verses" and the crisis chapter in Mill's *Autobiography* can be assigned as illustrations. How had a social world been impoverished by the atrophy of feeling? Why was a poet so sorely needed to "make us feel"? What "healing power" did Arnold see in him? Such questions lead us to the center of Wordsworth's sense of vocation, a word that had new meaning for his epoch in the history of labor. The end of poetry was to cultivate true power and feeling in a world that impoverished both. How did the world do this? Why was the poetic vocation vitally linked to what Wordsworth calls nature and the natural self? Our students are familiar (or think they are) with the "return to nature," but this seemingly changeless impulse had special and problematic meaning for Wordsworth's historical moment. (A. N. Whitehead, ch. 5, and Raymond Williams, *Country*, chs. 13–14, are helpful here.) Integrally related is the idea—some call it the archetype—of the child. Our students are surprised to learn that the special idea of the child is not eternal; as Philippe Ariès has shown us, it was largely a creation of the Enlightenment (see esp. 128–33, 398–404). Wordsworth's sense of vocation is imaginatively linked to the historically generated idea or myth of the child: the presexual anima or muse of the true poet, the opposing image to the world.

In pursuit of the historicity of such central ideas I want to sketch briefly the scenario for two or three class sessions in the introductory course in

British authors, major poets, or British Romanticism. The sessions center on a small group of poems published in *Poems, in Two Volumes* and follow discussion of *The Prelude*. At the end of the essay, I will list the readings and suggest questions for study and discussion.

First we must acknowledge a major obstacle: our students know little of the historic past, and our literature courses allow little time for remedy. Chapters in historical surveys (e.g., Hobsbawm) assume much knowledge and are written for historians. Modern background essays are specialized interpretations that offer little access to the experience of living in Wordsworth's world. We had better sketch our own broad strokes. Here, ready for filling in, are mine. (In giving them first, I mean to leave open the issue of when they should be offered—perhaps, best, after the discussion of texts has generated the questions such a sketch might answer.)

All history is the record of change, but between the 1780s and the 1830s many sensed a rapid acceleration and awakened to being involved in history. Political change is the mere tip of the iceberg, and it does not help to call this period "the industrial revolution," for that phrase summons up too narrow an image. For a while, in America and France, politics seemed uppermost; but political change seemed to end in terrorism and consequently in increased imperialism, reaction, social and economic change. In Britain during George III's half century, the population doubled, radically shifting from village to town; by 1832, perhaps half lived in urban conditions. At the time of the Westminster Bridge sonnet, Wordsworth was looking at a city of one million people. Foreign trade caused port towns to mushroom, and midland towns became factory centers. Cities set the styles, and village life and custom visibly waned or became pathetic imitations of city life. The rhythms of natural life gave way to clock time, work time. "Speed" (see Hazlitt's "Fight," De Quincey's "Mail Coach") was born, a generation before the railway.

As time changed, so did space. Wordsworth's life saw a revolution in transport and communications; the world was much larger, much closer. Canals crossed the countryside, dirt roads were macadamized, and rapid coach travel linked towns with the remotest areas. A new era of commuting and tourism opened. Becoming closer, country and city seemed more distinct. A transformed postal service led the way to ever quicker communications. Stamp-tax records show a jump from seven million newspapers in 1753 to fifteen million in 1792; new magazines and quarterlies prospered, popular "knowledge" became an industry, and educational reform was hotly debated. The "great world" became more familiar, more menacing. A world of extravagant and confused foreign styles—in architecture, landscaping, interior decor, dress—replaced tradition with "fashion" and "tone," mysteries dictated by the world of wealthy bourgeois imitation.

We needn't be Marxists to see what is central to the process of change:

the growth of wealth, prodigious and largely untaxed. Numerous enclosure acts, rationalized as "improvements," had turned small farming into a system of large, prosperous farms and gentrified farmers and had created a new class of landless agricultural workers, many of whom became industrial labor (see Williams, *Culture and Society*, on the birth of the idea of class, and E. P. Thompson on working-class consciousness). Banks spread all over the countryside; paper money came into being; the great jump in the national debt during the Napoleonic wars created hundreds of thousands of "fund holders," living on income from government bonds. A credit economy grew by leaps and bounds; one gets the impression that everyone borrowed, everyone lived in debt. The "dismal science" of economics had been born, and the meanings of "wealth" and "value" were public issues. Shortly, Carlyle would rant against the "cash-nexus," and England would be observed by Engels and Marx. But we needn't look so far. A few paragraphs from Burke will show our students the traditional humanist's anxieties at new political-economic images of human nature. Two or three letters from Cobbett (esp. 20 Oct. 1825, 31 Oct. 1825, 4 Sept. 1826) will sketch the radical response to the corrupting gentrification of the countryside; the social poisons of paper money, credit, and fashion; the dehumanizing horror of "the Great Wen" (the city). And for our purposes, there are texts much closer to Wordsworth.

Coleridge's "Lay Sermon" was written at a time of economic crisis just after Waterloo, but it reflects back over the war years. The relevance of the brief excerpts I will list is in his diagnosis of the effects on mind and society of what he calls the overbalance of the commercial spirit, his redefinition of the world. By the time he wrote this work, the breach with Wordsworth had occurred, but they had still been close enough (in 1809, the year of *The Friend*) for Coleridge to influence and partly revise the prose work in which Wordsworth's own reformulated ideas of social life and value had been most fully expressed.

The Convention of Cintra (also 1809) and the event that inspired it deserve brief introduction. In the year of Wordsworth's collected *Poems* (1807), Napoleon invaded the Iberian peninsula and was met by what Wordsworth and other cultural nationalists saw as a genuine popular uprising. A French army was trapped. But instead of exploiting the victory, British expeditionary leaders and "statesmen" at home negotiated a treaty and "betrayed" the resistance. In the betrayal Wordsworth saw an epitome of what had gone wrong in the world, saw how the world had given away the very powers of mind and imagination, the very powers of genius called for at such a moment in history (Owen and Smyser 1: 256, 291). Without genius, without the same powers possessed and cultivated by the true poet and poetry, national leaders are mere "spectators" who "neither see nor feel" (Owen and Smyser 1: 306).

They have purchased knowledge without power. They lack "that knowledge which is founded not upon things but upon sensations . . . not upon things which may be *brought*; but upon sensations which must be *met*" (304–05). The decline of such powers—the "fading" of the "splendour of the Imagination," the chasing away of "Sensibility, which was formerly a generous nursling of rude Nature"—he blames on the spread of "Mechanic Arts, Manufactures, Agriculture, Commerce, and all those products of knowledge which are confined to gross—definite—and tangible objects" (324–25). Such is "the world" that the poems we are concerned with confront.

> The world is too much with us. Late and soon,
> Getting and spending, we lay waste our powers;
> Little we see in nature that is ours.
> We have given our hearts away, a sordid boon.

Semantically, the opening lines of Wordsworth's famous sonnet appear simple enough, but they are not. The terms carry contextual weight; the elliptical connections are crucial. *Line 1.* "The world"—we have seen already what special currency the term had—is personified; it is "with" us, a separate, active agency, while we are passive, objectified. *Line 2.* The subject shifts: "we" are now in time, and time is filled with "getting and spending." The acts are economic, commercial; what we get and spend is not named, nor need it be. The acts of possession and dispossession are a "waste" of "powers"; "the world's" economies are a waste. How so? *Line 3.* The paradox of economy and waste clarifies. In wasting our powers in the world's commerce, we reach the condition of being dispossessed of "nature"; the world and nature are antithetical domains of possession. We discover dispossession in the act of seeing. The eye truly used is the organ of powers. If we waste our powers, we cannot see truly, and if we cannot see truly, we possess nothing real, nothing "in nature." *Line 4.* The effect—or is it the cause?—of being dispossessed of nature is revealed. We have "given away"—spent without recompense—our hearts. Our powers are of the "heart"—affect, organic feeling. Without them, no true seeing is possible, and so we are dispossessed. Such is the world: the world and the true self are alienated; the true self lives in powers and hearts linked affectively to the life of nature.

Three other poems—"Westminster Bridge," "The Solitary Reaper," and "I wandered lonely as a cloud"—help us pursue the historicity of the theme words heart, nature, power, and world. Recalling how the city is "seen" in *The Prelude*, what of its "sight" from Westminster Bridge? In the sonnet the city is seen only in terms of an affective unity with nature, and thus the "mighty heart" is not given away. True value is possessed only through the heart's powers. Likewise, the solitary reaper is seen and heard, but the value is truly possessed only when borne away by "my heart." And again, the lonely wanderer possesses the true "wealth" of the "show" of daffodils only when "my heart with pleasure fills." Wordsworth's response to the world of getting and spending is to redefine the very meaning of value. The final stanzas of "The Solitary Reaper" open a further perspective. The poet asks for knowledge, but "no one" is there to give it. No communication occurs between poet and reaper; no knowledge is exchanged. For what is exchanged is not knowledge but power. Or rather, knowledge is not gained—the line in the Boy of Winander passage (*Prelude* 5.425) uses the commercial term "purchased"—at the expense of power. The boy saw things in nature that were "his." He did not give his heart away, but like Lucy he remained separate and whole. Interaction with the reaper takes nothing, gives nothing away, respects the separate wholeness of both singers, reaper and poet.

This curious interaction, so familiar in Wordsworth, is sure to provoke troubled discussion. Why did Wordsworth see true power and wealth as such solitary, "antisocial" things, possessed only in "the bliss of solitude"? We might turn to the "Ode: Intimations of Immortality" for a historical answer. Reviewing it, one wonders whether any historical context applies: image and reflection seem fixed to pastoral and personal universals. But this sense is deceptive. Adopting Erik Erikson's model, Patricia Spacks reminds us that each historical moment focuses its sense of identity on a certain stage in the life cycle. The ode offers a statement of one historic person's idea of continuity and discontinuity in integrity and power. It translates a political idiom, formerly public and institutional, into terms of the individual life cycle. "Freedom" now applies to a stage of life, a state of being. What is "natural piety" if not a translated political value? And note the figure for the process of socialization: "shades of the prison-house begin to close" (67). Foucault, in *Discipline and Punish*, can unpack for us the grim historicity of that figure. Note especially the satiric seventh stanza and what it says about "communication" and self-presentation in society: the boy will "fit" his tongue "to dialogues of business, love, or strife," and then this stage too will be "thrown aside" as "the little Actor cons another part." The stanza closes with the meaningfully ironic rhyme of "vocation" and "imitation."

We are discovering a moment in social history when the world is "Society" and when the unnatural life of "Society" is seen—as it is seen variously by Rousseau, Blake, Byron, Austen—as an inevitable and pathetic hypocrisy, a yoking to role and custom, a prison house of inauthenticity (see Trilling's *Sincerity and Authenticity*), where hearts are given away in getting and spending. The idea of the child emerges as an opposing myth to the world. The child invokes and recalls a presocietal (domestic but "free") state when human nature still possesses its own powers, close to "natural" powers and elements that the world will conquer and destroy unless the poet, out of "natural piety," recovers them. The problem is still revolutionary: the loss of freedom, the loss of power. The enemy, however, is no longer political but social. This is the great shift described by Mill at the start of *On Liberty*. How did it happen? What did it feel like? The questions are historical, and history and poetry illuminate each other as we seek the answers.

Primary Readings

Poems assigned: "Elegiac Stanzas . . . Peele Castle" (1806/1807); "I wandered lonely as a cloud" (1804/1807); "Ode: Intimations of Immortality" (1804/1807); "The Solitary Reaper" (1805/1807); "Composed upon Westminster Bridge" (1802/1807); "The world is too much with us" (1802?/1807).

Prose selections assigned:
S. T. Coleridge, "Lay Sermon" (1816); selections in *Collected Works* 6: 161–62, 169–70, 173–74, 188–89, 204, 209–11.
W. Wordsworth, *Concerning . . . the Convention of Cintra* (1809); selections in Owen and Smyser 1: 256, 291–94, 304–06, 324–26.

Summary of Discussion Questions (Distributed Ahead to the Class)

1.   What is the "world" that is "too much with us"? What "powers" do we "waste"? How is our seeing of nature tied to our "hearts"? Explain how your answers to these questions are connected.

2.   How is this "giving away" of hearts related to the "mighty heart" of "Westminster Bridge," and to "my heart" in "The Solitary Reaper" and "I wandered lonely"? What "powers" has the poet here, and what "wealth" does he gain?

3.   Why, in such a "world," would the idea of the child have acquired such force? How did that idea affect the idea of a "return to nature"?

4.   Is Wordsworth's response to "the world" an antisocial one? How does Wordsworth see the pressures of socialization on human development in the ode? How do his views here compare with those of Mill in *On Liberty*, chapter 1? What historical explanation might there be for this celebration of solitude?

5.   Do Wordsworth's critical reactions to this changing world seem closer to Burke's or to Cobbett's? Why, in light of such reactions, did Wordsworth see the poet as an important social force?

Sympathy and Imagination: Wordsworth and English Romantic Poetry

John Hodgson

In the typical Major English Romantic Poets course Wordsworth's poetry comes early, looms high, bulks large, and, if we teach it at all well, persists stubbornly and vividly—it functions, then, rather as one of his own spots of time does. Coleridge, Shelley, Keats, even Byron—they all bear witness to Wordsworth's power, but as we try to cram their great riches into the little room of a basic undergraduate syllabus, we are not likely to dwell overlong on their explicit responses to him. For Wordsworth is most relevant to the other major Romantic poets not as the polemicist whom they mistake or debate or reject but as an efficacious spirit, the great poetic original whom they inevitably experience and absorb.

In these few pages I shall concentrate on two preeminent themes of Wordsworth's work as natural foci for a course in English Romantic poetry: his relation to human life and his attention to the growth of a poet's mind. These two themes have much to do with each other, as "Tintern Abbey," the Immortality Ode, and *The Prelude* all repeatedly proclaim; each in fact entails and partly defines the other, so that sympathy and imagination, as poet after Romantic poet discovers, prove inseparable.

Both Coleridge and Hazlitt expressed notable reservations about the aloofness of Wordsworth's ostensibly sympathetic poetry, but the most famous such characterization is probably that of Keats. In an 1818 letter contemporary with his early work on *Hyperion*, Keats distinguishes two contrary sorts of "the poetical Character." There is first his own sort, and especially Shakespeare's—that of "the camelion Poet," which "is not itself—it has no self—it is every thing and nothing—it has no character . . . he has no Identity" (1: 387). Alternatively, there is "the wordsworthian or egotistical sublime; which is a thing per se and stands alone" (1: 387), imposing itself on other things (1: 223). The fundamental distinction Keats here draws between his own poetry and Wordsworth's closely corresponds to Coleridge's analysis of Wordsworth in *Biographia Literaria* and *Table-Talk* as an essentially undramatic poet—for example, "Wordsworth and Goethe . . . both have this peculiarity of utter non-sympathy with the subjects of their poetry. They are always . . . spectators *ab extra*,—feeling *for*, but never *with*, their characters" (*Table-Talk* 193, 16 Feb. 1833; cf. 172, 21 July 1832). Coleridge's criticisms in the *Biographia* of "The Thorn" and "Gipsies" (Engell and Bate 2: 49–52, 137–38) afford some practical illustrations of his point (see also Keats 1: 173–74 on the latter poem).

But this didactically stark and easy categorization has heuristic potential: it cannot satisfy, it raises questions. Wordsworth himself, for one, certainly disagrees with it and had already denied it. His remarks on the subject in his Preface to *Lyrical Ballads* sound, in fact, positively Keatsian (and so help remind us that the notion was actually a critical commonplace; see Owen and Smyser 1: 177–78): "[I]t will be the wish of the Poet to bring his feelings near to those of the persons whose feelings he describes, nay, for short spaces of time, perhaps, to let himself slip into an entire delusion, and even confound and identify his own feelings with theirs . . ." (Owen and Smyser 1: 138). And most of his lyrical ballads are in fact more or less dramatic in form. Again, a poem added to the 1800 *Lyrical Ballads* volume, "A Narrow Girdle of Rough Stones," anecdotally recounting an initial failure of sympathy belatedly recognized, makes a particularly instructive comparison for Coleridge's censure of "Gipsies," for it seems proleptically to make and then respond to all Coleridge's points.

Yet if we cannot simply accept Keats's and Coleridge's sense of "the wordsworthian or egotistical sublime," neither can we simply reject it. There are odd hedgings on both sides. Coleridge's characterization of the Wordsworthian spectator *ab extra* as "feeling *for*, but never *with*, [his] characters" is a case in point (in the *Biographia* he explains this as "a sympathy with man as man; the sympathy indeed of a contemplator, rather than a fellow-sufferer or co-mate" [Engell and Bate 2: 150]). Keats, similarly, praises the egotistical Wordsworth (in direct contrast to the egotistical Milton, with his "apparently less anxiety for Humanity") for "think[ing] into the human heart" (1: 278, 282). Wordsworth, on the other hand, strangely yokes egotism and sympathy in his semiautobiographical Pedlar, whose heart, "Unoccupied by sorrow of its own, . . . lay open":

> He had no painful pressure from without
> Which made him turn aside from wretchedness
> With coward fears. He could *afford* to suffer
> With those whom he saw suffer.   (*Excursion* 1. 361–62, 368–71)

Perhaps the truer issue here, then, is not sympathy itself so much as the degree and duration of actual identification with another—a state temporary and controlled in Wordsworth's experience (cf. his intriguing comments on "To Joanna" [de Selincourt and Darbishire 2: 487]), potentially uncontrolled and overwhelming in Keats's ("the identity of every one in the room begins so to press upon me that, I am in a very little time anhilated" [1: 387]; cf. "Ode to a Nightingale"). So Wordsworth shrewdly diagnoses Coleridge's blocked poetic potential as the sad negation of the Pedlar's strength: "It was poor dear Coleridge's constant infelicity that prevented him from being the poet that Nature had given him the power to be. He had always too much personal and domestic discontent to paint the sorrows of mankind. He could not afford to suffer with those whom he saw suffer" (de Selincourt and Darbishire 5: 412–13). This crucial insight bears tellingly, for example, not simply on the "Resolution and Independence"-"Dejection"-Immortality Ode dialogue between Wordsworth and Coleridge but also on Moneta's "dreamer"-"poet" opposition in *The Fall of Hyperion* and on Prometheus's sufferings and strength in *Prometheus Unbound*.

Wordsworth's own poetic strength in this respect verges closely on what Keats calls "negative capability," notwithstanding some critics' arrogation of this quality and phrase to the chameleon poet exclusively. By negative capability, after all, Keats means the capability "of being in uncertainties, Mysteries, doubts, without any irritable reaching after fact & reason" (1:193). Keats meditates often in both his letters and his poetry on this condition of imperfect knowledge, and his customary epistolary phrase for it is in fact Wordsworth's poetical one—"the burden of the mystery." "[T]he World is full of Misery and Heartbreak, Pain, Sickness and oppression. . . . We see not the ballance of good and evil. . . . We feel the 'burden of the Mystery,' To this point was Wordsworth come . . . when he wrote 'Tintern Abbey' . . ." (1: 281). Negative capability, in these terms, is simply the ability to bear the burden of the mystery; if Coleridge perhaps could not bear it ("He could not afford to suffer with those whom he saw suffer"), Wordsworth most certainly could. How to bear this burden, in fact, becomes a central question of English Romanticism. Wordsworth's thoughtful responses in "Tintern Abbey," the Immortality Ode, and *The Prelude* compare interestingly with Byron's narrational speculations in *Don Juan*, Prometheus's and Demogorgon's formulations in *Prometheus Unbound*, and Apollo's and the poet's experiences in the *Hyperion* fragments.

If Keats's notion of imaginative sympathy with others seems initially an aesthetic, amoral principle, by the time of the *Hyperion* poems it takes on strongly moral implications: now in Keats, as long since in Wordsworth, the poet is recognized as "the rock of defence for human nature" (Owen and Smyser 1: 141). In Shelley, the aesthetic and the moral implications of imaginative sympathy are explicit and inseparable early on: they figure largely, for example, in "Alastor," where "self-centered seclusion" brings not only the spirit of solitude but vacancy of spirit and proves the ruin of poetry. Perhaps the strongest Romantic manifestos of this theme appear in Shelley's *Defence of Poetry* and *Prometheus Unbound*. As Shelley famously affirms in the *Defence*, imaginative sympathy, the putting of oneself "in the place of another and of many others," is "the great instrument of moral good," of love (7: 118). Hence in *Prometheus Unbound* the ascendancy of love over selfishness naturally entails and accompanies the apotheosis of poetry and all the arts (see 3.3.58–60, 4.415–17).

Shelley's changes of emphasis from Wordsworth are significant and instructive. Like Keats, but with a far more moral tone, Shelley stresses poetry's value as an antidote to the corruption of selfishness: "Poetry and the principle of Self . . . are the God and Mammon of the world," and poetry can lift men "out of the dull vapours of the little world of self" (7: 134). Wordsworth is far less dualistic on this score: he will not so quickly or absolutely divorce poetry from self, for he knows that "We have no sympathy but what is propagated by pleasure . . . no knowledge . . . but what has been built up by pleasure, and exists in us by pleasure alone" (Owen and Smyser 1: 140). And the two poets' striking divergences of subject matter (Wordsworth's "incidents and situations from common life," Shelley's mythic and abstract ones), imagery, tone, and even verse form exaggerate their philosophical differences. The underlying agreements that unite them, however, seem ultimately more important.

Shelley shares Wordsworth's fundamental conception of the poet as "an upholder and preserver, carrying everywhere with him relationship and love," who writes "in order to excite rational sympathy" (Owen and Smyser 1: 141, 143). To help my students confront these apparent contrasts and deeper affinities between the two poets, I find it particularly effective to juxtapose two pairs of corresponding theoretical and poetical texts—Shelley's *Defence* with Wordsworth's 1802 Preface and Shelley's *Prometheus Unbound* (especially act 3, scene 4, and the lyrics of act 4) with Wordsworth's *Lyrical Ballads*. In these works the characteristic differences are so pronounced that the likenesses stand out all the more emphatically.

At its end, Shelley's dialectic with Wordsworth takes a sober coloring from an eye that, in its very different way, had like Wordsworth's "kept watch o'er man's mortality" (Immortality Ode 198). For the devastated Rousseau of "The Triumph of Life" is, as many critics have noted, a pointedly Wordsworthian figure whose biography derives from the Immortality Ode. And in this Rousseau no less than in the deadly triumph that has victimized him, Shelley darkly envisions the doom and failure of the sympathetic imagination, the irreconcilability of "Good and the means of good" (231), love and imagination. Perhaps, though, we err in regarding Shelley's Rousseau as simply a surrogate Wordsworth. For this poet figure is no Keatsian "physician to all men" (*Fall of Hyperion* 1.190) but on the contrary a contagious sufferer:

See the great bards of old, who inly quelled

The passions which they sung, as by their strain
   May well be known: their living melody
   Tempers its own contagion to the vein

> Of those who are infected with it—I
> Have suffered what I wrote, or viler pain!—
> And so my words were seeds of misery—   (274-80)

This contagious, Rousseauvian poet seems the converse of Keats's chameleon; yet the Romantics' Wordsworth belongs with neither of these types but with the contrasted, egotistically sublime bards "who inly quelled / The passions which they sung."

If it will not quite do to speak of a Byronic egotistical sublime in such poems as the verse tales, *Childe Harold*, and *Manfred*, nevertheless the temptation to do so is natural and instructive. Much more properly than Wordsworth, the egotistical Byronic hero—generally aloof, unsympathetic, proud—stands as the prototypal opposite of the chameleon poet. How then does his egotism or his sublimity differ from Wordsworth's? The location of the Byronic hero relative to the Wordsworthian and Keatsian poets is all the more problematic in that the former's pose of reserve or even antipathy ostensibly derives from a rich history of suffering. But from this suffering, too commonly felt as victimization, proceeds no sympathy; it is as if his suffering from others has prevented or hindered his suffering with them. Hence those melodramatic withdrawals from society, centrifugal "pilgrimages," and fortified isolations so characteristic of Lara, Harold, Manfred, and their kind.

Yet beneath their proud, aristocratic trappings, these Byronic figures are sadly like a familiar, humbler type of Wordsworthian character: the yew-tree seat builder withdrawn into his "circling bower" (11); Margaret in "The Ruined Cottage," who nourishes her heartsickness but neglects her duties to others; or the Solitary in *The Excursion*, who deliberately chooses the isolation he is far from idealizing. These no less than Byron's dark figures are characters whom suffering has impoverished spiritually, made selfish. But Wordsworth, unlike the early Byron, typically provides the instructive, corrective contrast—the narrator of "Lines Left upon a Seat in a Yew-Tree," the Pedlar-Wanderer of *The Excursion*.

The transition from this egotistical Byron to that greater one who gives us *Don Juan*—a transition we can trace in his new appreciation for familial alliances and sympathies in *Childe Harold*, canto 3, and his sympathetic ennobling of the Abbot in *Manfred*, act 3—signals Byron's growth into a genuine imaginative sympathy with another and with many others. As Michael Cooke aptly notes with reference to *Don Juan*, "The fact is that, as much as Keats would oppose this, Byron is his consummate chameleon poet" (*Acts* 226). And if his dark heroes seem to have been effectively preempted by Wordsworth's earlier sympathetic studies of lapsed sympathies (a judgment we might also apply to Shelley's "Alastor"), in his comic-epic persona

Byron achieves a more fortunate relation to the earlier poet, showing us yet another way of bearing the burden of the mystery.

As the foregoing discussion suggests, imaginative sympathy had for the Romantic poets vocational no less than social and moral implications; hence the growth of a Romantic poet's mind is in important part an education in sympathy and negative capability. For some distinctive parallels and alternatives to Wordsworth's self-analysis here we may turn especially to Shelley and Keats.

For Shelley, poetry is "the expression of the Imagination," and so the growth (or rebirth) of a poet's mind is no less than the development (or reawakening) of the imagination, the agent of love. Shelley experiments with the theme in the "Hymn to Intellectual Beauty" and again in the dedication to *Laon and Cythna*, taking Wordsworth's Immortality Ode as his model. "Alastor" and "The Triumph of Life," in dark contrast, evoke Wordsworth's great ode only to depart antithetically from it and present instead the death of a poet's mind. But *Prometheus Unbound*, while also representing this fall in the bondage of Prometheus, nevertheless celebrates the resurrection and triumph of imagination and love as the divine essence of human potential. M. H. Abrams has ably discussed the plot of *Prometheus Unbound* in the context of the Wordsworthian plot form of self-education and self-discovery (*Natural Supernaturalism* 299–307), so I shall limit myself here to a narrower and more specific application.

Just as time in Shelley's myth is a series of cycles (apparently entropic in "The Triumph" but potentially ever-renewable, as Demogorgon's valediction teaches, in *Prometheus*), of which Prometheus's apotheosis figures but one ascendant curve, so too *The Prelude* gives us a redundant plot (I refer to the 1805 *Prelude* in Wordsworth, Abrams, and Gill). Thus the healing of Wordsworth's imagination in books 10–12, as I have noted elsewhere, simply repeats the processes of its shaping in books 1–4 and again in books 7–8 (Hodgson 136); his life is a series of strengthenings, healings, unbindings, to each of which Prometheus is figuratively relevant. Wordsworth tells us, for example, that for a crucial stage of his youth he was bound much as Prometheus is. His oppressor, his Jupiter, was an extreme rationalism, and in books 10 and 11 he tells of his subjugation to this power. Relying too exclusively on abstract reasoning, in however noble a cause, he unknowingly undertook the "work / Of false imagination, placed beyond / The limits of experience and truth" (10.846–48). The result was strikingly Jovian, even as Shelley's bound Prometheus is strikingly like his oppressor, Jupiter. Wordsworth's misguided attempt to liberate humanity—motivated by what, after Keats, we might well call a negative *in*capability—became a blind violation and degradation of his own human nature, until finally, losing "all feeling of conviction," he "yielded up moral questions in despair"(10.898–900). And the power that, together with the workings of his still vital imagination, helped rescue him from this bondage was a dual figure consisting of Dorothy and nature, who together, "maintain[ing] for me a saving intercourse / With my true self" (10.914–15), played Asia to Wordsworth's Prometheus.

Keats gives us several accounts of the growth of a poet's mind, most notably in his letter on the "vale of Soul-making" (2: 101–04), *Hyperion*, and *The Fall of Hyperion*. Particularly in *Hyperion* the redundancies of plot—for Keats's plot builds on repetition, just as do Wordsworth's and Shelley's— help distinguish the truly poetic: thus the poet-god Apollo reenacts but goes beyond the experiences of the titans; the disanointing mortal oil poured on Saturn (2.97–98) yields to the anointing mortality that pours into Apollo (3.115–20); and Apollo's song and music surpass and overwhelm Clymene's.

Among the many points of comparison with Wordsworth that *Hyperion* suggests, let me single out Keats's careful reinversion of Wordsworth's re-visionary insight, "The Child is father of the Man." Apollo may be younger than the titans, but they are developmentally his juniors. In the terms of the "Soul-making" letter, they are intelligences—sparks of the divinity, like little children or childlike adults—while he, now being schooled more suc-cessfully than they by experience and suffering (theirs no less than his), is acquiring an identity, becoming a soul. Apollo's epiphanic schooling, a sud-den and intense consciousness and appreciation of mortality (it is thus yet another shouldering of the burden of the mystery), suggests a mythic version of a Wordsworthian spot of time but also clarifies Keats's divergence from Wordsworth: for not in childhood, Keats finds, but in the leaving it does man's greatness originate, and not by his origins but by his destiny shall you know him.

Wordsworth and Modern Poetry

Allan Chavkin

In my courses on Wordsworth, I consider him as the founder of a tradition that includes such twentieth-century poets as Wallace Stevens, Theodore Roethke, and even at times William Butler Yeats; my approach enables students to overcome their prejudices and appreciate his importance as one of the first modern poets. In these courses, I argue that modern literature begins not with the twentieth-century modernists Eliot and Pound but with the nineteenth-century English Romantics. Relating Wordsworth to the giants of twentieth-century poetry has been received with enthusiasm by my students, but a colleague has raised an objection to my approach. He considers time devoted to twentieth-century poets during the unit on Wordsworth "unfair to the Romantic poet." Moreover, he argues that one should not discuss American poets in a course on British masterpieces. I respond that my focus is always on Wordsworth, not on the twentieth-century poets, and that my approach shows the interdependence of modern British and American literature, as well as of nineteenth- and twentieth-century poetry. Most important, this comparative approach not only shows the importance of the tradition that Wordsworth established but also illuminates better than any other that I have seen the ideas and the methods of his poetry.

In a course on nineteenth- and twentieth-century British masterpieces, my unit on Wordsworth is divided into three parts. The text is Jack Stillinger's Riverside edition, which provides a large selection of poems, an excellent introduction, and detailed notes. In the first part of the unit, I lecture on Romanticism as a modern tradition and summarize and comment on the theories of M. H. Abrams, Harold Bloom, George Bornstein, Robert Langbaum, Morse Peckham, Jack Stillinger, and others who argue for the continuity of English Romanticism in the twentieth century. In the second part, by focusing on several key selections from Wordsworth's canon, especially from *The Prelude*, the class attempts to delineate how his imagination operates. Finally, in the third part, the class examines four of Wordsworth's poems in conjunction with twentieth-century poems that can be seen as extending the tradition of Wordsworthian Romanticism.

The first part of the unit is brief and consists primarily of lecture. I suggest that literature beginning with the English Romantics is qualitatively different from literature before them and, moreover, that nineteenth-century Romantic views of art, the writer, and the imagination have dominated literature for the last two centuries. The modern sensibility was born at the end of the eighteenth century when the Romantic problem of "dejection," what twentieth-century writers often call "alienation," emerged. This problem was precipitated by the "new science" of the Enlightenment, which destroyed the stable worldview of humanity.

I use Keats's remarks in his 3 May 1818 letter to John Hamilton Reynolds to introduce the class to Wordsworth's sensitivity to this problem. When Keats notes that in "Tintern Abbey" Wordsworth explores "the dark passages" of his psyche, he is observing Wordsworth's major contribution to modern poetry (*Letters* 1: 280–81). He creates a new kind of poem, a discursive meditation that can explore the dark passages of the mind and regenerate the individual. Keats does not name or delineate this new genre, which developed from the neoclassic descriptive-meditative poem (the "local descriptive" poem); the twentieth-century Romantic poet Wallace Stevens provides both the best appellation and the most concise description of it in his "Of Modern Poetry," which defines "The poem of the mind in the act of finding / What will suffice." The class examines Stevens's poem to understand this genre.

To see how Wordsworth's imagination functions in this genre that he largely invented, in the second part of the unit the class focuses on several crucial passages from *The Prelude* and then analyzes in detail "Resolution and Independence." Typically, Wordsworth's imagination is anchored in the world of the senses, and while it colors, modifies, and interprets reality by projecting feelings and ideas on the external world, it does not transcend everyday existence. In the transaction between the imagination and reality, the poet's goal is "a balance, an ennobling interchange / Of action from without and from within" (*Prelude* 13.375–76).

This "ennobling interchange" between the mind and nature frequently occurs in heightened moments of illumination, what the poet calls "spots of time." Therefore, the class examines carefully the "spots of time" passage in book 12 of *The Prelude*, which is crucial for understanding Wordsworth's emphasis on the importance of one's mental powers. Scrutiny of the text enables us to see several key Wordsworthian themes: the power of the imagination fading with age; the heightening of an ordinary scene by endowing it with feeling; the importance of memory as a necessary storehouse for past spots of time that the poet can use in the present; and the importance of "spots of time" for spiritual growth.

Next, the class examines the discharged-soldier episode of *The Prelude* (4.370–469) to see how a spot of time can renovate the individual who has become overwhelmed by what Wordsworth in "Tintern Abbey" calls "the dreary intercourse of daily life" (131). In this heightened moment, Wordsworth is transformed by a chance occurrence in a bleak landscape that suddenly exudes a visionary dreariness. A close reading reveals that the imagination deliberately endows the solitary discharged soldier with meaning, making him an emblem of the dignity and the endurance of the common person's life in order to awaken the self-absorbed poet.

The renovating power of the imagination with its capacity to create spots of time is seen in "Resolution and Independence," which the class examines in detail. In this prototypal Wordsworthian "act of the mind," the imagination confronts a solitary man and creates a heightened moment in which the isolated Leech Gatherer becomes a symbol of noble, enduring humankind, once again awakening the poet from his self-absorption. This discursive meditation reveals the gradual process of reconciliation as the mind seeks to find what will suffice to overcome its problem.

As the class begins to understand the basic functioning of Wordsworth's imagination in an act of the mind, we proceed to the third part of the unit. We explore the complexities of Wordsworth's imagination by focusing on four important poems and comparing them to modern poems in the Wordsworthian tradition. Using the comparative method, the class tests the ideas presented in the preceding two sections. Because the complex transformations of Wordsworthian tradition in the twentieth-century poems require detailed analysis, I shall only be able to indicate briefly my basic reasons for linking the various pairs of poems.

The first poems that the class examines are "Tintern Abbey" and William Butler Yeats's "The Wild Swans at Coole." "Tintern Abbey" is an excellent example of an act of the mind: the poet revisits a specific landscape, and the contrast between the present and the remembered landscape results in a "sad perplexity" (60), which his subsequent meditation attempts to alleviate. The situation in Yeats's poem is similar. The poet returns to the same landscape nineteen years later and like the poet of "Tintern Abbey" is prompted by a sense of loss to meditate on how he has changed. In both meditations the poet is aware of the permanence of nature, with which in his youth he had felt at one but with which he now does not, having become conscious of his own mortality.

Blake and Shelley are the most important influences on Yeats, of course. The Irish poet usually rejects the Wordsworthian idea of "ennobling interchange" for the notion of an autonomous imagination that is not anchored in the external world. Yet Wordsworth and Yeats can be profitably compared at times, for in some poems they explore the theme of memory in all its complexities and ponder how much the imagination compensates for the loss of feelings of spontaneous joy in nature.

There is little question that Wordsworth was a most important influence on Stevens's work, and it is quite possible that "The Idea of Order at Key West" was inspired by "The Solitary Reaper." The dramatic situations of the two poems are the same: a speaker overhears a singing woman in nature, and the experience has a powerful and lasting effect on him. Yet there are significant differences: in Wordsworth's poem the overheard song will be a future stimulus to imagination, in Stevens's the song immediately prompts an act of the mind. In general, despite the poets' similar views of the imagination, their canons do reveal some differences. In contrast to Wordsworth, Stevens displays an acute awareness of nothingness and a pervasive skepticism of the power of the imagination to humanize the desolate landscape, despite temporary triumphs.

Wordsworth was certainly a primary influence on Roethke, who considered the English poet one of his literary ancestors and borrowed lines from *The Prelude* and *The Excursion* for titles of his own works. There are a number of important parallels between the two poets, of which the most important may be the idea of an imaginative excursion into the past as essential for authentic growth. Childhood represents the time of organic harmony with nature, and much value is placed on memory, which enables the poet to gain a meaningful insight into the past and into its relation to the present.

The class compares two poems based on a childhood memory of desecrating nature—Wordsworth's "Nutting" and Roethke's "Moss-Gathering." Roethke's poem may have been prompted by Wordsworth's. In both the solitary child ventures into the woods in search of a particular plant, destroys the "natural order of things," and feels guilty because of his act of profanation. The poems reveal that this experience is one of education, in which the child moves from egotism to an awareness that there is a world outside the self. In both poems the child becomes aware of a spiritual order that pervades the universe, although, in general, Roethke tends to be more mystical than Wordsworth.

Finally, the class grapples with the difficult "Ode: Intimations of Immortality" by comparing it with Roethke's "Meditations of an Old Woman." Both of these landscape meditations lament a loss of vision, of a feeling of unity with nature that the poet possessed in the past but that has been replaced by a disturbing awareness of mortality and impermanence. Both poets ponder the compensations for the loss and seek to overcome the doubts, anxieties, and self-questionings that haunt them. The works are essentially metaphoric systems that may be penetrated only at a few key points. Roethke's poem is more difficult to penetrate than Wordsworth's because it contains a number of visions that the poet conveys in his "psychic shorthand," as he calls it; this elliptical style, so different from Wordsworth's, makes large demands on the student trying to understand Roethke's mystical proclivities.

By the end of the unit, most of the students who had preconceived Wordsworth as an obsolete nature poet whose head was in the clouds abandon their banal view; they come to see that the poet's primary concern is for humanity's coming to terms with, and eventually affirming, the transient everyday world—"The world / Of all of us,—the place where, in the end, / We find our happiness, or not at all!" (*Prelude* 11.142–44). In discursive meditations, acts of the mind often organized around spots of time, Wordsworth shows the ability of the imagination to create values and renovate the alienated poet. In so doing, he establishes the dominant genre of modern poetry.

THEORETICAL PERSPECTIVES

Teaching Wordsworth and Women

Anne K. Mellor

What questions do I, as a feminist critic teaching Wordsworth's poetry, wish to pursue? First, I ask my classes to analyze Wordsworth's conception of the female. How does he portray women in his poetry? What does he associate with the feminine as opposed to the masculine? Second, I raise the issue of Wordsworth's personal relationships with women. In particular, we explore the roles played in his life and work by his lover Annette Vallon, his wife Mary Hutchinson, and his sister Dorothy Wordsworth. And finally, we try to determine the extent to which sexuality or gender as such is central to Wordsworth's creative processes. Finding it necessary to begin with a working definition of feminist criticism, I propose the following: a feminist critic sees sex roles and gender definitions as socially relative rather than biologically determined and thus as subject to critique and change. In relation to a literary text, the feminist critic studies the ways in which the meaning of the text is influenced by the sex of the author, the gender expectations of the author's society, the author's responses to those expectations, and the sex and gender expectations of the reader.

In teaching Wordsworth's poetry and life from a feminist perspective, I typically focus on a few representative texts: "Nutting"; *The Prelude*, especially the boat-stealing and Mount Snowdon episodes; the Lucy poems; "Tintern Abbey" and "The Thorn"; "The Ruined Cottage"; and selected passages from Dorothy Wordsworth's letters and journals.

I begin by asking the class to explore the following text for what it reveals of Wordsworth's concept of the female.

> . . . But I believe
> That Nature, oftentimes, when she would frame
> A favor'd Being, from his earliest dawn
> Of infancy doth open out the clouds,
> As at the touch of lightning, seeking him
> With gentlest visitation; not the less
> Though haply aiming at the self-same end,
> Does it delight her sometimes to employ
> Severer interventions, ministry
> More palpable, and so she dealt with me.
>
> (1805 *Prelude* 1.362–71)

My students quickly recognize that for Wordsworth nature is female. Nature is the mother who fosters her son with both beauty and fear, with both loving nurturance and disciplining frustration. We go on to point out that Wordsworth's conception is based on a traditional patriarchal identification of the female with the body, with earth. But in Wordsworth's case, I suggest, drawing on Richard Onorato's psychoanalytic study, this identification also functioned as a powerful strategy for coping with the early death of his own mother. In substituting a female, maternal nature for his dead mother, Wordsworth projected outward onto the landscape his ambivalent responses to the mother who both provided and withdrew nourishment and love.

I then ask the class to analyze the consequences of Wordsworth's identification of nature as the mother or female, focusing particularly on such texts as "Nutting" and the Mount Snowdon episode of *The Prelude*. My students usually interpret the "Nutting" episode as a rape of nature by the male poet. From this perception they come to the recognition that, for Wordsworth, identifying nature as the female and the mother constitutes nature as an other that must be both possessed and exploited, specifically through the agency of language or poetic discourse. In other words, Wordsworth uses his poetry to force nature to give up her "quiet being," her secrets and her creative powers, to his imagination. More critically sophisticated students here often move in the direction suggested by Geoffrey Hartman and other deconstructive critics to argue that Wordsworth substitutes the linguistic creations of his own imagination for a genuine participation in nature or in the female. Wordsworth remains trapped in a male gender identity, a self-enclosed linguistic universe that can conceive of nature or the objective universe only as the other, as the mysterious female.

This point can be clarified by looking at the Mount Snowdon episode in *The Prelude*, where Wordsworth further attempts to usurp the shaping power of nature by defining that power, in a remarkable gender contradiction, as male, as "the Counterpart and Brother" of the poet's imagination (1805 *Prelude* 13.88–89). Finally, for Wordsworth, nature is female and the poetic imagination male. The act of poetically imagining nature is thus an act of sexual penetration and possession, as the overtly erotic imagery of the boat-stealing episode in *The Prelude* reveals:

> . . . lustily
> I dipp'd my oars into the silent Lake,
> And, as I rose upon the stroke, my Boat
> Went heaving through the water, like a Swan.
> (1805 *Prelude* 1.401–04)

Consciousness itself—or what Wordsworth in the Immortality Ode calls the "philosophic mind"—is grounded in a masculine penetration and appropriation of female nature.

If nature is female, is the converse also true? Are women identified with nature in Wordsworth's poetry? A reading of the Lucy poems, "The Thorn," and "The Ruined Cottage" establishes that the answer to this question is yes. My women students frequently comment that Wordsworth never presents his female figures as distinct individuals with complex, changing personalities. Instead, they seem to exist only as embodiments of an undifferentiated life cycle that moves inexorably from birth to death. Margaret's powerful suffering and decline are marked not by her own words but by the gradual decay of her cottage garden. Lucy is entirely a child of nature, "sportive as the fawn" while alive, "rolled round . . . / With rocks and stones and trees" when dead. Even Wordsworth's dear sister Dorothy figures in "Tintern Abbey" not as an autonomous identity but as a vicarious projection of the poet's own earlier passions and appetites:

> . . .in thy voice I catch
> The language of *my* former heart, and read
> *My* former pleasures in the shooting lights
> Of thy wild eyes. (116-19; emphasis added)

Since Wordsworth's female figures embody nature or his former, closer-to-nature self, they cannot exist as self-conscious, autonomous human beings with minds as capable as the poet's. In this sense, all of Wordsworth's poetic women are dead, either literally (Lucy, Margaret, Martha Ray) or figuratively (Dorothy, Ruth, his numerous mad mothers and vagrants).

At this point I make the polemical feminist argument that Wordsworth has not only embraced the patriarchal construction of the female as nature—and its attendant association of femininity with passivity, emotionality, irrationality, and corporeality—but also carried it one step further; he has denied to the female both her own language and the opportunity to speak. In short, he has constituted the female as not human. When my male students protest that Wordsworth's masculine figures are also nonindividuated projections of his own ego, anxieties, mental states, or philosophical concerns, I emphasize that Wordsworth's male characters are literally permitted to speak: Matthew, the Leech Gatherer, the old soldier, Michael—all speak their own words in Wordsworth's texts. But his women—Lucy, Margaret, Martha Ray, Dorothy—do not speak *in propria persona*; the words assigned to them are literally spoken by male narrators.

Turning now to the topic of Wordworth's relationships with women, I rely on biographical and historical evidence to support the assertion that he was clearly capable of feeling and articulating a strong, deep concern for the women he loved. The Vaudracour and Julia episode in *The Prelude* manifests his intense feelings for Annette Vallon; the recently published love letters between Wordsworth and Mary Hutchinson document his powerful and enduring love for his wife; and Dorothy Wordsworth's letters and journals frequently record moments of intense emotional communion between them and instances of brotherly support and sympathy. Moreover, Wordsworth provided a home for his sister for her entire adult life, at real financial cost to himself.

The lifelong relationship between Dorothy and William was both intense and mutually supportive. Wordsworth from time to time based poems on the observations made by Dorothy in her journals: detailed descriptions of natural phenomena in Somerset and the Lake District. Wordsworth's use of Dorothy's journals must be judiciously presented to a class. Too often feminist readers have accused Wordsworth of "stealing" Dorothy's material or even of silencing her own poetic identity and career (Margaret Homans takes this line). Against this interpretation must be placed Dorothy's own letter to Lady Beaumont of 20 April 1806, in which she insists that she has "no command of language, no power of expressing my ideas, and no one was ever more inapt at molding words into regular metre" (Hill 77).

Placing a passage from Dorothy's journal beside a poem by Wordsworth based on that passage—the obvious comparison is Dorothy's description of the daffodils in Gowbarrow Park recorded for 15 April 1802 with Wordsworth's "I wandered lonely as a cloud"—affords students an ideal opportunity to discuss poetry as such. When my classes have compared these two texts, they readily acknowledge Dorothy's gift for precise, vivid description: she makes you see what she has seen. But in contrast to Wordsworth's poem,

Dorothy's observations do not reveal the significance of what she sees. She does not mention her emotional or intellectual responses to her observations, nor does she generalize from this particular event to universal meaning.

Wordsworth in contrast brings to the scene a charged imaginative realization of what it means, in both the present ("A poet could not but be gay / In such a jocund company") and the future:

> For oft, when on my couch I lie
> In vacant or in pensive mood,
> They flash upon that inward eye
> Which is the bliss of solitude;
> And then my heart with pleasure fills,
> And dances with the daffodils.

Wordsworth adds to what Dorothy sees the presence of a self-conscious human mind, judging, evaluating, treasuring, mourning. Dorothy is a tourist, recording her travels; William is a poet, creating meaning through language. Dorothy explicitly wrote her journals for William's pleasure and benefit, and he repaid her devotion by using her eyes to write some of the finest poems in the English language.

While we must give Wordsworth full credit for genuinely loving and respecting Dorothy and his wife, I end the class by reminding students that he entirely dominated his own household, using its female resources to further his own poetic craft and career. Borrowing from Dorothy's journals, dictating his compositions to Dorothy, Mary, or Sara Hutchinson, relying on their admiration and devotion, Wordsworth fully appropriated their female identities into his own male egotistical sublime.

A Psychobiographical Approach to Wordsworth's Goslar Poetry

Richard E. Matlak

The goal of the psychobiographical approach to Wordsworth is to discover the motivating (un)consciousness of the poet's work and to discern its influence on form and development. As distinguished from biography, which creates an inclusive narrative of life, times, and works but reads the works more for information about the life than to consider critical problems (Pachter), psychobiography addresses specific, related cruxes of text and life. Like psychohistory, it requires a standard narrative account of its subject so that it may be free to address specific issues (de Mause). If biography is narrative without a thesis, psychobiography is a capacious analytic structure embodying theoretical application, close readings, narrative, and persuasion in support of a unifying argument or solution to the question it has raised. As distinguished from the psychological critic, who might seek to identify impersonal, ahistorical, psychological patterning in a text, the psychobiographer will create a personal historical context. The psychobiographical approach establishes a corroboration among biographical data, psychological theory, and poetic text. The question underlying the approach is, How did the poet's state of mind and being predetermine the poem?

Generally, the psychology applied in answering this question is psychoanalytic. As Murray Schwartz and David Willbern have recently said, psychoanalytic theory "connects deep human motives to specific human actions and thereby uniquely attends to emotional and linguistic aspects of literature, through careful analysis of the language, image, and metaphor of a text" (207). To many, this preference does not presume that the poet is neurotic or that the resolution to biographical and textual matters resides exclusively in the dawn of infantile states. Rather, motivation is understood as having both dynamic and genetic components, the former referring to present circumstances that stimulate behavior, the latter referring to the influence of early experiences on the same behavior (Silverman). Both imply the functioning of a dynamic unconscious, influencing fantasy and linguistic behavior through primal desires and fears.

An especially creative period that illustrates the value of the psychobiographical approach in teaching Wordsworth's poetry is his Goslar period (October 1798–February 1799). During this brief, though intense, interlude in Germany, Wordsworth composed the Matthew poems, the Lucy lyrics (except for "I travelled among unknown men"), and the first part of the two-part *Prelude* of 1799, which concludes with the spots of time—the scene at the murderer's gibbet and the wait for the ponies during the holiday when the poet's father dies. The thematic emphasis of these works is a complex of separation, death, and chastisement. As in all research, one begins with questions: What anxiety or mood stimulated this productive gloom? What caused the anxiety? How does it affect the development of the poetry? Critics have considered these groups of poems separately, especially the Lucy poems, but the psychobiographical context reveals them as deriving from a common, troubled source.

In its biographical dimension, the Goslar period immediately succeeds the annus mirabilis at Alfoxden, the most joyful period of the great decade because of Coleridge's daily inspiration and, above all, his influence on Wordsworth's high vocational ambitions. Coleridge boldly identified the still obscure Wordsworth as the heir apparent to Milton. The trip to Germany, prompted by Coleridge's desire to study philosophy in preparation for his own life's work, finally caused a separation between the friends, because the Wordsworths could not afford Coleridge's preferences for towns of social and educational consequence. The Wordsworths retreated to the affordable village of Goslar in the Harz Mountains, where they remained in near isolation during the coldest winter of the century, while Coleridge spent his time in a social whirl at Ratzeburg, where he learned the language and customs, and then at Göttingen, where he studied at the university. It did not take anyone long to realize that the added expense of keeping Dorothy caused the separation between the poets. Wordsworth pined for Coleridge's guidance and adulation.

Wordsworth describes his emotional condition in a letter to Coleridge written shortly after arrival at Goslar:

> As I have had no books I have been obliged to write in self-defence. I should have written five times as much as I have done but that I am prevented by an uneasiness at my stomach and side, with a dull pain about my heart. I have used the word pain, but uneasiness and heat are words which more accurately express my feeling. . . . When I do not read I am absolutely consumed by thinking and feeling and bodily exertions of voice or of limbs, the consequence of those feelings.   (de Selincourt, *Letters* 1: 236)

It is difficult for a layperson to know what specific ailment Wordsworth is diagnosing, but clearly he feels besieged by anxieties. It is commonly understood that anxiety results from uncertainty vis-à-vis an object of endearment—a loved one, an ideal, a sense of self-esteem, or a state of well-being. Wordsworth's well-being had certainly been disturbed by this venture to Germany, and, furthermore, he was probably experiencing some distress and ambivalence about both of his relationships: were it not for Dorothy, he could be with Coleridge; were it not for Coleridge's newfound self-interest, they could be back in England, where Coleridge had been devoted to him. Wordsworth's Goslar poetry seems to stem from such related complications. The Lucy poems reveal ambivalence toward Dorothy; the Matthew poems and part 1 of the 1799 *Prelude* manifest the anxiety and distress caused by Coleridge's waning devotion.

Within this context, then, the Lucy poems can be taught as fantasies of Dorothy's death, written not to ward off incestuous feelings, as Bateson argued, but to be rid of her inconvenient presence. The vented hostility arouses attendant guilt, however, which the lover of the poems dissipates through mourning. In fact, the lover figure goes through the entire psychological process of mourning over time in correspondence with the poet's response to his sister's presence. He mourns most at the outset of the fantasy, when feelings of hostility and guilt would have been strongest—immediately after parting from Coleridge and shortly thereafter—in "Strange fits of passion," "She dwelt among the untrodden ways," and "A slumber did my spirit seal." His grief seems less intense as he recalls Lucy's death in "Three years she grew," written shortly before Wordsworth was to rejoin Coleridge after their winter-long separation (apparently, Wordsworth would have preferred to be alone with Coleridge). Finally, grief and hostility are spent by the final poem of the cycle, "I travelled among unknown men," composed two years later—in 1801—in England but prompted by another threat of separation from Coleridge. Thus, just as in an actual process of mourning—in which grief is most intense in initial response to loss and inevitably wanes with time, to be finally (if ever) extinguished when love has been transferred to another (Freud)—the lover grieves, later recalls his loss, and finally confesses a newfound love for England in his final poem. Throughout, grief has been atonement for the fantasy.

The lover's guilt-grief complex is intriguingly manifested in "A slumber did my spirit seal," where grief seems perfectly controlled by understatement and an absence of textual affect, except for a closing exclamation point, which was finally eliminated.

> No motion has she now, no force;
>   She neither hears nor sees
> Roll'd round in earth's diurnal course
>   With rocks and stones and trees!

Critical response has divided on the narrator's response: Is this a muted cry of distress over the frailty of the mortal vessel? Or is it a pantheistic affirmation of an almost fortunate return to a spiritually infused universe? We, however, read the lover's peculiar response more skeptically. The text is void of affect, indeed, unacceptably void of humane response; thus the reader sympathetically grants the lover an overwhelming measure of sorrow presumably controlled through understatement. The poet cannot lose: he can treat Lucy with guarded hostility and have it interpreted as magnificent management of grief. Of course, he intends sorrow, just as the reader expects sorrow and amplifies it to overcome its absence, but the unconscious, to achieve its purposes, works within the scope of the conscious intention. The complex interaction of text with emotion perfectly expresses the poet's ambivalence even as it relieves his grief. The tone of understatement becomes the vehicle of the poet's released hostility (Matlak, "Lucy Poems").

A second result of Wordsworth's anxiety and depression during the Goslar period is his elegiac reflection on the series of father surrogates that had loved yet also disappointed him during his adolescence. The Matthew poems recall the frustration of Wordsworth's search for a father when Matthew, who represents at least three men of Wordsworth's youth at Hawkshead, rejected his offer of filial affection. The biographical reality was indeed dismal. When Wordsworth required an adult male's love and guidance in his adolescence, five men he had befriended either died or left Hawkshead: Thomas Cowperthwaite, the Matthew of "The Fountain," died in 1782; John Harrison, the Matthew figure of "The Two April Mornings," left Hawkshead in 1783; John Wordsworth, the poet's father, died in 1783; Hugh Tyson, who boarded the Wordsworth brothers at Hawkshead, died in 1784; and the Reverend William Taylor, the probable Matthew of "Matthew" and "Address to the Scholars of the Village School of———," died in 1786. Separation from Coleridge now seemed to provoke interest in this pattern of loss, undoubtedly out of fear and foreboding of its continuance.

Two Matthew poems, "The Two April Mornings" and "The Fountain," explore the motivation of Matthew's rejection of the narrator's adolescent love. In "Two April Mornings," Matthew associates an April morning of thirty years back, when he met a "blooming Girl" (43) near his daughter's grave, with the present April morning, when he and the narrator are out for a holiday. A "purple cleft" (71) in the clouds triggers an association between the days and, indirectly, between the dewy girl of the past and the young narrator. Both represent a temptation to accept a surrogate for the departed child. "A day like this," which Matthew thought he "left / Full thirty years behind" (23–24), is another day of painful awareness that he still mourns for his daughter. The purpose of revealing his silent suffering is to imply his rejection of the narrator; when he saw the "blooming Girl" beside his daughter's grave, he discovered something:

> There came from me a sigh of pain
> Which I could ill confine;
> I looked at her, and looked again:
> And did not wish her mine!   (53–56)

The narrator, a motherless boy with an absent father, and Matthew, a melancholy (because childless) man, only seem to be a perfect pair. At Goslar, Wordsworth ruminates on the enduring relevance of the rejection:

> Matthew is in his grave, yet now,
> Methinks I see him stand,
> As at that moment, with a bough
> Of wilding in his hand.   (57–60)

"The Fountain" more explicitly reveals the same emotional paradox: the adult cannot be satisfied by surrogate filial love, while the child cannot help but seek it (Matlak, "Men").

Wordsworth's exploration of the foundations of self in the "spots of time" section of the two-part *Prelude* finally takes us to the bottom of his anxiety. After an ordered series of chastisements amid retributive winds and peaks, the poet places the solitary child of his memory in the valley he has never forgotten because of the distress he has never quite understood (1.248-58). Freud identified self-reproach as the distinguishing symptom of depression, and the poet's posture of self-reproach and even his selection of incidents seem the results of depressive anxiety.

The scene at the murderer's gibbet has special status in this emotional milieu as an earliest memory. Earliest memories, therapists strongly believe, "reveal, probably more clearly than any other single psychological datum, the central core of each person's psychodynamics. . . . This is an empirical observable fact" (Saul 229). The gibbet scene is fraught with a pattern of oedipal detail that re-creates the emotional world of the young boy on the day of his trauma: the aspiration to manhood that riding the horse represents ("We were a pair of horsemen" [302]); the terror of abandonment as the servant, James, somehow parts from the child (it's coincidental that Oedipus was also abandoned by a servant); the dashing of the pretense to manhood as the child dismounts after realizing he is lost; the transformation of "A *girl* who bore a pitcher on her head" to "The *woman* and her garments vexed and tossed" (317, 326; emphasis added) as the boy fantasizes the presence of an adult woman, surely revealing a desire for—if not a hallucination of—the mother; the lordly beacon on the summit that commands the scene of the vulnerable "naked pool" (315), the terrified child, and the woman struggling against the wind; and, at the center of all, the detail that the gibbet was the scene of the execution of a wife murderer. Except that it wasn't. The gibbet Wordsworth had seen as a boy marked the spot where a Thomas Parker had been murdered by one Thomas Nicholson in 1766. The crime of wife murder had occurred in the area in 1672 and then again in 1789. Wordsworth did not learn of the latter until 1797. Regardless of which wife murder he alludes to, the imposition of this specific crime on a memory of his earliest past indicates that Wordsworth was feeling for the detail that would provide an emotional correlative of the child's irrational fears. This scene of paternal abandonment and projected power underlies the anxiety awakened by Coleridge. This child was indeed the father of the man at Goslar.

I might now suggest, in conclusion, that the psychobiographical approach is useful for teaching because of its completeness. It offers the student a narrative structure with which to unify seemingly disparate analyses of poems and, further, a heuristic with which to approach other poems in pursuing unified understanding. By recalling a story, students more readily retain even the details of close readings; by pursuing the motivation of a story in relation to problems of the text, they experience an analytically oriented empathy. They feel they know the poet as well as his works. Although undergraduates will be responsive to the integration of psychology, biographical data, and poetic text, most will be unable to apply the approach independently without a great deal of guidance; three days on Wordsworth in a survey will not prepare the student to do psychobiography. On the other hand, the approach will probably assist the student in recalling the three days on Wordsworth.

Teaching Wordsworth's Poetry from the Perspective of a Poetics of Speech

Don H. Bialostosky

What students make of Wordsworth's poems will depend on what they expect the poems to be. The questions teachers ask and the features they name and notice always shape students' expectations. Theory gives an explicit account of the implicit relations among the questions we ask and the features we notice and makes those relations available for critical scrutiny. To teach from a theory of the poems, then, is not to interfere with an otherwise innocent reading process but to take responsibility for the model or models of poetry that guide our questions and direct our attention.

Wordsworth himself anticipated, from the Advertisement to the 1798 *Lyrical Ballads* until his last critical pronouncement, that many of his poems would not satisfy the probable expectations of his readers, and his challenge to those expectations made reading his poems a theoretical problem from the beginning. As John Danby puts it, Wordsworth confronts the reader "with the need to be aware of what he is judging with as well as what he is judging" (38). I would add that theory attempts to make explicit what readers are "judging with" so that they can take responsibility for their expectations and neither automatically blame the poet if the poem does not seem to work nor uncritically praise the poet if it does.

Just as students can be led to share the implicit expectations of their teachers, so they can be led to recognize explicitly the role of their expectations in the constitution of their poetic (and other) experiences. Theory in this view is not just for theorists or even just for teachers but for students as well. The invitation to reflect on the model of poetry implicit in the expectations with which we read is an invitation to make reading poetry a liberal discipline in which the poet's work, the teacher's presuppositions, and the students' responses are all subject to critical scrutiny and in which none receives permanent privilege over the others.

The theoretical perspective I have called a poetics of speech makes explicit the implications of expecting poems to be *scripts for the pleasurable re-creation of utterances*. I have argued elsewhere that this perspective is especially appropriate to Wordsworth's poetry, and I shall confine myself here to saying what it leads us to guide our students to look for in his poems. (Those desiring a fuller exposition of the theory should consult Bakhtin, Bialostosky, and Barbara Herrnstein Smith.)

Utterance implies a speaker, first of all. In this view, the words of a poem are to be read as someone's words, though not necessarily or simply the poet's. The poet who produces the script of an utterance may choose, as Wordsworth sometimes does, to make himself the character whose words he inscribes, but he need not always do so. In either case, we must always ask who is represented as speaking or what identifies the speaker.

Of the many ways to identify or characterize a person in answer to such a question, the most common may be psychological, but the most appropriate is to identify him or her in terms of a twofold orientation toward a listener and toward an object or hero of the discourse. Wordsworth presents his speakers in a wide array of relations to their listeners and heroes: from the domestic address of brother to sister about the restorative powers of nature to the inscribed address of poet to stranger about Sir William's architectural ambitions; from the shepherd Andrew's fireside tale of the oak and the broom for his youngest son to Lucy's lover's tale of his own strange fit of passion for "the lover's ear alone." Speakers addressing public figures in public tones and those addressing a particular friend or small circle of friends treat subjects ranging from personal recollections to universal principles of being. The principal genres of Wordsworth's experimental poems—inscriptions, personal anecdotes, tales, exhortations, and others—can be distinguished as different determinations of these relations.

To recognize that the question "Who is presented as speaking?" always involves the further questions "To whom?" and "About whom or what?" is to discover a richer and more specific range of goings on in Wordsworth's poetry than one would find by looking solely for the expression of a subject's feelings, for the depiction of a mind's relation to nature, or for the manipulation of a reader's responses. But the answers to these three questions are interesting not just because they point to the presence of various kinds of speakers, listeners, and heroes but because these presences determine the tone and dynamic development of individual utterances. That is, the relations of speaker to listener, speaker to hero, and listener to hero are charged with value in ways that are reflected in the utterance itself. To re-create a given poem as an utterance is to recover the values of these relations as they impinge on the speaker and determine the unfolding of his or her utterance.

In other words, tone in Wordsworth's poetry is almost never set; instead, it is almost always shifting, as the speakers come under the influence of different aspects of their subject or shift attention from subject to listener or from listener and subject to self. Inquiry into tone thus opens up not only the speaker's situation but the active movement of the utterance. Further, though the locus of activity is the speaker, speech registers the independent activities of the implied listener and the hero of the utterance, interrupting, redirecting, interfering with or cooperating with the speaker's intentions.

We are perhaps most familiar with how this implied listener's activity affects the direction of an utterance. The questioning voice in "The Thorn" manifestly redirects the poem's principal speaker to tell what he knows of

Martha Ray even though his own interest is in the uncanny spot to which she goes. Less obviously, an inner listener in the speaker of "Tintern Abbey" may be imagined to suggest that "these beauteous forms" have indeed been "as is a landscape to a blind man's eye" or the speaker would not need to deny it, just as the same voice may be imagined to declare that the speaker's elevated tribute is "but a vain belief" (22, 24, 50). Again, the development of the poem turns on these interruptions, and its shape as a movement of the speaker's mind incorporates them.

We are less familiar with the idea of an active hero's voice—with a subject of discourse who talks back to the speaker and modifies the speaker's utterance. This activity is manifest in certain lyrical ballads where the reported words of the hero transform or contradict the speaker's effort to characterize him or her—the old man's words in "Old Man Travelling," for example, or the little girl's persistent declaration in "We Are Seven." The power of the hero's voice can be felt, however, even in poems that report no words but adopt a perspective that contrasts with the speaker's and represents, through the speaker's imaginative identification, the hero's own voice. Thus the poet-narrator's evocation of Sir Walter's voice in the first part of "Hart-Leap Well" identifies the poet more closely with Sir Walter than with the shepherd from whom he has learned the history of the spot, and the narrator's response in "Simon Lee" to the voice of Simon Lee's pleasure in the hunt complicates his attempt to tell a pathetic tale and prevents his fulfilling his promise to his reader. The activity of the hero in Wordsworth's poetry, one of its least explored and richest areas of inquiry, is opened by the perspective of a poetics of speech.

Tone, understood in these terms, is not a static disposition of relations to be characterized but a dynamic interplay of speaker, hero, and listener to be followed "through many of its more subtle windings." We do not ask merely how the speaker "stands" toward listener and hero but how the speaker moves in relation to them, registering their initiatives and incorporating those initiatives into the overall trajectory of the utterance.

For Mikhail Bakhtin, whose outline of a poetics of speech (he calls it a "sociological poetics") I have been elaborating, the problem of such a poetics would be resolved "if each factor of form could be explained as the active expression of evaluation in these two directions—toward the listener and toward the object of utterance, the hero." He goes on fruitfully to analyze the factors of form that carry this evaluative activity into the "rhythm and other formal elements of verse," "the very evaluative impetus of epithet and metaphor," and "the manner of the unfolding of the depicted event" (Bakhtin 107–08).

In guiding us to attend from these formal features of the poems to the relations of speaker, hero, and listener, Bakhtin identifies a teachable common function for them. Instead of considering only metaphorical language as poetically functional, he also directs attention to how the choice of epithets can carry the evaluative weight of the speaker's relations to subject and listener. Thus the set of epithets in "Anecdote for Fathers"—"my boy," "little Edward," "my little Edward," and "the boy"—trace an important dynamic in the speaker-father's relation to his son. Instead of treating metrical arrangement as always poetically elevating, Bakhtin invites attention to the way in which the play of sense against form reveals the passions and pleasures that move the speaker's utterance. As discomposed facial expressions reveal the effect of feeling, so enjambed lines often betray passion, just as lines composed within their proper bounds show minds enjoying at least momentary composure (see Johnson). Finally, the order of presentation itself—the movement from present reliving to narration of past experience or from anecdote to sententious interpretation or from sharing the perspective of one character to sharing that of another—follows the movement of the speaker's thought and feeling and provides evidence from which to recreate it.

A theoretical paradigm that treats all these aspects of literary form as functions of the relations among persons has considerable value in the classroom. It allows us to appeal to the "human and dramatic imagination" of our students to examine not only the choice of words but the order of presentation and the formal organization of language in a poem. By asking how changes in these features reflect developments in the speaker's relation to hero or listener, we direct our students' attention to the human working of these formal elements, not just to their conformity or nonconformity with conventional patterns. By treating diction, meter, and arrangement in this way we may bring our students closer to discovering the pleasures of recognizing "human passions, human characters, and human incidents" in Wordsworth's poetry.

Deconstructing Wordsworth

Tilottama Rajan

I teach Wordsworth in two contexts: second- and third-year survey courses on Romantic poetry and honors and graduate seminars on poststructuralism and its alternatives. I begin by exploring the Derridean proposition that language is difference, that the process of articulation is also one of disarticulation, in which what we say/write/think becomes different from itself, perpetually deferring a stable self-identical meaning. A useful point to make is that deconstruction often involves the dismantling of binary oppositions in which one term is privileged over the other, by showing how each term is inhabited by the other and how their relation is thus "undecidable." One must also point out that the aporias and hiatuses in a text where this undecidability becomes manifest go far beyond the "ambiguities" explored by the New Criticism. Inevitably it is the disclosure of thematic ruptures in a text that proves most accessible to second-year students, and one must leave to a more advanced stage the semiotic dismantling of voice and authority characteristic of an approach that grounds differences in the very process of articulation. At some point too one must ask whether deconstruction and poststructuralism are synonymous and whether one can confine Romantic poetry to the poststructuralist sense that the only identity of the text is a grammatological and linguistic rather than an ontological and psychological one.

Remembering the above caveat, I find it useful to approach the Romantics through figures like Nietzsche and De Quincey, who anticipate the concerns of deconstruction while translating them into mythological and psychological rather than purely semiotic terms. The dismantling of binary oppositions goes back to Schopenhauer's *The World As Will and Representation*, which explores, on the level of epistemology and metapsychology, the problematical status of mental representations. But *The Birth of Tragedy* is one of the earliest works to dehomogenize the *text* and to see it as undecidable, a product of the difference between the logocentric Apollonian impulse and the differential energy of Dionysus. Similarly De Quincey in *Suspiria de profundis* is one of the first writers to see the growth of the mind as a series of textual constructions. In imaging consciousness as a palimpsest whose layers are related through repetition and displacement, he breaks with the Hegelian model of *Geistesgeschichte* and the organic analogy used by Schelling and Coleridge. Instead he views the psyche as a location for different writings, each inhabited by the voice of the other and hence different from itself. At the same time, however, in "Levana" and "The Dark Interpreter," he presents these voices through myth and personification, thus figuratively endowing them with ontological as well as linguistic status.

Book 1 of *The Excursion* and its textual antecedents as traced by Jonathan Wordsworth (*Music*) and James Butler provide a convenient starting-point, because they allow me to link the idea of a text as a palimpsest of rewritings to a problem in conventional bibliography: that of the "correct" text. Ms. A of the poem is a fragment, embryonically similar to other short, bare narratives of unrelieved distress that Wordsworth was writing at the time, but more single-mindedly bleak because of its monadic brevity. Ms. B greatly expands the narrative and adds to its "objective" reporting of naturalistic facts the "subjective" and pantheist voice of the Pedlar, who tries to provide a consoling gloss on Margaret's suffering. In subsequent texts Wordsworth tries unsuccessfully to synthesize these two voices, splitting them apart in Ms. D (where "The Pedlar" becomes a mere addendum) and uneasily recombining them thereafter. But this attempt to homogenize the text, like the attempt of orthodox bibliographers to privilege one version as correct, is continuously challenged by the archaeology of the poem. For desedimenting that archaeology reveals a process in which expanding the first text unweaves its single-minded pessimism by adding a countervoice that also unweaves itself by virtue of its supplementarity. The diachronic series of differences evident in a variorum edition simply clarifies the discrepancies simultaneously at work in any one text of the poem. For rewriting could not occur if traces of what is added did not exist in the preceding version, and yet an addition per se supplements and displaces as well as completes. Similarly, the textual history of this poem simply places in relief the intersection of voices in Wordsworth's work as a whole.

While I do not approach *The Prelude* by way of its variants, this poem too can be seen as palimpsestic. As a poem of memory it is inhabited by "two consciousnesses" (2.32), which repeat and textualize each other as do the layers of De Quincey's palimpsest. Attempts at unified self-representation on the level of what Lacan calls the Imaginary, whether this imaginary ego be located in the original experience or in the later clarification of it, are thus problematized by the fact that both experience and memory exist in language—a fact we become aware of when there are gaps between them. In other ways too the poem repeats and doubles itself and acquires a reflexive structure intrinsic to its reflective mode. Passages of narration alternate with passages of retrospective commentary, and the two are not always symmetrical. A striking example is the account of the discharged soldier in the 1850 text, where the prefatory comment that allegorizes him as a hermit (4.354–70) is disrupted by the encounter with the soldier, who exists in a world where God is absent and charity supplementary. Similar discrepancies develop as the poem repeats episodes in different and mutually complicating ways: the dredging up of the corpse from the lake, for instance, can be viewed as a refiguring of the boating scene. Finally, Wordsworth's communication of the poem to Coleridge (and by extension to the reader) is a form of repetition and may well function not as rhetorical self-confirmation that guarantees the self-identity of the poem's meaning but rather as disconfirmation. As I shall suggest, *repetition* (be it Wordsworth's through memory, self-commentary, and communication or ours through reading) functions not to fix the identity of the text by doubling and strengthening a univocal meaning but rather to complicate that identity.

Such concerns can be explored only obliquely in a second-year class. Here I concentrate on the groundwork for a deconstructive reading of *The Prelude*, which has been laid by early critics like David Ferry and Geoffrey Hartman (*Wordsworth's Poetry*), who focus on shifts in voice between the humanitarian and the apocalyptic and on thematic breaks between the portrayal of nature as complementing and opposing imagination. Where earlier criticism sought to rewrite these ungrammaticalities using a New Critical grammar of ambiguity or a psychological grammar of manifest and latent content, we would now see them as aporias that mark the poem's difference from itself and inhibit its resolution into a complex whole or a repressed subtext.

A useful paradigm for analyzing the disarticulation that occurs in long poetic structures is the passage on the Boy of Winander. In its earliest form (Ms. JJ, 1799) the lines celebrate the communion of the boy with nature through a music (whistling) completely without artifice, and though they refer to a past it is one of eternal recurrence. The closing lines confirm this communion, as the boy and the visible scene resume on a reflective level their interrupted sensory conversation. But the addition of the lines on the boy's death (*Lyrical Ballads*, 1800) and the subsequent absorption of the passage into *The Prelude*, where it is surrounded by narratives about drowning and placed in a book that focuses on the anxiety rather than the power of imagination, subtly unweave our earlier reading. As I have suggested elsewhere ("Romanticism" 198–200), shifts in tense from the draft to the final version and ambiguities in book 5, lines 381-88, about whether key words are to be taken literally or metaphorically may suggest that the closing lines describe how the "uncertain" metaphoric heaven constructed in the boy's imagination is "received" (literally) into the lake as he drowns. In retropsect we are uncertain whether the passage commemorates or deconstructs its use of the boy as a figure for the capable imagination, makes his life "merely" metaphoric or his death "merely" literal. Thus the passage comes to contain its own double or shadow, as the "heaven" received into the lake ceases to be purely literal and the "receiving" ceases to be entirely figurative.

I suggest that extended poetic structures are more likely to elicit deconstructive reading than are brief lyrics read in isolation, because such structures refer the individual unit of meaning to a larger context, a network of

differences that destabilizes it by making the layers of the palimpsest dia-
chronically available to us. Intrinsic to larger structures, similarly, is a dia-
logizing of poetic voice. In the present case, the closed world of lyric time
is absorbed into a universe of psychological narrative where things change,
and the disturbance of the generic boundary complicates our sense that the
voice behind the passage ever really was homogeneous.

In more advanced teaching I try to focus explicitly on problems in voice
and authority and to combine deconstruction and reader-response theory,
taking up rhetorical approaches that restore through reading a logocentrism
disrupted in the text itself. I lead up to the semiotic problem in *The Prelude*
through the more familiar terrain of genre and literary history. Wordsworth's
poem marks its difference from *Paradise Lost* by taking a structure often
described as a bright center with a dark border and replacing it by one in
which the dark passages are seemingly encircled by the early flowering and
later regaining of imaginative power. If the structural inversion is an index
of a shift from a Puritan to a Romantic worldview, then the rereading is
inevitably complicated by the anxiety of influence. Is Wordsworth's argument for the imagination as a means of grace subtended purely by a subjective
and lyrical voice, or does it truly have epic dimensions and authority? And
can we have a generic *Gesamtkunstwerk* that unifies subjective and objective, lyric and narrative, personal and public voices? Or do we have a text
fractured by the differences between these voices? The expansion of the
two-part *Prelude* is an attempt to create just such a thematic and generic
totality, to expand lyric and pastoral into epic by including a war. But the
war is then presented as a digression to reduce its disruptiveness, and yet
it transgresses its marginality by virtue of its length. Finally these problems
are reflected in the uncertain status of the poem's discourse. Unlike Blake's
later prophecies, *The Prelude* combines an egotistically sublime tone in-
herited from Milton with a conversational voice. As discourse in the high
style it speaks with authority to an unquestioning reader. As conversation
it is more tentative, oriented toward and penetrated by the understanding
of a *different* person even as it seeks to minimize that difference.

Once again earlier criticism recognizes parenthetically the potential dis-
establishing of authority in Wordsworth's poetry. Donald Davie points to
the problematizing of signification characteristic of Wordsworth's philosophic
poetry, which hovers between the concrete and the abstract and creates a
suspension between sense and sound. He suggests that the poem persuades
by using its words as "fiduciary" symbols that, like coins as values of monetary
exchange, possess their value as a result of a social contract and "have
meaning" only "so long as we trust them" (106–07). Michael Cooke in *Acts
of Inclusion* focuses on the use of Coleridge as a way of acknowledging yet
containing doubt and disagreement, by remaining aware of utterances as

dialogically addressed to another person, yet making this "other" a kindred spirit. "Coleridge" represents what we would now call the implied reader, the reader desired by the author. While acknowledging that the communicative process may jeopardize the self-presence of the text, both approaches remain rhetorical in assuming that authors are not themselves inscribed in the text but maintain a paternal and authoritative relation to text and reader.

In arguing against this essentially traditional view of the reader-text relation, I suggest that the text is inhabited by and not simply vulnerable to the disarticulating pressures of the communicative process. The conversation poem, the subgenre expanded in the poem to Coleridge, is itself a problematic form. Designed to create authority for the text by addressing it to an auditor/reader whose sympathetic assent will make its acts of imagination the constructions of a visionary company rather than of a sole self, the form also lays itself open to the withholding of this assent dramatized in a poem like "The Eolian Harp." Wordsworth's encoding of an implied reader through the figure of Coleridge is not necessarily at one with his narration of dialogical situations or relations. To begin with, "Coleridge" as characterized in more extended addresses is not simply an embodiment of Wordsworth's desire for self-confirmation but also a projection of his doubt. Initially Wordsworth suggests that he and Coleridge "by different roads . . . have gained / The self-same bourne" (2.453-54). But by book 11 their "converse strong and sanative" (1.396) has become infiltrated by the anxieties of therapy, and the model of conversation/reading as self-confirmation has been disrupted.

More significant, the poem contains "reading interludes," intratextual allegories that reflect on the uncertainties of communication. Encounters between Wordsworth and figures like the discharged soldier or the blind beggar disrupt the earlier model of reading as conversation. As someone marginal to the rural economy and indifferent to the world outside him, the soldier poses a challenge to Wordsworth's belief in nature as an organic unity that knows no waste or vacancy. This challenge, registered in the uneasiness with which their conversation proceeds, raises the larger problem of whether the conversation of text and reader will necessarily be a communion between like minds. Behind the fiction of restored communication created as he finds a place for the soldier with neighboring cottagers is the awareness that Wordsworth does not really know how his intentions (and the view of life that informs them) are being read by the other person. Even more disturbing is the encounter with the beggar, who must convey the story of his life through the signs on a placard. Through the image of the placard the poem explores the disruption of the relation between voice and word, the possibility that the text of the self may become no more than a collection of signs, a grammatological construct.

Whether this reduction of voice to text sums up *The Prelude* is, however, problematical. Recently Vincent Leitch has raised the question of whether deconstruction is opposed to all varieties of phenomenology or is a moment within the long history of hermeneutics, a way of arriving at the identity of the text. The issue is between Derridean and Heideggerian deconstruction: between the poststructuralist view that there is nothing outside the infinitely self-deferring play of language and the phenomenological view that the process of language dis-closes truth and being, the truth of a being that is always different from itself.

I find support for a deconstructive but, paradoxically, not poststructuralist reading of *The Prelude* in J. Hillis Miller's discussion of the Arab dream in book 5. Using the Sartrean opposition of *en-soi* and *pour-soi*, Miller argues that the Arab's quest for permanence rather than difference through the lodging of the originary prophetic voice in a stone (*en-soi*) is dismantled by the related image of the shell, which is hollowed out and different from itself (*pour-soi*). Yet in Miller's own words, the episode suggests that the "original voice is already double" (258), not that voice and origin are fictions. Similarly in book 7 the voice of the beggar does speak through the placard, but it speaks as an emptiness and dis-closes a being grounded in nothingness. That he is a dis-figured version of the blind seer is obvious, even as he deconstructs the Miltonic substitution of the presence of voice for the absence of sight. I suggest in conclusion that there are limits to viewing Romantic poetry poststructurally, that *The Prelude* denies us a being outside the desedimentations of language but also grants reader and author a being enmeshed in language.

PARTICIPANTS IN SURVEY OF WORDSWORTH INSTRUCTORS

James H. Averill, Princeton Univ.; Roland Bartel, Univ. of Oregon; Ernest Bern-hardt-Kabisch, Indiana Univ., Bloomington; Carol L. Bernstein, Bryn Mawr Coll.; Werner Beyer, Butler Univ.; Don H. Bialostosky, State Univ. of New York, Stony Brook; George Bornstein, Univ. of Michigan, Ann Arbor; Allan Chavkin, Southwest Texas State Univ.; Samuel Coale, Wheaton Coll.; Sue Coffman, Univ. of Texas, Arlington; Ralph Cohen, Univ. of Virginia; John Combs, Kentucky Wesleyan Coll.; Jared Curtis, Simon Fraser Univ.; Edward Duffy, Marquette Univ.; W. Dumbleton, State Univ. of New York, Albany; Mary L. Fawcett, George Mason Univ.; Laraine Fergenson, Bronx Community Coll., City Univ. of New York; Anthony Franzese, Oklahoma City Univ.; Michael H. Friedman, Ripon Coll.; William Galperin, Rutgers Univ.; Wayne Glausser, DePauw Univ.; Jack H. Haeger, San Jose State Univ.; James Hafley, St. John's Univ.; Anthony John Harding, Univ. of Saskatchewan; Tori Haring-Smith, Brown Univ.; F. R. Hart, Univ. of Massachusetts, Boston; Robert Hartley, St. Mary's Coll., IN; Donald Hassler, Kent State Univ.; John O. Hayden, Univ. of California, Davis; Robert J. Heaman, Wilkes Coll.; John Hodgson, Univ. of Georgia; William Craig Howes, Univ. of Hawaii, Manoa; Edward A. Hungerford, Southern Oregon State Coll.; Kenneth Johnston, Indiana Univ., Bloomington; Frank Jordan, Miami Univ.; John Kearney, Lebanon Valley Coll.; Katherine Kernberger, Linfield Coll.; J. Douglas Kneale, Bishop's Univ.; Paul Lacey, Earlham Coll.; W. B. Lambert, Univ. of Lethbridge; David J. Leigh, Gonzaga Univ.; Herbert S. Lindenberger, Stanford Univ.; Dwight W. Lindley, Hamilton Coll.; Paul Magnuson, New York Univ.; John Mahoney, Boston Coll.; Peter Manning, Univ. of Southern California; Richard Matlak, Coll. of the Holy Cross; James McDonough, Univ. of Guam; Juliet McMaster, Univ. of Alberta; Anne K. Mellor, Stanford Univ.; Muriel J. Mellown, North Carolina Central Univ.; A. M. Miller, New Coll. Univ. of South Florida; John Milstead, Oklahoma State Univ.; John R. Nabholtz, Loyola Univ. of Chicago; Virgil Nemoianu, Catholic Univ.; John T. Ogden, Univ. of Manitoba; W. J. B. Owen, McMaster Univ.; Satya S. Pachori, Univ. of North Florida; Judith Page, Millsaps Coll.; Anna Sue Parrill, Southeastern Louisiana Univ.; Rosa Penna, Universidad de Buenos Aires; Stuart Peterfreund, Northeastern Univ.; M. Byron Raizis, Univ. of Athens; Tilottama Rajan, Univ. of Wisconsin, Madison; Jonathan Ramsey, Skidmore Coll.; Donald H. Reiman, Carl H. Pforzheimer Lib.; Mark Reynolds, Jefferson Davis State Junior Coll.; Donald Ross, Univ. of Minnesota, Minneapolis; Jill Rubenstein, Univ. of Cincinnati; Charles J. Rzepka, Boston Univ.; Ben Ross Schneider, Jr., Lawrence Univ.; Patricia L. Skarda, Smith Coll.; Lisa M. Steinman, Reed Coll.; Eugene L. Stelzig, State Univ. of New York Coll., Geneseo; Frank W. Stevenson, Fu Jen Catholic Univ., Taiwan; Gordon K. Thomas, Brigham Young Univ., Provo; Richard Tobias, Univ. of Pittsburgh; Nicholas O. Warner, Claremont McKenna Coll.; Donald Wesling, Univ. of California, San Diego; Jonathan Wordsworth, St. Cath-erine's Coll., Oxford Univ.

WORKS CITED

Books and Articles

Abrams, M. H. "The Correspondent Breeze: A Romantic Metaphor." *Kenyon Review* 19 (1957): 113–30. Rpt. in Abrams, *Correspondent Breeze* 25–43, and in Abrams, *English Romantic Poets* 37–54.

———. *The Correspondent Breeze: Essays on English Romanticism.* New York: Norton, 1984.

———. "English Romanticism: The Spirit of the Age." Frye, *Romanticism Reconsidered* 26–72.

———, ed. *English Romantic Poets: Modern Essays in Criticism.* Rev. ed. New York: Oxford UP, 1975.

———. *The Mirror and the Lamp: Romantic Theory and the Critical Tradition.* 1953. New York: Norton, 1958.

———. *Natural Supernaturalism: Tradition and Revolution in Romantic Literature.* New York: Norton, 1971.

———, gen. ed. *The Norton Anthology of English Literature.* 4th ed. 2 vols. New York: Norton, 1979.

———, gen. ed. *The Norton Anthology of English Literature: Third Major Authors Edition.* New York: Norton, 1975.

———. "Structure and Style in the Greater Romantic Lyric." *From Sensibility to Romanticism: Essays Presented to Frederick A. Pottle.* Ed. Frederick W. Hilles and Harold Bloom. New York: Oxford UP, 1965. 527–60.

———, ed. *Wordsworth: A Collection of Critical Essays.* Englewood Cliffs: Prentice, 1972.

Ariès, Philippe. *Centuries of Childhood.* Trans. R. Baldick. New York: Vintage, 1962.

Averill, James H., ed. *An Evening Walk.* Cornell Wordsworth. Ithaca: Cornell UP, 1984.

———. "Teaching the Whole of *Lyrical Ballads.*" *Wordsworth Circle* 9 (1978): 365–66.

———. *Wordsworth and the Poetry of Human Suffering.* Ithaca: Cornell UP, 1980.

Baker, Carlos, ed. *William Wordsworth: The Prelude and Selected Poems and Sonnets.* New York: Holt, 1954.

Baker, Jeffrey. *Time and Mind in Wordsworth's Poetry.* Detroit: Wayne State UP, 1980.

Bakhtin, Mikhail. "Discourse in Life and Discourse in Art." *Freudianism: A Marxist Critique*. Trans. I. R. Titunik. Ed. Neal H. Bruss. New York: Academic, 1976. 93–115. (Though translated under the name of V. N. Voloshinov, both the essay and the volume in which it appears are now generally attributed to Bakhtin.)

Barker, Arthur E. "Structural Pattern in *Paradise Lost*." *Philological Quarterly* 28 (1949): 17–30. Rpt. in *Milton: Modern Essays in Criticism*. Ed. Arthur E. Barker. New York: Oxford UP, 1965. 142–55.

Bate, Walter Jackson. *The Burden of the Past and the English Poet*. Cambridge: Belknap–Harvard UP, 1970.

———. *From Classic to Romantic: Premises of Taste in Eighteenth-Century England*. 1946. New York: Harper, 1961.

Bateson, F. W. *Wordsworth: A Reinterpretation*. 2nd ed. London: Longmans, 1956.

Bauer, N. S. *William Wordsworth: A Reference Guide to British Criticism, 1793–1899*. London: Hall, 1978.

Bayley, John. *The Romantic Survival: A Study of Poetic Evolution*. London: Constable, 1957.

Beach, Joseph Warren. *The Concept of Nature in Nineteenth-Century English Poetry*. 1936. New York: Pageant, 1956.

Beatty, Arthur. *William Wordsworth: His Doctrine and Art in Their Historical Relations*. 1922. 3rd ed. Madison: U of Wisconsin P, 1960.

Beer, John. *Wordsworth and the Human Heart*. New York: Columbia UP, 1978.

———. *Wordsworth in Time*. London: Faber, 1979.

Ben-Porat, Ziva. "The Poetics of Allusion." *A Semiotic Landscape*. Ed. Seymour Chatman, Umberto Eco, and Jean-Marie Klinkenberg. The Hague: Mouton, 1979. 588–93.

Betz, Paul F., ed. *Benjamin the Waggoner*. Cornell Wordsworth. Ithaca: Cornell UP, 1981.

Bialostosky, Don H. *Making Tales: The Poetics of Wordsworth's Narrative Experiments*. Chicago: U of Chicago P, 1984.

Bicknell, Peter, ed. *The Illustrated Wordsworth's* Guide to the Lakes. New York: Congdon, 1984.

Birdsall, Eric, ed. *Descriptive Sketches*. Cornell Wordsworth. Ithaca: Cornell UP, 1984.

Blanshard, Frances. *Portraits of Wordsworth*. London: Allen, 1959.

Bleich, David. *Readings and Feelings: An Introduction to Subjective Criticism*. Urbana: NCTE, 1975.

———. *Subjective Criticism*. Baltimore: Johns Hopkins UP, 1978.

"Bloodsuckers from France." *Time* 14 Dec. 1981: 100.

Bloom, Harold. *The Anxiety of Influence: A Theory of Poetry*. New York: Oxford UP, 1973.

———. "The Internalization of Quest-Romance." Bloom, *Romanticism and Consciousness* 3–24.

————. *A Map of Misreading.* New York: Oxford UP, 1975.

————. *Poetry and Repression: Revisionism from Blake to Stevens.* New Haven: Yale UP, 1976.

————. *The Ringers in the Tower: Studies in Romantic Tradition.* Chicago: U of Chicago P, 1971.

————, ed. *Romanticism and Consciousness: Essays in Criticism.* New York: Norton, 1970.

————. *The Visionary Company: A Reading of English Romantic Poetry.* Rev. ed. Ithaca: Cornell UP, 1971.

Bloom, Harold, and Lionel Trilling, eds. *Romantic Poetry and Prose.* Vol. 4 of *The Oxford Anthology of English Literature.* 6 vols. London: Oxford UP, 1973.

Bloom, Harold, et al., eds. *Deconstruction and Criticism.* New York: Seabury, 1979.

Bostetter, Edward E. *The Romantic Ventriloquists: Wordsworth, Coleridge, Keats, Shelley, Byron.* Seattle: U of Washington P, 1963.

Brantley, Richard. *Wordsworth's "Natural Methodism."* New Haven: Yale UP, 1975.

Brett, R. L., and A. R. Jones, eds. *Lyrical Ballads: Wordsworth and Coleridge; The Text of the 1798 Edition with the Additional 1800 Poems and the Prefaces.* Rev. ed. 1963. New York: Barnes, 1968.

Briggs, Asa. *The Age of Improvement, 1783–1867.* London: Longmans, 1959.

Brisman, Leslie. *Milton's Poetry of Choice and Its Romantic Heirs.* Ithaca: Cornell UP, 1973.

————. *Romantic Origins.* Ithaca: Cornell UP, 1978.

Brooks, Cleanth. *The Well Wrought Urn: Studies in the Structure of Poetry.* New York: Harcourt, 1947.

Burke, Edmund, and Thomas Paine. Reflections on the Revolution in France *and* The Rights of Man. Garden City: Doubleday, 1961.

Bush, Douglas. *Mythology and the Romantic Tradition in English Poetry.* 1937. New York: Norton, 1963.

Butler, James, ed. *"The Ruined Cottage" and "The Pedlar."* Cornell Wordsworth. Ithaca: Cornell UP, 1979.

Butler, Marilyn. *Romantics, Rebels, and Revolutionaries: English Literature and Its Background, 1760–1830.* New York: Oxford UP, 1982.

Cappon, Alexander. *Aspects of Wordsworth and Whitehead: Philosophy and Certain Continuing Life-Problems.* New York: Philosophical Lib., 1983.

Chandler, James K. *Wordsworth's Second Nature: A Study of the Poetry and Politics.* Chicago: U of Chicago P, 1984.

Clark, Kenneth. *Landscape into Art.* 1949. New York: Harper, 1976.

Clarke, C. C. *Romantic Paradox: An Essay on the Poetry of Wordsworth.* London: Routledge, 1962.

Clarkson, Thomas. *The History of the Rise, Progress and Accomplishment of the Abolition of the African Slave Trade.* London, 1808.

Clubbe, John, and Ernest J. Lovell, Jr. *English Romanticism: The Grounds of Belief.* De Kalb: Northern Illinois UP, 1983.

Cobbett, William. *Rural Rides*. Harmondsworth: Penguin, 1967.

Coleridge, Samuel Taylor. *The Collected Works*. 13 vols. to date. Gen. ed. Kathleen Coburn. Bollingen Series 75. Princeton: Princeton UP, 1969–

———. *The Table-Talk and Omniana of Samuel Taylor Coleridge*. Ed. T. Ashe. London: Bell, 1905.

Cooke, Michael G. *Acts of Inclusion: Studies Bearing on an Elementary Theory of Romanticism*. New Haven: Yale UP, 1979.

———. *The Romantic Will*. New Haven: Yale UP, 1976.

Cooper, Lane, ed. *A Concordance to the Poems of William Wordsworth*. New York: Dutton, 1911.

Cosgrove, Brian. *Wordsworth and the Poetry of Self-Sufficiency: A Study of the Poetic Development, 1796–1814*. Salzburg Studies in English Literature: Romantic Reassessment 93. Atlantic Highlands: Humanities, 1982.

Crawley, C. W., ed. *War and Peace in an Age of Upheaval, 1793–1830*. New Cambridge Modern History 9. Cambridge: Cambridge UP, 1965.

Culler, Jonathan. *The Pursuit of Signs: Semiotics, Literature, Deconstruction*. Ithaca: Cornell UP, 1981.

Curtis, Jared R., ed. Poems, in Two Volumes, *and Other Poems, 1800–1807*. Cornell Wordsworth. Ithaca: Cornell UP, 1983.

———. *Wordsworth's Experiments with Tradition: The Lyric Poems of 1802*. Ithaca: Cornell UP, 1971.

Danby, John F. *The Simple Wordsworth: Studies in the Poems, 1797–1807*. London: Routledge, 1960.

Darbishire, Helen. *The Poet Wordsworth*. 1950. Westport: Greenwood, 1980.

Darlington, Beth, ed. *Home at Grasmere*. Cornell Wordsworth. Ithaca: Cornell UP, 1977.

———, ed. *The Love Letters of William and Mary Wordsworth*. Ithaca: Cornell UP, 1982.

Davie, Donald. "Syntax in the Blank Verse of Wordsworth's *Prelude*." *Articulate Energy*. London: Routledge, 1955. 106–16.

Davis, Jack M., ed. *Discussions of William Wordsworth*. Boston: Heath, 1964.

Davis, Philip. *Memory and Writing: From Wordsworth to Lawrence*. Liverpool English Texts and Studies 21. Totowa: Barnes, 1983.

de Man, Paul. "Intentional Structure of the Romantic Image." Bloom, *Romanticism and Consciousness* 65–77.

———. "The Rhetoric of Temporality." *Interpretation: Theory and Practice*. Ed. Charles S. Singleton. Baltimore: Johns Hopkins UP, 1969. 173–209.

———. "Symbolic Landscape in Wordsworth and Yeats." *In Defense of Reading*. Ed. R. A. Brower and Richard Poirier. New York: Dutton, 1962. 22–37.

de Mause, Lloyd. "The Independence of Psychohistory." *The New Psychohistory*. Ed. de Mause. New York: Psychohistory, 1975. 7–27.

Derrida, Jacques. "White Mythology." *Margins of Philosophy*. Trans. Alan Bass. Chicago: U of Chicago P, 1983. 207–72.

de Selincourt, Ernest. *Dorothy Wordsworth: A Biography*. Oxford: Clarendon, 1933.

———, ed. *Journals of Dorothy Wordsworth*. 2 vols. London: Macmillan, 1941.

———, ed. *The Letters of William and Dorothy Wordsworth*. 6 vols. Oxford: Clarendon, 1935–39. Rev. Chester Shaver, Mary Moorman, and Alan G. Hill. 1967–

———, ed. *The Prelude, or Growth of a Poet's Mind*. [1805 version.] Oxford Paperbacks. Corr. by Stephen Gill. London: Oxford UP, 1970.

———, ed. *The Prelude, or Growth of a Poet's Mind*. 1926. Rev. Helen Darbishire. Oxford: Clarendon, 1959.

———, ed. *Wordsworth's* Guide to the Lakes. 1906. London: Oxford UP, 1970. Paperback ed., 1977.

de Selincourt, Ernest, and Helen Darbishire, eds. *The Poetical Works of William Wordsworth*. 5 vols. Oxford: Clarendon, 1940–49.

Devlin, D. D. *Wordsworth and the Poetry of Epitaphs*. London: Macmillan, 1980.

Durrant, Geoffrey. *William Wordsworth*. Cambridge: Cambridge UP, 1969.

Empson, William. *Seven Types of Ambiguity*. Rev. ed. New York: New Directions, 1966.

Engell, James. *The Creative Imagination: Enlightenment to Romanticism*. Cambridge: Harvard UP, 1981.

Engell, James, and W. Jackson Bate, eds. *Biographia Literaria*. Vol. 7 of *The Collected Works of Samuel Taylor Coleridge*. 13 vols. to date. Bollingen Series 75. 1983. 2 vols. Princeton: Princeton UP, 1984.

Erdman, David, ed. *The Romantic Movement: A Selective and Critical Bibliography*. Vols. 211, 213, 216, 217. New York: Garland, 1979–

Ferguson, Frances. *Wordsworth: Language as Counter-Spirit*. New Haven: Yale UP, 1977.

Ferry, David. *The Limits of Mortality: An Essay on Wordsworth's Major Poems*. Middletown: Wesleyan UP, 1959.

Fogle, Richard Harter, ed. *Romantic Poets and Prose Writers*. New York: Appleton, 1967.

Foucault, Michel. *Discipline and Punish*. Trans. A. Sheridan. New York: Pantheon, 1977.

Freud, Sigmund. "Mourning and Melancholia." *The Standard Edition of the Complete Psychological Works of Sigmund Freud*. Trans. and ed. James Strachey. 24 vols. London: Hogarth, 1953–76. 14: 239–58.

Friedman, Michael H. *The Making of a Tory Humanist: William Wordsworth and the Idea of Community*. New York: Columbia UP, 1979.

Frye, Northrop. "The Drunken Boat: The Revolutionary Element in Romanticism." Frye, *Romanticism Reconsidered* 1–25.

———, ed. *Romanticism Reconsidered: Selected Papers from the English Institute*. New York: Columbia UP, 1963.

———. *A Study of English Romanticism*. New York: Random, 1968.

Garber, Frederick. *Wordsworth and the Poetry of Encounter*. Urbana: U of Illinois P, 1971.

Gérard, Albert. *English Romantic Poetry: Ethos, Structure, and Symbol in Coleridge, Wordsworth, Shelley, and Keats*. Berkeley: U of California P, 1968.

Gill, Stephen, ed. *The Salisbury Plain Poems of William Wordsworth*. Cornell Wordsworth. Ithaca: Cornell UP, 1975.

———, ed. *William Wordsworth*. Oxford Authors. Oxford: Oxford UP, 1984.

Gleckner, Robert F., and Gerald E. Enscoe, eds. *Romanticism: Points of View*. 1962. Englewood Cliffs: Prentice, 1970.

Glen, Heather. *Vision and Disenchantment: Blake's* Songs *and Wordsworth's* Lyrical Ballads. Cambridge: Cambridge UP, 1983.

Grob, Alan. *The Philosophic Mind: A Study of Wordsworth's Poetry and Thought, 1797–1805*. Columbus: Ohio State UP, 1973.

Hagstrum, Jean. *The Sister Arts: The Tradition of Literary Pictorialism and English Poetry from Dryden to Gray*. Chicago: U of Chicago P, 1958.

Halliday, F. E. *Wordsworth and His World*. London: Thames, 1970.

Harper, George McLean. *William Wordsworth: His Life, Works, and Influence*. 1916. 3rd ed. New York: Scribner's, 1929.

Hartman, Geoffrey H. *Beyond Formalism*. New Haven: Yale UP, 1970.

———, ed. *New Perspectives on Coleridge and Wordsworth: Selected Papers from the English Institute*. New York: Columbia UP, 1972.

———. "A Poet's Progress: Wordsworth and the *Via naturaliter negativa*." *Modern Philology* 59 (1962): 214–24.

———. "Romanticism and Antiself-Consciousness." *Centennial Review* 6 (1962): 553–65.

———, ed. *The Selected Poetry and Prose of Wordsworth*. 1970. New York: NAL, 1980.

———. *The Unmediated Vision: An Interpretation of Wordsworth, Hopkins, Rilke, and Valéry*. 1954. New York: Harcourt, 1966.

———. *Wordsworth's Poetry, 1787–1814*. 1964. New Haven: Yale UP, 1971.

Harvey, A. D. *English Poetry in a Changing Society, 1780–1825*. New York: St. Martin's, 1980.

Harvey, W. J., and Richard Gravil, eds. *Wordsworth: The Prelude; A Casebook*. New York: Macmillan, 1972.

Havens, Raymond Dexter. *The Mind of a Poet: A Study of Wordsworth's Thought with Particular Reference to* The Prelude. Baltimore: Johns Hopkins UP, 1941.

Hayden, Donald E. *Wordsworth's Walking Tour of 1790*. U of Tulsa Monograph Series 19. Tulsa: U of Tulsa P, 1983.

Hayden, John O., ed. *William Wordsworth: The Poems*. 2 vols. 1977. New Haven: Yale UP, 1981.

Heath, William, ed. *Major British Poets of the Romantic Period*. New York: Macmillan, 1973.

Heffernan, James. *Wordsworth's Theory of Poetry: The Transforming Imagination.* Ithaca: Cornell UP, 1969.

Henley, Elton F., and David H. Stam. *Wordsworthian Criticism 1945–1964: An Annotated Bibliography.* Rev. ed. New York: New York Public Lib., 1965.

Hertz, Neil H. "Wordsworth and the Tears of Adam." *Studies in Romanticism* 7 (1967): 15–33.

Hill, Alan G., ed. *The Letters of Dorothy Wordsworth: A Selection.* Oxford: Oxford UP, 1981.

——, ed. *The Letters of William Wordsworth: A New Selection.* Oxford: Oxford UP, 1984.

Hilles, Frederick, and Harold Bloom, eds. *From Sensibility to Romanticism.* New York: Oxford UP, 1965.

Hirsch, E. D. *Wordsworth and Schelling: A Typological Study.* New Haven: Yale UP, 1960.

Hobsbawm, E. J. *The Age of Revolution, 1789–1848.* New York: NAL, 1964.

Hodgson, John. *Wordsworth's Philosophical Poetry.* Lincoln: U of Nebraska P, 1980.

Holt, Ted, and John Gilroy. *A Commentary on Wordsworth's* Prelude *Books I–V.* London: Routledge, 1983.

Homans, Margaret. *Women Writers and Poetic Identity—Dorothy Wordsworth, Emily Brontë and Emily Dickinson.* Princeton: Princeton UP, 1980.

Hutchinson, Thomas, ed. *Wordsworth: Poetical Works.* 1895. Rev. Ernest de Selincourt. London: Oxford UP, 1950.

Jacobus, Mary. *Tradition and Experiment in Wordsworth's* Lyrical Ballads *(1798).* Oxford: Clarendon, 1976.

Jay, Paul. *Being in the Text: Self-Representation from Wordsworth to Roland Barthes.* Ithaca: Cornell UP, 1984.

Johnson, Lee M. *Wordsworth's Metaphysical Verse: Geometry, Nature, and Form.* Toronto: U of Toronto P, 1982.

Johnston, Kenneth R. *Wordsworth and* The Recluse. New Haven: Yale UP, 1984.

Jones, Alun R., and William Tydeman, eds. *Wordsworth:* Lyrical Ballads: *A Casebook.* London: Macmillan, 1972.

Jones, John. *The Egotistical Sublime: A History of Wordsworth's Imagination.* London: Chatto, 1954.

Jordan, Frank, ed. *The English Romantic Poets: A Review of Research and Criticism.* 4th ed. New York: MLA, 1985.

Jordan, John E. *Why the* Lyrical Ballads? *The Background, Writing, and Character of Wordsworth's 1798* Lyrical Ballads. Berkeley: U of California P, 1974.

Keats, John. *The Letters of John Keats.* 2 vols. Ed. Hyder E. Rollins. Cambridge: Harvard UP, 1958.

Kermode, Frank. *Romantic Image.* London: Routledge, 1957.

Knight, G. Wilson. *The Starlit Dome: Studies in the Poetry of Vision.* 1941. London: Methuen, 1959.

Kroeber, Karl, ed. *Backgrounds to British Romantic Literature.* San Francisco: Chandler, 1968.

——. "Constable: Millais/Wordsworth: Tennyson." *Articulate Images: The Sister Arts from Hogarth to Tennyson.* Ed. Richard Wendorf. Minneapolis: U of Minnesota P, 1983. 216–42.

——. *Romantic Landscape Vision: Constable and Wordsworth.* Madison: U of Wisconsin P, 1975.

——. *Romantic Narrative Art.* Madison: U of Wisconsin P, 1960.

Kumar, Shiv K., ed. *British Romantic Poets: Recent Revaluations.* New York: New York UP, 1966.

Langbaum, Robert. *The Modern Spirit: Essays on the Continuity of Nineteenth and Twentieth Century Literature.* New York: Oxford UP, 1970.

——. *The Poetry of Experience: The Dramatic Monologue in Modern Literary Tradition.* 1957. New York: Norton, 1963.

Legouis, Émile. *The Early Life of William Wordsworth, 1770–1798: A Study of* The Prelude. Trans. J. W. Matthews. 3rd ed. New York: Dutton, 1932.

Leitch, Vincent. *Deconstructive Criticism: An Advanced Introduction and Summary.* New York: Columbia UP, 1982.

Lindenberger, Herbert. *On Wordsworth's* Prelude. Princeton: Princeton UP, 1963.

——. *Saul's Fall: A Critical Fiction.* Baltimore: Johns Hopkins UP, 1979.

——. "Toward a New History in Literary Study." *Profession 84.* New York: MLA, 1984. 16–23.

Logan, James V. *Wordsworthian Criticism: A Guide and Bibliography.* 1947. New York: Gordian, 1974.

Lovejoy, Arthur O. *The Great Chain of Being: A Study of the History of an Idea.* 1936. New York: Harper, 1960.

Mack, Maynard, gen. ed. *The Norton Anthology of World Masterpieces.* 4th ed. 2 vols. New York: Norton, 1979.

Mahoney, John L., ed. *The English Romantics: Major Poetry and Critical Theory.* Lexington: Heath, 1978.

Margoliouth, H. M. *Wordsworth and Coleridge, 1795–1834.* London: Oxford UP, 1953.

Matlak, Richard E. "The Men in Wordsworth's Life." *Wordsworth Circle* 9 (1978): 391–97.

——. "Wordsworth's Lucy Poems in Psychobiographical Context." *PMLA* 95 (1978): 46–65.

Maxwell, J. C., ed. *William Wordsworth:* The Prelude, *A Parallel Text.* 1971. New Haven: Yale UP, 1981.

McConnell, Frank D. *The Confessional Imagination: A Reading of Wordsworth's* Prelude. Baltimore: Johns Hopkins UP, 1974.

McCracken, David. *Wordsworth and the Lake District: A Guide to the Poems.* Oxford: Oxford UP, 1984.

McFarland, Thomas. *Romanticism and the Forms of Ruin: Wordsworth, Coleridge, and the Modalities of Fragmentation*. Princeton: Princeton UP, 1981.

McGann, Jerome J. *The Romantic Ideology: A Critical Investigation*. Chicago: U of Chicago P, 1983.

McMaster, Graham, ed. *William Wordsworth: A Critical Anthology*. Harmondsworth: Penguin, 1972.

Mellor, Anne K. *English Romantic Irony*. Cambridge: Harvard UP, 1980.

Mill, John Stuart. Autobiography *and Other Writings*. Ed. Jack Stillinger. Boston: Houghton, 1969.

Miller, J. Hillis. "The Stone and the Shell: The Problem of Poetic Form in Wordsworth's 'Dream of the Arab.' " *Untying the Text: A Poststructuralist Anthology*. Ed. Robert Young. London: Routledge, 1981. 244–65.

Milton, John. *Complete Poems and Major Prose*. Ed. Merritt Y. Hughes. New York: Odyssey, 1957.

Monk, Samuel H. *The Sublime: A Study of Critical Theories in Eighteenth-Century England*. 1935. Ann Arbor: U of Michigan P, 1960.

Moorman, Mary, ed. *Journals of Dorothy Wordsworth*. Oxford Paperbacks. London: Oxford UP, 1971.

———. *William Wordsworth: A Biography*. 2 vols. Oxford: Clarendon, 1957–65.

Murray, Roger N. *Wordsworth's Style: Figures and Themes in the* Lyrical Ballads *of 1800*. Lincoln: U of Nebraska P, 1967.

Noyes, Russell, ed. *English Romantic Poetry and Prose*. New York: Oxford UP, 1956.

———. *Wordsworth and the Art of Landscape*. Bloomington: Indiana UP, 1968.

Ogden, John T., ed. "On the Teaching of Wordsworth." *Wordsworth Circle* 9 (1978): 325-90.

Onorato, Richard J. *The Character of the Poet: Wordsworth in* The Prelude. Princeton: Princeton UP, 1971.

Osborn, Robert, ed. *The Borderers*. Cornell Wordsworth. Ithaca: Cornell UP, 1982.

Owen, W. J. B. "Annotating Wordsworth." *Editing Texts of the Romantic Period*. Ed. John D. Baird. Toronto: Hakkert, 1972. 47–71.

———, ed. *Preface to* Lyrical Ballads. 1957. Westport: Greenwood, 1979.

———, ed. *Wordsworth and Coleridge:* Lyrical Ballads *1798*. 2nd ed. 1967. London: Oxford UP, 1969.

———. *Wordsworth as Critic*. Toronto: U of Toronto P, 1969.

———, ed. *Wordsworth's Literary Criticism*. London: Routledge, 1974.

Owen, W. J. B., and Jane Worthington Smyser, eds. *The Prose Works of William Wordsworth*. 3 vols. Oxford: Clarendon, 1974.

Pachter, Marc. "The Biographer Himself: An Introduction." *Telling Lives: The Biographer's Art*. Ed. Marc Pachter. Washington: New Republic, 1979. 2–15.

Parker, Reeve. " 'Finer Distance': The Narrative Art of Wordsworth's 'The Wanderer.' " *ELH* 39 (1972): 87–111.

Parrish, Stephen Maxfield. *The Art of the* Lyrical Ballads. Cambridge: Harvard UP, 1973.

———, ed. The Prelude, *1798–1799.* Cornell Wordsworth. Ithaca: Cornell UP, 1977.

Paulson, Ronald. *Literary Landscape: Turner and Constable.* New Haven: Yale UP, 1982.

Peckham, Morse. "Toward a Theory of Romanticism." *PMLA* 66 (1951): 5–23. Rpt. in Peckham, *The Triumph of Romanticism* 3–26.

———. "Toward a Theory of Romanticism: II. Reconsiderations." *Studies in Romanticism* 1 (1961): 1–8. Rpt. in Peckham, *The Triumph of Romanticism* 27–35.

———. *The Triumph of Romanticism.* Columbia: U of South Carolina P, 1970.

Perkins, David, ed. *English Romantic Writers.* New York: Harcourt, 1967.

———. *The Quest for Permanence: The Symbolism of Wordsworth, Shelley, and Keats.* Cambridge: Harvard UP, 1959.

———. *Wordsworth and the Poetry of Sincerity.* Cambridge: Harvard UP, 1964.

Piper, H. W. *The Active Universe: Pantheism and the Concept of Imagination in the English Romantic Poets.* London: Athlone, 1962.

Pirie, David B. *William Wordsworth: The Poetry of Grandeur and of Tenderness.* London: Methuen, 1982.

Pottle, Frederick A. "The Eye and the Object in the Poetry of Wordsworth." *Yale Review* 40 (1950): 27–42.

Potts, Abbie F. *Wordsworth's* Prelude: *A Study of Its Literary Form.* Ithaca: Cornell UP, 1953.

Prickett, Stephen. *Coleridge and Wordsworth: The Poetry of Growth.* Cambridge: Cambridge UP, 1970.

———, ed. *The Romantics: The Context of English Literature.* New York: Holmes, 1981.

———. *Wordsworth and Coleridge: The* Lyrical Ballads. London: Arnold, 1975.

Proffitt, Edward. " 'This pleasant lea': Waning Vision in 'The World Is Too Much with Us.' " *Wordsworth Circle* 11 (1980): 75–78.

Quennell, Peter. *Romantic England: Writing and Painting, 1717–1851.* New York: Macmillan, 1970.

Rader, Melvin. *Wordsworth: A Philosophical Approach.* Oxford: Clarendon, 1967.

Rajan, Tilottama. *Dark Interpreter: The Discourse of Romanticism.* Ithaca: Cornell UP, 1980.

———. "Romanticism and the Death of Lyric Consciousness." *Lyric Poetry: Beyond New Criticism.* Ed. Chaviva Hošek and Patricia Parker. Ithaca: Cornell UP, 1985.

Reed, Mark L. *Wordsworth: The Chronology of the Early Years, 1770–1799.* Cambridge: Harvard UP, 1967.

———. *Wordsworth: The Chronology of the Middle Years, 1800–1815.* Cambridge: Harvard UP, 1975.

Rehder, Robert. *Wordsworth and the Beginnings of Modern Poetry*. New York: Barnes, 1981.

Reiman, Donald H. "The Beauty of Buttermere as Fact and Romantic Symbol." *Criticism* 26 (1984): 139–70.

———."Poetry of Familiarity: Wordsworth, Dorothy, and Mary Hutchinson." Reiman, Jaye, and Bennett 142–77.

———, ed. *The Romantics Reviewed: Contemporary Reviews of British Romantic Writers*. 9 vols. New York: Garland, 1972.

Reiman, Donald H., Michael C. Jaye, and Betty T. Bennett, eds. *The Evidence of the Imagination: Studies of Interactions between Life and Art in English Romantic Literature*. New York: New York UP, 1978.

Salvesen, Christopher. *The Landscape of Memory: A Study of Wordsworth's Poetry*. Lincoln: U of Nebraska P, 1965.

Saul, Leon J., Thoburn R. Snyder, Jr., and Edith Sheppard. "On Earliest Memories." *Psychoanalytic Quarterly* 25 (1956): 228–37.

Schneider, Ben Ross, Jr. *Wordsworth's Cambridge Education*. Cambridge: Cambridge UP, 1957.

Schwartz, Murray M., and David Willbern. "Literature and Psychology." *Interrelations of Literature*. Ed. Jean-Pierre Barricelli and Joseph Gibaldi. New York: MLA, 1982. 205–24.

Sheats, Paul D. *The Making of Wordsworth's Poetry, 1785–1798*. Cambridge: Harvard UP, 1973.

———, ed. *The Poetical Works of Wordsworth*. Cambridge Edition. 1904. Rev. ed. Boston: Houghton, 1982.

Shelley, Percy Bysshe. *The Complete Works*. Ed. Roger Ingpen and Walter E. Peck. 10 vols. New York: Gordian, 1965.

Sherry, Charles. *Wordsworth's Poetry of the Imagination*. New York: Oxford UP, 1980.

Silverman, Lloyd H. "Psychoanalytic Theory: 'The Reports of My Death Are Greatly Exaggerated.' " *American Psychologist* 31 (1976): 621–37.

Simpson, David. *Irony and Authority in Romantic Poetry*. Totowa: Rowman, 1979.

———. *Wordsworth and the Figurings of the Real*. Atlantic Highlands: Humanities, 1982.

Smith, Barbara Herrnstein. *On the Margins of Discourse*. Chicago: U of Chicago P, 1978.

Spacks, Patricia. "Stages of Self." *Boston University Journal* 25 (1977): 7–17.

Sperry, Willard. *Wordsworth's Anti-Climax*. Cambridge: Harvard UP, 1935.

Stallknecht, Newton. *Strange Seas of Thought: Studies in William Wordsworth's Philosophy of Man and Nature*. 1945. 2nd ed. Durham: Duke UP, 1958.

Stam, David H. *Wordsworthian Criticism 1964–1973: An Annotated Bibliography*. New York: New York Public Lib., 1974.

Stedman, J. G. *Narrative of a Five Years' Expedition against the Revolted Negroes of Surinam.* Illus. with 80 engravings, 16 by William Blake. London, 1796.

Stillinger, Jack, ed. *William Wordsworth: Selected Poems and Prefaces.* Boston: Houghton, 1965.

Swingle, L. J. "Wordsworth's 'Picture of the Mind.'" *Images of Romanticism: Verbal and Visual Affinities.* Ed. Karl Kroeber and William Walling. New Haven: Yale UP, 1978. 81–90.

Thomas, Gordon, ed. *William Wordsworth's* Convention of Cintra: *A Facsimile of the 1809 Tract.* Provo: Brigham Young UP, 1983.

Thompson, A. W., ed. *Wordsworth's Mind and Art.* Edinburgh: Oliver, 1969.

Thompson, E. P. *The Making of the English Working Class.* 1964. New York: Random, 1966.

Thompson, T. W. *Wordsworth's Hawkshead.* Ed. R. S. Woof. Oxford: Oxford UP, 1970.

Thomson, James. *The Complete Poetical Works.* Ed. J. Logie Robertson. London: Oxford UP, 1908.

Thorpe, Clarence D., Carlos Baker, and Bennett Weaver, eds. *The Major English Romantic Poets: A Symposium in Reappraisal.* Carbondale: Southern Illinois UP, 1957.

Thorslev, Peter, Jr. *Romantic Contraries: Freedom versus Destiny.* New Haven: Yale UP, 1984.

Tinker, Chauncey Brewster. *Painter and Poet: Studies in the Literary Relations of English Painting.* Cambridge: Harvard UP, 1938.

Trawick, Leonard M., ed. *Backgrounds of Romanticism: English Philosophical Prose of the Eighteenth-Century.* Bloomington: Indiana UP, 1967.

Trevelyan, G. M. *British History of the Nineteenth Century and After.* 2nd ed. New York: Longmans, 1938.

———. *English Social History: A Survey of Six Centuries, Chaucer to Queen Victoria.* New York: Longmans, 1942.

Trilling, Lionel. "The Immortality Ode." *The English Institute Annual, 1941.* New York: Columbia UP, 1942. 1–28. Rpt. in Trilling, *Liberal Imagination* 125–54.

———. *The Liberal Imagination: Essays on Literature and Society.* 1950. Garden City: Anchor-Doubleday, 1953.

———. "The Sense of the Past." *Partisan Review* 9 (1942): 229–41. Rpt. in Trilling, *Liberal Imagination* 181–97.

———. *Sincerity and Authenticity.* Cambridge: Harvard UP, 1972.

Tuveson, Ernest. *The Imagination as a Means of Grace: Locke and the Aesthetics of Romanticism.* Berkeley: U of California P, 1960.

Twitchell, James B. *Romantic Horizons: Aspects of the Sublime in English Poetry and Painting, 1770–1850.* Columbia: U of Missouri P, 1983.

Van Doren, Mark, ed. *William Wordsworth: Selected Poetry.* Modern Lib. New York: Random, 1950.

Vendler, Helen. "Lionel Trilling and the 'Immortality Ode.' " *Salmagundi* 41 (1978): 66–86.

Vogler, Thomas. *Preludes to Vision: The Epic Venture in Blake, Wordsworth, Keats, and Hart Crane.* Berkeley: U of California P, 1971.

Watson, J. R. *Wordsworth's Vital Soul: The Sacred and Profane in Wordsworth's Poetry.* Atlantic Highlands: Humanities, 1982.

Webb, Robert K. *Modern England: From the Eighteenth Century to the Present.* 2nd ed. New York: Harper, 1980.

Weiskel, Thomas. *The Romantic Sublime: Studies in the Structure and Psychology of Transcendence.* Baltimore: Johns Hopkins UP, 1976.

Wesling, Donald. *Wordsworth and the Adequacy of Landscape.* New York: Barnes, 1970.

White, R. J. *Life in Regency England.* New York: Putnam's, 1963.

Whitehead, A. N. *Science and the Modern World.* New York: Macmillan, 1925.

Wilkie, Brian. *Romantic Poets and Epic Tradition.* Madison: U of Wisconsin P, 1965.

Wilkie, Brian, and James Hurt, eds. *Literature of the Western World.* 2 vols. New York: Macmillan, 1984.

Willey, Basil. *The Eighteenth Century Background: Studies on the Idea of Nature in the Thought of the Period.* 1940. Boston: Beacon, 1961.

Williams, E. Neville. *Life in Georgian England.* New York: Putnam's, 1962.

Williams, Raymond. *The Country and the City.* New York: Oxford UP, 1973.

———. *Culture and Society, 1780–1950.* New York: Columbia UP, 1958.

Wimsatt, William K., Jr. "The Structure of Romantic Nature Imagery." *The Age of Johnson: Essays Presented to Chauncey Brewster Tinker.* Ed. Frederick Hilles. New Haven: Yale UP, 1949. 291–303. Rpt. in Wimsatt, *The Verbal Icon: Studies in the Meaning of Poetry.* Lexington: UP of Kentucky, 1954. 103–16.

Wlecke, Albert O. *Wordsworth and the Sublime: An Essay on Romantic Self-Consciousness.* Berkeley: U of California P, 1973.

Woodring, Carl. *Politics in English Romantic Poetry.* Cambridge: Harvard UP, 1970.

———. *Wordsworth.* 1965. Cambridge: Harvard UP, 1968.

Wordsworth, Christopher. *Memoirs of William Wordsworth.* 2 vols. Ed. Henry Reed. Boston, 1851.

Wordsworth, Jonathan, ed. *Bicentenary Wordsworth Studies in Memory of John Alban Finch.* Ithaca: Cornell UP, 1970.

———. *The Music of Humanity: A Critical Study of Wordsworth's "Ruined Cottage."* New York: Harper, 1969.

———. *William Wordsworth: The Borders of Vision.* 1982. Oxford: Oxford UP, 1984.

Wordsworth, Jonathan, M. H. Abrams, and Stephen Gill, eds. The Prelude, *1799, 1805, 1850.* Norton Critical Editions. New York: Norton, 1979.

Wordsworth, William. *A Guide through the District of the Lakes in the North of England.* 1822. New York: Greenwood, 1968.

Wüscher, Hermann J. *Liberty, Equality, and Fraternity in Wordsworth: 1791–1800.* Studia Anglistica Upsaliensa 39. Uppsala, Swed.: Almquist, 1980.

Zall, Paul M., ed. *Literary Criticism of William Wordsworth.* Lincoln: U of Nebraska P, 1966.

Audiovisual Aids

Films and Sound Filmstrips

Blake, Wordsworth and Coleridge. Sound filmstrip. Films for the Humanities. FFH 348, 1982.

Clark, Kenneth, writ. and narr. "The Worship of Nature." *Civilisation.* Dir. Michael Gill and Peter Montagnon. 12 programs. BBC, 1969. (Videocassette available Time-Life Films.)

Coleridge: The Fountain and the Cave. 16mm film. Pyramid Film Productions, 1974.

English Romantic Poetry and Painting—A Series. Sound filmstrip. United Learning, 1974.

Ketcham, Carl H., writ. and dir. *Wordsworth.* 16mm film. Radio-TV Bureau, U of Arizona, 1961.

The Romantic Age. Sound filmstrip. Thomas S. Klise, 1976.

The Romantic Era. Sound filmstrip. Educational Audio-Visual, 1970.

Romanticism: The Revolt of the Spirit. 16mm film. Learning Corp. of America, 1971.

The Time, the Life, the Works, and Selected Poems of William Wordsworth. Sound filmstrip. Educational Audio-Visual, 1969.

Wordsworth. Sound filmstrip. Thomas S. Klise, 1975.

The Wordsworth Country. 16mm film. Universal Education and Visual Arts, 1952.

Wordsworth's Lake Country: Image of Man and Nature. 16mm film. Perfection Form, 1971.

Readings

Bloom, Claire, Anthony Quayle, et al. *English Romantic Poetry.* Caedmon, TC 3005, 1971.

Fletcher, Bramwell. *English Romantic Poets.* Audiotape cassette. Listening Library, LL 305 CX, 1971.

Hardwicke, Cedric. *Poetry of Wordsworth.* 1957. Caedmon, TC 1026, 1963. Audiotape cassette, CDL 51026.

Speaight, Robert. *Treasury of William Wordsworth.* Spoken Arts, SA 860, 1964. Audiotape cassette, SAC 8023, 1969.

Recorded Criticism

Easson, Angus, and Terence Wright. *Wordsworth: The* Lyrical Ballads. Audiocassette program. Audio Learning, ELA 063.

———. *Wordsworth's* The Prelude. Audiocassette program. Audio Learning, ELA 066.

Gill, Stephen, and Mary Jacobus. *Wordsworth.* Audiocassette program. Gould Media, A27.

Martin, Graham, and Mark Storey. *English Romantic Poetry 1780–1820s.* Audiocassette program. Audio Learning, ELA 067.

Pricket, Stephen. *William Wordsworth.* 4 audiocassette programs. *Ode: Intimations of Immortality* (3503). *Tintern Abbey* (3504). *The Prelude* (3502). *The Sonnets* (3501). Gould Media.

Salvesen, Christopher, and William Walsh. *The Romantics.* Audiocassette program. Gould Media, A4.

INDEX